# Mastering JavaS
# Design Patterns

## *Second Edition*

Write reliable code to create powerful applications by
mastering advanced JavaScript design patterns

**Simon Timms**

BIRMINGHAM - MUMBAI

# Mastering JavaScript Design Patterns
## *Second Edition*

First published: November 2014

Second published: June 2016

Production reference: 1240616

Published by Packt Publishing Ltd.
Livery Place
35 Livery Street
Birmingham B3 2PB, UK.

ISBN 978-1-78588-216-6

www.packtpub.com

# Credits

**Author**
Simon Timms

**Reviewer**
Dobrin Ganev

**Commissioning Editor**
Wilson D'souza

**Acquisition Editor**
Tushar Gupta

**Content Development Editor**
Onkar Wani

**Technical Editor**
Dhiraj Chandanshive

**Copy Editor**
Safis Editing

**Project Coordinator**
Ulhas Kambli

**Proofreader**
Safis Editing

**Indexer**
Monica Ajmera Mehta

**Production Coordinator**
Aparna Bhagat

**Cover Work**
Aparna Bhagat

# About the Author

**Simon Timms** is a developer who loves writing code. He writes in a variety of languages and using a number of tools. Mostly, he develops web applications with .NET backends. Simon is very interested in visualizations and cloud computing. A background in builds and system administration keeps him on the straight and narrow when it comes to DevOps.

He is the author of *Social Data Visualization with HTML5 and JavaScript*, *Packt Publishing*. He blogs on `blog.simontimms.com`, and he is also a frequent contributor to the Western Devs (`http://westerndevs.com`), which is a loose collaboration of developers mostly located in Canada. Twice a week, he participates in a videocast called *The ASP.NET Monsters* about the future of ASP.NET, which is one of the most popular series on Microsoft's Channel 9 video service (`https://channel9.msdn.com/Series/aspnetmonsters`).

Simon is the president of the Calgary .Net user group and a member of half a dozen other groups. He speaks on a variety of topics from DevOps to how the telephone system works. He works as a principal software developer for Clear-Measure located in Austin, Texas. He is currently working on a new title about ASP.NET Core.

I would like to thank my wonderful wife for all her support and my kids for providing a welcome distraction from writing. I would also like to thank the Western Devs for being a constant sounding board for insane ideas.

# About the Reviewer

**Dobrin Ganev** is a software developer with years of experience in various development environments from finance to business process management. In recent years, he has focused on geospatial development and data analytics using languages such as JavaScript, Java, Python, Scala, and R. He has extensive knowledge about the open source geospatial and the Esri platforms. Currently, he is focused on Big Data, and its applications across broad industries and sectors.

chorStream Inc. (http://www.chorstream.com/) is a software development firm focused on the use of Big Data and Big Data technologies to help clients work with and leverage large and diverse volumes of data, which was founded in 2015. As a co-founder, Mr. Ganev has worked with an accomplished team of professionals to create and bring to market an application's framework that end users are able to use to build custom and focused applications without needing any development skills.

He has reviewed the book *ArcGIS for JavaScript Developers by Example*, by *Packt Publishing*.

# www.PacktPub.com

## eBooks, discount offers, and more

Did you know that Packt offers eBook versions of every book published, with PDF and ePub files available? You can upgrade to the eBook version at www.PacktPub.com and as a print book customer, you are entitled to a discount on the eBook copy. Get in touch with us at customercare@packtpub.com for more details.

At www.PacktPub.com, you can also read a collection of free technical articles, sign up for a range of free newsletters and receive exclusive discounts and offers on Packt books and eBooks.

https://www2.packtpub.com/books/subscription/packtlib

Do you need instant solutions to your IT questions? PacktLib is Packt's online digital book library. Here, you can search, access, and read Packt's entire library of books.

## Why subscribe?

- Fully searchable across every book published by Packt
- Copy and paste, print, and bookmark content
- On demand and accessible via a web browser

# Table of Contents

## Part 2: Other Patterns

# Preface

JavaScript is starting to become one of the most popular languages in the world. However, its history as a bit of a toy language means that developers are tempted to ignore good design. Design patterns are a great tool to suggest some well-tried solutions.

## What this book covers

This book is divided into two main halves, each of which contains a number of chapters. The first half of the book, which we'll refer to as *Part 1*, covers the classical design patterns, which are found in the GoF book.

*Chapter 1, Designing for Fun and Profit*, introduces what design patterns are and why we are interested in using design patterns. We will also talk about some of the history of JavaScript to give you a historical context.

*Chapter 2, Organizing Code,* looks at how to create the classical structures that are used to organize code, namespaces, or modules and classes, as JavaScript lacks these constructs as first class citizens.

*Chapter 3, Creational Patterns*, covers the creational patterns outlined in the Gang of Four book. We'll discuss how these patterns apply to JavaScript, as opposed to the languages that were popular at the time when the Gang of Four wrote their book.

*Chapter 4, Structural Patterns*, looks at creational patterns. We'll examine the structural patterns from the Gang of Four book.

*Chapter 5, Behavioral Patterns*, discusses behavioral patterns. These are the final set of patterns from the Gang of Four book that we'll examine. These patterns govern different ways to link classes together.

*Part 2* looks at patterns that are either not covered in the GoF book or that are specific to JavaScript.

*Chapter 6, Functional Programming,* covers some of the patterns that can be found in functional programming languages. We'll look at how these patterns can be used in JavaScript to improve code.

*Chapter 7, Reactive Programming,* explores the problems associated with the callback model of programming in JavaScript. It presents Reactive programming, a stream-based approach to events, as a possible solution.

*Chapter 8, Application Patterns,* examines the confusing variety of different patterns to create single page applications. We'll provide clarity and look at how to use libraries which use each of the existing patterns, as well as create our own lightweight framework.

*Chapter 9, Web Patterns,* looks at a number of patterns that have specific applicability to web applications. We'll also look at some patterns around deploying code to remote runtimes, such as the browser.

*Chapter 10, Messaging Patterns,* covers how messaging is a powerful technique to communicate inside and even between applications. In this chapter, we'll look at some common structures around messaging and discuss why messaging is so useful.

*Chapter 11, Microservices,* covers microservices, which are growing in popularity at a tremendous rate. This chapter examines the ideas behind this approach to programming and suggests a number of patterns to keep in mind when building using this approach.

*Chapter 12, Patterns for Testing,* discusses how building software is hard, and how building good software is doubly so. This chapter provides some patterns which can make the testing process a little bit easier.

*Chapter 13, Advanced Patterns,* explains how some patterns such as aspect-oriented programming are rarely applied in JavaScript. We'll look at how these patterns can be applied in JavaScript and discuss whether we should apply them.

*Chapter 14, ECMAScript-2015/2016 Solutions Today,* covers some of the tools available to allow you to use features from future versions of JavaScript today. We'll examine Microsoft's TypeScript as well as Traceur.

# What you need for this book

There is no specialized software needed for this book. JavaScript runs on all modern browsers. There are standalone JavaScript engines written in C++ (V8) and Java (Rhino), and these are used to power all sorts of tools, such as Node.js, CouchDB, and even Elasticsearch. These patterns can be applied to any of these technologies.

# Who this book is for

This book is ideal for JavaScript developers who want to gain expertise in object-oriented programming with JavaScript and the new capabilities of ES-2015 to improve their web development skills and build professional-quality web applications.

# Conventions

In this book, you will find a number of text styles that distinguish between different kinds of information. Here are some examples of these styles and an explanation of their meaning.

Code words in text, database table names, folder names, filenames, file extensions, pathnames, dummy URLs, user input, and Twitter handles are shown as follows: "You'll notice that we explicitly define the name field."

A block of code is set as follows:

```
let Castle = function(name){
 this.name = name;
}
Castle.prototype.build = function(){ console.log(this.name);}
let instance1 = new Castle("Winterfell");
instance1.build();
```

When we wish to draw your attention to a particular part of a code block, the relevant lines or items are set in bold:

```
let Castle = function(name){
 this.name = name;
}
Castle.prototype.build = function(){ console.log(this.name);}
let instance1 = new Castle("Winterfell");
instance1.build();
```

Any command-line input or output is written as follows:

```
ls -1| cut -d \. -f 2 -s | sort |uniq
```

**New terms** and **important words** are shown in bold. Words that you see on the screen, for example, in menus or dialog boxes, appear in the text like this: "To access them there is a menu item, which is located under **Tools | Developer Tools in Chrome | Tools | Web Developer in Firefox.**"

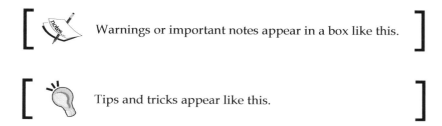

> Warnings or important notes appear in a box like this.

> Tips and tricks appear like this.

# Reader feedback

Feedback from our readers is always welcome. Let us know what you think about this book—what you liked or disliked. Reader feedback is important for us as it helps us develop titles that you will really get the most out of.

To send us general feedback, simply e-mail feedback@packtpub.com, and mention the book's title in the subject of your message.

If there is a topic that you have expertise in and you are interested in either writing or contributing to a book, see our author guide at www.packtpub.com/authors.

# Customer support

Now that you are the proud owner of a Packt book, we have a number of things to help you to get the most from your purchase.

# Downloading the example code

You can download the example code files for this book from your account at http://www.packtpub.com. If you purchased this book elsewhere, you can visit http://www.packtpub.com/support and register to have the files e-mailed directly to you.

You can download the code files by following these steps:

1. Log in or register to our website using your e-mail address and password.
2. Hover the mouse pointer on the **SUPPORT** tab at the top.
3. Click on **Code Downloads & Errata**.
4. Enter the name of the book in the **Search** box.
5. Select the book for which you're looking to download the code files.
6. Choose from the drop-down menu where you purchased this book from.
7. Click on **Code Download**.

You can also download the code files by clicking on the **Code Files** button on the book's webpage at the Packt Publishing website. This page can be accessed by entering the book's name in the **Search** box. Please note that you need to be logged in to your Packt account.

Once the file is downloaded, please make sure that you unzip or extract the folder using the latest version of:

- WinRAR / 7-Zip for Windows
- Zipeg / iZip / UnRarX for Mac
- 7-Zip / PeaZip for Linux

The code bundle for the book is also hosted on GitHub at `https://github.com/PacktPublishing/Mastering-JavaScript-Design-Patterns-Second-Edition`. We also have other code bundles from our rich catalog of books and videos available at `https://github.com/PacktPublishing/`. Check them out!

# Errata

Although we have taken every care to ensure the accuracy of our content, mistakes do happen. If you find a mistake in one of our books—maybe a mistake in the text or the code—we would be grateful if you could report this to us. By doing so, you can save other readers from frustration and help us improve subsequent versions of this book. If you find any errata, please report them by visiting `http://www.packtpub.com/submit-errata`, selecting your book, clicking on the **Errata Submission Form** link, and entering the details of your errata. Once your errata are verified, your submission will be accepted and the errata will be uploaded to our website or added to any list of existing errata under the Errata section of that title.

To view the previously submitted errata, go to `https://www.packtpub.com/books/content/support` and enter the name of the book in the search field. The required information will appear under the **Errata** section.

# Piracy

Piracy of copyrighted material on the Internet is an ongoing problem across all media. At Packt, we take the protection of our copyright and licenses very seriously. If you come across any illegal copies of our works in any form on the Internet, please provide us with the location address or website name immediately so that we can pursue a remedy.

Please contact us at `copyright@packtpub.com` with a link to the suspected pirated material.

We appreciate your help in protecting our authors and our ability to bring you valuable content.

# Questions

If you have a problem with any aspect of this book, you can contact us at `questions@packtpub.com`, and we will do our best to address the problem.

# Designing for Fun and Profit

JavaScript is an evolving language that has come a long way from its inception. Possibly more than any other programming language, it has grown and changed with the growth of the World Wide Web. The exploration of how JavaScript can be written using good design principles is the topic of this book. The preface of this book contains a detailed explanation of the sections of the book.

In the first half of this chapter, we'll explore the history of JavaScript and how it came to be the important language that it is today. As JavaScript has evolved and grown in importance, the need to apply rigorous methods to its construction has also grown. Design patterns can be a very useful tool to assist in developing maintainable code. The second half of the chapter will be dedicated to the theory of design patterns. Finally, we'll look briefly at anti-patterns.

The topics in this chapter are as follows:

- History of JavaScript
- What is a design pattern?
- Anti-patterns

# The road to JavaScript

We'll never know how language first came into being. Did it slowly evolve from a series of grunts and guttural sounds made during grooming rituals? Perhaps it developed to allow mothers and their offspring to communicate. Both of these are theories, all but impossible to prove. Nobody was around to observe our ancestors during that important period. In fact, the general lack of empirical evidence led the Linguistic Society of Paris to ban further discussions on the topic, seeing it as unsuitable for serious study.

# The early days

Fortunately, programming languages have developed in recent history and we've been able to watch them grow and change. JavaScript has one of the more interesting histories of modern programming languages. During what must have been an absolutely frantic 10 days in May of 1995, a programmer at Netscape wrote the foundation for what would grow up to be modern JavaScript.

At the time, Netscape was involved in the first of the browser wars with Microsoft. The vision for Netscape was far grander than simply developing a browser. They wanted to create an entire distributed operating system making use of Sun Microsystems' recently-released Java programming language. Java was a much more modern alternative to the C++ Microsoft was pushing. However, Netscape didn't have an answer to Visual Basic. Visual Basic was an easier to use programming language, which was targeted at developers with less experience. It avoided some of the difficulties around memory management that make C and C++ notoriously difficult to program. Visual Basic also avoided strict typing and overall allowed more leeway. Here is an illustration of the timeline of JavaScript:

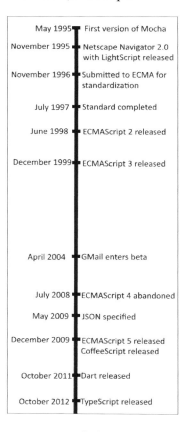

| | |
|---|---|
| May 1995 | First version of Mocha |
| November 1995 | Netscape Navigator 2.0 with LightScript released |
| November 1996 | Submitted to ECMA for standardization |
| July 1997 | Standard completed |
| June 1998 | ECMAScript 2 released |
| December 1999 | ECMAScript 3 released |
| April 2004 | GMail enters beta |
| July 2008 | ECMAScript 4 abandoned |
| May 2009 | JSON specified |
| December 2009 | ECMAScript 5 released CoffeeScript released |
| October 2011 | Dart released |
| October 2012 | TypeScript released |

Brendan Eich was tasked with developing Netscape repartee to VB. The project was initially codenamed Mocha, but was renamed LiveScript before Netscape 2.0 beta was released. By the time the full release was available, Mocha/LiveScript had been renamed JavaScript to tie it into the Java applet integration. Java Applets were small applications which ran in the browser. They had a different security model from the browser itself and so were limited in how they could interact with both the browser and the local system. It is quite rare to see applets these days, as much of their functionality has become part of the browser. Java was riding a popular wave at the time and any relationship to it was played up.

The name has caused much confusion over the years. JavaScript is a very different language from Java. JavaScript is an interpreted language with loose typing, which runs primarily on the browser. Java is a language that is compiled to bytecode, which is then executed on the Java Virtual Machine. It has applicability in numerous scenarios, from the browser (through the use of Java applets), to the server (Tomcat, JBoss, and so on), to full desktop applications (Eclipse, OpenOffice, and so on). In most laypersons' minds, the confusion remains.

JavaScript turned out to be really quite useful for interacting with the web browser. It was not long until Microsoft had also adopted JavaScript into their Internet Explorer to complement VBScript. The Microsoft implementation was known as JScript.

By late 1996, it was clear that JavaScript was going to be the winning web language for the near future. In order to limit the amount of language deviation between implementations, Sun and Netscape began working with the **European Computer Manufacturers Association** (**ECMA**) to develop a standard to which future versions of JavaScript would need to comply. The standard was released very quickly (very quickly in terms of how rapidly standards organizations move), in July of 1997. On the off chance that you have not seen enough names yet for JavaScript, the standard version was called **ECMAScript**, a name which still persists in some circles.

Unfortunately, the standard only specified the very core parts of JavaScript. With the browser wars raging, it was apparent that any vendor that stuck with only the basic implementation of JavaScript would quickly be left behind. At the same time, there was much work going on to establish a standard **Document Object Model** (**DOM**) for browsers. The DOM was, in effect, an API for a web page that could be manipulated using JavaScript.

For many years, every JavaScript script would start by attempting to determine the browser on which it was running. This would dictate how to address elements in the DOM, as there were dramatic deviations between each browser. The spaghetti of code that was required to perform simple actions was legendary. I remember reading a year-long 20-part series on developing a **Dynamic HTML (DHTML)** drop down menu such that it would work on both Internet Explorer and Netscape Navigator. The same functionally can now be achieved with pure CSS without even having to resort to JavaScript.

 DHTML was a popular term in the late 1990s and early 2000s. It really referred to any web page that had some sort of dynamic content that was executed on the client side. It has fallen out of use, as the popularity of JavaScript has made almost every page a dynamic one.

Fortunately, the efforts to standardize JavaScript continued behind the scenes. Versions 2 and 3 of ECMAScript were released in 1998 and 1999. It looked like there might finally be some agreement between the various parties interested in JavaScript. Work began in early 2000 on ECMAScript 4, which was to be a major new release.

# A pause

Then, disaster struck. The various groups involved in the ECMAScript effort had major disagreements about the direction JavaScript was to take. Microsoft seemed to have lost interest in the standardization effort. It was somewhat understandable, as it was around that time that Netscape self-destructed and Internet Explorer became the de-facto standard. Microsoft implemented parts of ECMAScript 4 but not all of it. Others implemented more fully-featured support, but without the market leader on-board, developers didn't bother using them.

Years passed without consensus and without a new release of ECMAScript. However, as frequently happens, the evolution of the Internet could not be stopped by a lack of agreement between major players. Libraries such as jQuery, Prototype, Dojo, and Mootools, papered over the major differences in browsers, making cross-browser development far easier. At the same time, the amount of JavaScript used in applications increased dramatically.

# The way of GMail

The turning point was, perhaps, the release of Google's GMail application in 2004. Although XMLHTTPRequest, the technology behind **Asynchronous JavaScript and XML (AJAX)**, had been around for about five years when GMail was released, it had not been well-used. When GMail was released, I was totally knocked off my feet by how smooth it was. We've grown used to applications that avoid full reloads, but at the time, it was a revolution. To make applications like that work, a great deal of JavaScript is needed.

AJAX is a method by which small chunks of data are retrieved from the server by a client instead of refreshing the entire page. The technology allows for more interactive pages that avoid the jolt of full page reloads.

The popularity of GMail was the trigger for a change that had been brewing for a while. Increasing JavaScript acceptance and standardization pushed us past the tipping point for the acceptance of JavaScript as a proper language. Up until that point, much of the use of JavaScript was for performing minor changes to the page and for validating form input. I joke with people that, in the early days of JavaScript, the only function name which was used was Validate().

Applications such as GMail that have a heavy reliance on AJAX and avoid full page reloads are known as **Single Page Applications** or **SPAs**. By minimizing the changes to the page contents, users have a more fluid experience. By transferring only a **JavaScript Object Notation (JSON)** payload instead of HTML, the amount of bandwidth required is also minimized. This makes applications appear to be snappier. In recent years, there have been great advances in frameworks that ease the creation of SPAs. AngularJS, backbone.js, and ember are all Model View Controller style frameworks. They have gained great popularity in the past two to three years and provide some interesting use of patterns. These frameworks are the evolution of years of experimentation with JavaScript best practices by some very smart people.

JSON is a human-readable serialization format for JavaScript. It has become very popular in recent years, as it is easier and less cumbersome than previously popular formats such as XML. It lacks many of the companion technologies and strict grammatical rules of XML, but makes up for it in simplicity.

At the same time as the frameworks using JavaScript are evolving, the language is too. 2015 saw the release of a much-vaunted new version of JavaScript that had been under development for some years. Initially called ECMAScript 6, the final name ended up being ECMAScript-2015. It brought with it some great improvements to the ecosystem. Browser vendors are rushing to adopt the standard. Because of the complexity of adding new language features to the code base, coupled with the fact that not everybody is on the cutting edge of browsers, a number of other languages that transcompile to JavaScript are gaining popularity. CoffeeScript is a Python-like language that strives to improve the readability and brevity of JavaScript. Developed by Google, Dart is being pushed by Google as an eventual replacement for JavaScript. Its construction addresses some of the optimizations that are impossible in traditional JavaScript. Until a Dart runtime is sufficiently popular, Google provides a Dart to the JavaScript transcompiler. TypeScript is a Microsoft project that adds some ECMAScript-2015 and even some ECMAScript-201X syntax, as well as an interesting typing system, to JavaScript. It aims to address some of the issues that large JavaScript projects present.

The point of this discussion about the history of JavaScript is twofold: first, it is important to remember that languages do not develop in a vacuum. Both human languages and computer programming languages mutate based on the environments in which they are used. It is a popularly held belief that the Inuit people have a great number of words for "snow", as it was so prevalent in their environment. This may or may not be true, depending on your definition for the word and exactly who makes up the Inuit people. There are, however, a great number of examples of domain-specific lexicons evolving to meet the requirements for exact definitions in narrow fields. One need look no further than a specialty cooking store to see the great number of variants of items which a layperson such as myself would call a pan.

The Sapir–Whorf hypothesis is a hypothesis within the linguistics domain, which suggests that not only is language influenced by the environment in which it is used, but also that language influences its environment. Also known as linguistic relativity, the theory is that one's cognitive processes differ based on how the language is constructed. Cognitive psychologist Keith Chen has proposed a fascinating example of this. In a very highly-viewed TED talk, Dr. Chen suggested that there is a strong positive correlation between languages that lack a future tense and those that have high savings rates (`https://www.ted.com/talks/keith_chen_could_your_language_affect_your_ability_to_save_money/transcript`). The hypothesis at which Dr. Chen arrived is that when your language does not have a strong sense of connection between the present and the future, this leads to more reckless behavior in the present.

Thus, understanding the history of JavaScript puts one in a better position to understand how and where to make use of JavaScript.

The second reason I explored the history of JavaScript is because it is absolutely fascinating to see how quickly such a popular tool has evolved. At the time of writing, it has been about 20 years since JavaScript was first built and its rise to popularity has been explosive. What more exciting thing is there than to work in an ever-evolving language?

# JavaScript everywhere

Since the GMail revolution, JavaScript has grown immensely. The renewed browser wars, which pit Internet Explorer and Edge against Chrome and against Firefox, have lead to building a number of very fast JavaScript interpreters. Brand new optimization techniques have been deployed and it is not unusual to see JavaScript compiled to machine-native code for the added performance it gains. However, as the speed of JavaScript has increased, so has the complexity of the applications built using it.

JavaScript is no longer simply a language for manipulating the browser, either. The JavaScript engine behind the popular Chrome browser has been extracted and is now at the heart of a number of interesting projects such as Node.js. Node.js started off as a highly asynchronous method of writing server-side applications. It has grown greatly and has a very active community supporting it. A wide variety of applications have been built using the Node.js runtime. Everything from build tools to editors have been built on the base of Node.js. Recently, the JavaScript engine for Microsoft Edge, ChakraCore, was also open sourced and can be embedded in Node.js as an alternative to Google's V8. SpiderMonkey, the Firefox equivalent, is also open source and is making its way into more tools.

JavaScript can even be used to control microcontrollers. The Johnny-Five framework is a programming framework for the very popular Arduino. It brings a much simpler approach to programming devices than the traditional low-level languages used for programming these devices. Using JavaScript and Arduino opens up a world of possibilities, from building robots to interacting with real-world sensors.

All of the major smartphone platforms (iOS, Android, and Windows Phone) have an option to build applications using JavaScript. The tablet space is much the same, with tablets supporting programming using JavaScript. Even the latest version of Windows provides a mechanism for building applications using JavaScript. This illustration shows some of the things possible with JavaScript:

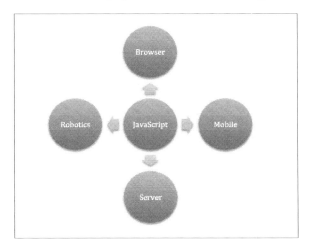

JavaScript is becoming one of the most important languages in the world. Although language usage statistics are notoriously difficult to calculate, every single source which attempts to develop a ranking puts JavaScript in the top 10:

| Language index | Rank of JavaScript |
| --- | --- |
| Langpop.com | 4 |
| Statisticbrain.com | 4 |
| Codeval.com | 6 |
| TIOBE | 8 |

What is more interesting is that most of of these rankings suggest that the usage of JavaScript is on the rise.

The long and short of it is that JavaScript is going to be a major language in the next few years. More and more applications are being written in JavaScript and it is the lingua franca for any sort of web development. Developer of the popular Stack Overflow website Jeff Atwood created Atwood's Law regarding the wide adoption of JavaScript:

> *"Any application that can be written in JavaScript, will eventually be written in JavaScript"* – Atwood's Law, Jeff Atwood

This insight has been proven to be correct time and time again. There are now compilers, spreadsheets, word processors—you name it—all written in JavaScript.

As the applications which make use of JavaScript increase in complexity, the developer may stumble upon many of the same issues as have been encountered in traditional programming languages: how can we write this application to be adaptable to change?

This brings us to the need for properly designing applications. No longer can we simply throw a bunch of JavaScript into a file and hope that it works properly. Nor can we rely on libraries such as jQuery to save ourselves. Libraries can only provide additional functionality and contribute nothing to the structure of an application. At least some attention must now be paid to how to construct the application to be extensible and adaptable. The real world is ever-changing and any application that is unable to change to suit the changing world is likely to be left in the dust. Design patterns provide some guidance in building adaptable applications, which can shift with changing business needs.

# What is a design pattern?

For the most part, ideas are only applicable in one place. Adding peanut butter is really only a great idea in cooking and not in sewing. However, from time to time it is possible to find applicability for a great idea outside of its original purpose. This is the story behind design patterns.

In 1977, Christopher Alexander, Sara Ishikawa, and Murray Silverstein authored a seminal book on what they called design patterns in urban planning, called *A Pattern Language: Towns, Buildings, Construction*.

The book described a language for talking about the commonalities of design. In the book, a pattern is described thusly:

> *"The elements of this language are entities called patterns. Each pattern describes a problem that occurs over and over again in our environment, and then describes the core of the solution to that problem, in such a way that you can use this solution a million times over, without ever doing it the same way twice."* – *Christopher Alexander*

These design patterns were such things as how to layout cities to provide a mixture of city and country living, or how to build roads in loops as a traffic-calming measure in residential areas, as is shown in the following picture taken from the book:

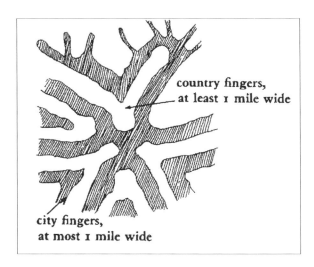

Even for those without a strong interest in urban planning, the book presents some fascinating ideas about how to structure our world to promote healthy societies.

Using the work of Christopher Alexander and the other authors as a source of inspiration, Erich Gamma, Richard Helm, Ralph Johnson, and John Vlissides wrote a book called *Design Patterns: Elements of Reusable Object-Oriented Software*. When a book is very influential in a computer science curriculum, it is often given a pet name. For instance, most computer science graduates will know of which book you mean if you talk about *The Dragon Book* (*Principles of Compiler Design*, 1986). In enterprise software, *The Blue Book* is well known to be Eric Evan's book on domain-driven design. The design patterns book has been so important that it is commonly referred do as the GoF book, or *Gang of Four* book, for its four authors.

This book outlined 23 patterns for use in object-oriented design. It is divided the patterns into three major groups:

- **Creational**: These patterns outlined a number of ways in which objects could be created and their lifecycles managed

- **Behavioral**: These patterns describe how objects interact with each other

- **Structural**: These patterns describe a variety of different ways to add functionality to existing objects

The purpose of design patterns is not to instruct you on how to build software, but rather to give guidance on ways in which to solve common problems. For instance, many applications have a need to provide some sort of an undo function. The problem is common to text editors, drawing programs, and even e-mail clients. Solving this problem has been done many times before so it would be great to have a common solution. The command pattern provides just such a common solution. It suggests keeping track of all the actions performed in an application as instances of a command. This command will have forward and reverse actions. Every time a command is processed it is placed onto a queue. When it comes time to undo a command it is as simple as popping the top command off of the command queue and executing the undo action on it.

Design patterns provide some hints about how to solve common problems like the undo problem. They have been distilled from performing hundreds of iterations of solving the same problem. The design pattern may not be exactly the correct solution for the problem you have, but it should, at the very least, provide some guidance to implement a solution more easily.

> A consultant friend of mine once told me a story about starting an assignment at a new company. The manager told them that he didn't think there would be a lot of work to do with the team because they had bought the GoF design pattern book for the developers early on and they'd implemented every last design pattern. My friend was delighted about hearing this because he charges by the hour. The misapplication of design patterns paid for much of his first-born's college education.

Since the GoF book, there has been a great proliferation of literature dealing with enumerating and describing design patterns. There are books on design patterns which are specific to a certain domains and books which deal with patterns for large enterprise systems. The Wikipedia category for software design patterns contains 130 entries for different design patterns. I would, however, argue that many of the entries are not true design patterns but rather programming paradigms.

For the most part, design patterns are simple constructs that don't need complicated support from libraries. While there do exist pattern libraries for most languages, you need not go out and spend a lot of money to purchase the libraries. Implement the patterns as you find the need. Having an expensive library burning a hole in your pocket encourages blindly applying patterns just to justify having spent the money. Even if you did have the money, I'm not aware of any libraries for JavaScript whose sole purpose is to provide support for patterns. Of course, GitHub is a wealth of interesting JavaScript projects, so there may well be a library on there of which I'm unaware.

There are some who suggest that design patterns should be emergent. That is to say, that by simply writing software in an intelligent way, one can see the patterns emerge from the implementation. I think that may be an accurate statement, however, it ignores the actual cost of getting to those implementations by trial and error. Those with an awareness of design patterns are much more likely to spot the emergent pattern early on. Teaching junior programmers about patterns is a very useful exercise. Knowing early on which pattern or patterns can be applied acts as a shortcut. The full solution can be arrived at earlier and with fewer missteps.

# Anti-patterns

If there are common patterns to be found in good software design, are there also patterns that can be found in bad software design? Absolutely! There are any number of ways to do things incorrectly, but most of them have been done before. It takes real creativity to screw up in a hitherto unknown way.

The shame of it is that it is very difficult to remember all the ways in which people have gone wrong over the years. At the end of many major projects, the team will sit down and put together a document called *Lessons Learned*. This document contains a list of things that could have gone better on the project and may even outline some suggestions as to how these issues can be avoided in the future. That these documents are only constructed at the end of a project is unfortunate. By that time, many of the key players have moved on and those who are left must try to remember lessons from the early stages of the project, which could be years ago. It is far better to construct the document as the project progresses.

Once complete, the document is filed away ready for the next project to make use of. At least, that is the theory. For the most part, the document is filed away and never used again. It is difficult to create lessons that are globally applicable. The lessons learned tend to only be useful for the current project or an exactly identical project, which almost never happens.

However, by looking at a number of these documents from various projects, patterns start to emerge. It was by following such an approach that William Brown, Raphael Malveau, Skip McCormick, and Tom Mowbray, collectively known as the Upstart Gang of Four in reference to the original Gang of Four, wrote the initial book on anti-patterns. The book, *AntiPatterns: Refactoring Software, Architectures, and Projects in Crisis*, outlined anti-patterns not just for issues in code, but also in the management process which surrounds code.

Patterns outlined include such humorously named patterns as *The Blob and Lava Flow*. The Blob, also known as the God object, is the pattern where one object grows to take on the responsibility for vast swathes of the application logic. Lava Flow is a pattern that emerges as a project ages and nobody knows if code is still used. Developers are nervous about deleting the code because it might be used somewhere or may become useful again. There are many other patterns described in the book that are worth exploring. Just as with patterns, anti-patterns are emergent from writing code, but in this case, code which gets out of hand.

This book will not cover JavaScript anti-patterns, but it is useful to remember that one of the anti-patterns is an over-application of design patterns.

# Summary

Design patterns have a rich and interesting history. From their origin as tools for helping to describe how to build the structures to allow people to live together, they have grown to be applicable to a number of domains.

It has now been a decade since the seminal work on applying design patterns to programming. Since then, a vast number of new patterns have been developed. Some of these patterns are general-purpose patterns such as those outlined in the GoF book, but a larger number are very specific patterns which are designed for use in a narrow domain.

JavaScript also has an interesting history and is really coming of age. With server-side JavaScript taking off and large JavaScript applications becoming common, there is a need for more diligence in building JavaScript applications. It is rare to see patterns being properly exploited in most modern JavaScript code.

Leaning on the teachings provided by design patterns to build modern JavaScript patterns gives one the best of both worlds. As Isaac Newton famously wrote:

> *"If I have seen further it is by standing on ye shoulders of Giants."*

Patterns give us easily-accessible shoulders on which to stand.

In the next chapter we will look at some techniques for building structure into JavaScript. The inheritance system in JavaScript is unlike that of most other object-oriented languages and that provides us both opportunities and limits. We'll see how to build classes and modules in the JavaScript world.

# Part 1

## Classical Design Patterns

Organizing Code

Creational Patterns

Structural Patterns

Behavioral Patterns

# 2
# Organizing Code

In this chapter we'll look at how to organize JavaScript code into reusable, understandable chunks. The language itself doesn't lend itself well to this sort of modularization but a number of methods of organizing JavaScript code have emerged over the years. This chapter will argue for the need to break down code and then work through the methods of creating JavaScript modules.

We will cover the following topics:

- Global scope
- Objects
- Prototype inheritance
- ECMAScript 2015 classes

## Chunks of code

The first thing anybody learns to program is the ubiquitous Hello World application. This simple application prints some variation of "hello world" to the screen. Depending on who you ask, the phrase hello world dates back to the early 1970s where it was used to demonstrate the B programming language or even to 1967 where it appears in a BCL programming guide. In such a simple application there is no need to worry about the structure of code. Indeed, in many programming languages, hello world needs no structure at all.

For Ruby, it is as follows:

```
#!/usr/bin/ruby
puts "hello world"
```

For JavaScript (via Node.js), it is as follows:

```
#!/usr/local/bin/node
console.log("Hello world")
```

Programming modern computers was originally done using brutally simplistic techniques. Many of the first computers had problems they were attempting to solve hard-wired into them. They were not general purpose computing machines like the ones we have today. Instead they were built to solve just one problem such as decoding encrypted texts. Stored program computers were first developed in the late 1940s.

The languages used to program these computers were complicated at first, usually very closely tied to the binary. Eventually higher and higher-level abstractions were created to make programming more accessible. As these languages started to take shape through the 50s and 60s it quickly became apparent that there needed to be some way to divide up large blocks of code.

In part this was simply to maintain the sanity of programmers who could not keep an entire, large program in their heads at any one time. However, creating reusable modules also allowed for code to be shared within an application and even between applications. The initial solution was to make use of statements, which jumped the flow control of the program from one place to another. For a number of years these GOTO statements were heavily relied upon. To a modern programmer who has been fed a continual stream of warnings about the use of GOTO statements this seems like insanity. However it was not until some years after the first programming languages emerged that structured programming grew to replace the GOTO syntax.

Structured programming is based on the Böhm-Jacopini theorem, which states that there is a rather large class of problems, the answer to which can be computed using three very simple constructs:

- Sequential execution of sub-programs
- Conditional execution of two sub-programs
- Repeated execution of a sub-program until a condition is true

Astute readers will recognize these constructs as being the normal flow of execution, a branch or `if` statement, and a loop.

Fortran was one of the earliest languages and was initially built without support for structured programming. However structured programming was soon adopted as it helped to avoid spaghetti code.

Code in Fortran was organized into modules. Modules were loosely coupled collections of procedures. For those coming from a modern object oriented language, the closest concept might be that a module was like a class that contains only static methods.

Modules were useful for dividing code into logical groupings. However, it didn't provide for any sort of structure for the actual applications. The structure for object-oriented languages, that is classes and subclasses, can be traced to a 1967 paper written by Ole-Johan Dahl and Kristen Nygaard. This paper would go on to form the basis of Simula-67, the first language with support for object oriented programming.

While Simula-67 was the first language to have classes, the language most talked about in relation to early object oriented programming is Smalltalk. This language was developed behind closed doors at the famous Xerox **Palo Alto Research Center (PARC)** during the 1970s. it was released to the public in 1980 as Smalltalk-80 (it seems like all historically relevant programming languages where prefixed with the year of release as a version number). What Smalltalk brought was that everything in the language was an object, even literal numbers like 3 could have operations performed on them.

Almost every modern programming language has some concept of classes to organize code. Often these classes will fall into a higher-level structure commonly called a namespace or module. Through the use of these structures, even very large programs can be divided into manageable and understandable chunks.

Despite the rich history and obvious utility of classes and modules, JavaScript did not support them as first class constructs until just recently. To understand why, one has to simply look back at the history of JavaScript from *Chapter 1*, *Designing For Fun and Profit*, and realize that for its original purpose having such constructs would have been overkill. Classes were a part of the ill-fated ECMAScript 4 standard and they finally became part of the language with the release of the ECMAScript 2015 standard.

In this chapter we'll explore some of the ways to recreate the well worn class structure of other modern programming languages in JavaScript.

# What's the matter with global scope anyway?

In browser based JavaScript every object you create is assigned to the global scope. For the browser, this object is simply known as **window**. It is simple to see this behavior in action by opening up the development console in your favorite browser.

**Opening the Development Console**

Modern browsers have, built into them, some very advanced debugging and auditing tools. To access them there is a menu item, which is located under **Tools | Developer Tools in Chrome | Tools | Web Developer in Firefox**, and directly under the menu as **F12 Developer Tools** in Internet Explorer. Keyboard shortcuts also exist for accessing the tools. On Windows and Linux, *F12* is standard and, on OSX, Option + Command + I is used.

Within the developer tools is a console window that provides direct access to the current page's JavaScript. This is a very handy place to test out small snippets of code or to access the page's JavaScript.

Once you have the console open, enter the following code:

```
> var words = "hello world"
> console.log(window.words);
```

The result of this will be hello world printed to the console. By declaring words globally it is automatically attached to the top level container: window.

In Node.js the situation is somewhat different. Assigning a variable in this fashion will actually attach it to the current module. Not including the var object will attach the variable to the global object.

For years you've likely heard that making use of global variables is a bad thing. This is because globals are very easily polluted by other code.

Consider a very commonly named variable such as index. It is likely that in any application of appreciable size that this variable name would be used in several places. When either piece of code makes use of the variable it will cause unexpected results in the other piece of code. It is certainly possible to reuse variables, and it can even be useful in systems with very limited memory such as embedded systems, but in most applications reusing variables to mean different things within a single scope is difficult to understand and a source of errors.

Applications that make use of global scoped variables also open themselves up to being attacked on purpose by other code. It is trivial to alter the state of global variables from other code, which could expose secrets like login information to attackers.

Finally global variables add a great deal of complexity to applications. Reducing the scope of variables to a small section of code allows developers to more easily understand the ways in which the variable is used. When the scope is global then changes to that variable may have an effect far outside of the one section of code. A simple change to a variable can cascade into the entire application.

As a general rule global variables should be avoided.

# Objects in JavaScript

JavaScript is an object oriented language but most people don't make use of the object oriented features of it except in passing. JavaScript uses a mixed object model in that it has some primitives as well as objects. JavaScript has five primitive types:

- undefined
- null
- boolean
- string
- number

Of these five, only two are what we would expect to be an object anyway. The other three, boolean, string, and number all have wrapped versions, which are objects: Boolean, String, and Number. They are distinguished by starting with uppercase. This is the same sort of model used by Java, a hybrid of objects and primitives.

JavaScript will also box and unbox the primitives as needed.

In this code you can see the boxed and unboxed versions of JavaScript primitives at work:

```
var numberOne = new Number(1);
var numberTwo = 2;
typeof numberOne; //returns 'object'
typeof numberTwo; //returns 'number'
var numberThree = numberOne + numberTwo;
typeof numberThree; //returns 'number'
```

Creating objects in JavaScript is trivial. This can be seen in this code for creating an object in JavaScript:

```
var objectOne = {};
typeof objectOne; //returns 'object'
var objectTwo = new Object();
typeof objectTwo; //returns 'object'
```

Because JavaScript is a dynamic language, adding properties to objects is also quite easy. This can be done even after the object has been created. This code creates the object:

```
var objectOne = { value: 7 };
var objectTwo = {};
objectTwo.value = 7;
```

Objects contain both data and functionality. We've only seen the data part so far. Fortunately in JavaScript, functions are first class objects. Functions can be passed around and functions can be assigned to variables. Let's try adding some functions to the object we're creating in this code:

```
var functionObject = {};
functionObject.doThings = function() {
  console.log("hello world");
}
functionObject.doThings(); //writes "hello world" to the console
```

This syntax is a bit painful, building up objects an assignment at a time. Let's see if we can improve upon the syntax for creating objects:

```
var functionObject = {
  doThings: function() {
    console.log("hello world");
  }
}
functionObject.doThings();//writes "hello world" to the console
```

This syntax seems, at least to me, to be a much cleaner, more traditional way of building objects. Of course it is possible to mix data and functionality in an object in this fashion:

```
var functionObject = {
  greeting: "hello world",
  doThings: function() {
    console.log(this.greeting);
  }
}
functionObject.doThings();//prints hello world
```

There are a couple of things to note in this piece of code. The first is that the different items in the object are separated using a comma and not a semi-colon. Those coming from other languages such as C# or Java are likely to make this mistake.The next item of interest is that we need to make use of the `this` qualifier to address the `greeting` variable from within the `doThings` function. This would also be true if we had a number of functions within the object as shown here:

```
var functionObject = {
  greeting: "hello world",
  doThings: function() {
    console.log(this.greeting);
    this.doOtherThings();
  },
  doOtherThings: function() {
    console.log(this.greeting.split("").reverse().join(""));
  }
}
functionObject.doThings();//prints hello world then dlrow olleh
```

The `this` keyword behaves differently in JavaScript than you might expect coming from other C-syntax languages. `this` is bound to the owner of the function in which it is found. However, the owner of the function is sometimes not what you expect. In the preceding example `this` is bound to the `functionObject` object, however if the function were declared outside of an object this would refer to the global object. In certain circumstances, typically event handlers, this is rebound to the object firing the event.

Let's look at the following code:

```
var target = document.getElementById("someId");
target.addEventListener("click", function() {
  console.log(this);
}, false);
```

`this` takes on the value of target. Getting used to the value of `this` is, perhaps, one of the trickiest things in JavaScript.

ECMAScript-2015 introduces the `let` keyword which can replace the `var` keyword for declaring variables. `let` uses block level scoping which is the scoping you're likely to use from most languages. Let's see an example of how they differ:

```
for(var varScoped =0; varScoped <10; varScoped++)
{
  console.log(varScoped);
}
console.log(varScoped +10);
```

```
for(let letScoped =0; letScoped<10; letScoped++)
{
  console.log(letScoped);
}
console.log(letScoped+10);
```

With the var scoped version you can see that the variable lives on outside of the block. This is because behind the scenes the declaration of varScoped is hoisted to the beginning of the code block. With the let scoped version of the code letScoped is scoped just within the for loop so, once we leave the loop, letScoped is undefined. When given the option of using let or var we would tend to err on the side of always using let. There are some cases when you actually would want to use var scoping but they are few and far between.

We have built up a pretty complete model of how to build objects within JavaScript. However, objects are not the same thing as classes. Objects are instances of classes. If we want to create multiple instances of our functionObject object we're out of luck. Attempting to do so will result in an error. In the case of Node.js the error will be as follows:

```
let obj = new functionObject();
TypeError: object is not a function
  at repl:1:11
  at REPLServer.self.eval (repl.js:110:21)
  at repl.js:249:20
  at REPLServer.self.eval (repl.js:122:7)
  at Interface.<anonymous> (repl.js:239:12)
  at Interface.EventEmitter.emit (events.js:95:17)
  at Interface._onLine (readline.js:202:10)
  at Interface._line (readline.js:531:8)
  at Interface._ttyWrite (readline.js:760:14)
  at ReadStream.onkeypress (readline.js:99:10)
```

The stack trace here shows an error in a module called repl. This is the read-execute-print loop that is loaded by default when starting Node.js.

Each time that a new instance is required, the object must be reconstructed. To get around this we can define the object using a function as can be seen here:

```
let ThingDoer = function(){
  this.greeting = "hello world";
  this.doThings = function() {
    console.log(this.greeting);
    this.doOtherThings();
  };
```

```
      this.doOtherThings = function() {
        console.log(this.greeting.split("").reverse().join(""));
      };
    }
    let instance = new ThingDoer();
    instance.doThings(); //prints hello world then dlrow olleh
```

This syntax allows for a constructor to be defined and for new objects to be created from this function. Constructors without return values are functions that are called as an object is created. In JavaScript the constructor actually returns the object created. You can even assign internal properties using the constructor by making them part of the initial function like so:

```
    let ThingDoer = function(greeting){
      this.greeting = greeting;
      this.doThings = function() {
        console.log(this.greeting);
      };
    }
    let instance = new ThingDoer("hello universe");
    instance.doThings();
```

# Build me a prototype

As previously mentioned, there was, until recently, no support for creating true classes in JavaScript. While ECMAScript-2015 brings some syntactic sugar to classes, the underlying object system is still as it has been in the past, so it remains instructive to see how we would have created objects without this sugar. Objects created using the structure in the previous section have a fairly major drawback: creating multiple objects is not only time consuming but also memory intensive. Each object is completely distinct from other objects created in the same fashion. This means that the memory used to hold the function definitions is not shared between all instances. What is even more fun is that you can redefine individual instances of a class without changing all of the instances. This is demonstrated in this code:

```
    let Castle = function(name){
      this.name = name;
      this.build = function() {
        console.log(this.name);
      };
    }
    let instance1 = new Castle("Winterfell");
    let instance2 = new Castle("Harrenhall");
```

```
instance1.build = function(){ console.log("Moat Cailin");}
instance1.build(); //prints "Moat Cailin"
instance2.build(); //prints "Harrenhall" to the console
```

Altering the functionality of a single instance or really of any already defined object in this fashion is known as **monkey patching**. There is some division over whether or not this is a good practice. It can certainly be useful when dealing with library code but it adds great confusion. It is generally considered better practice to extend the existing class.

Without a proper class system JavaScript, of course, has no concept of inheritance. However, it does have a prototype. At the most basic level an object in JavaScript is an associative array of keys and values. Each property or function on an object is simply defined as part of this array. You can even see this in action by accessing members of an object using array syntax as is shown here:

```
let thing = { a: 7};
console.log(thing["a"]);
```

Accessing members of an object using array syntax can be a very handy way to avoid using the eval function. For instance, if I had the name of the function I wanted to call in a string called funcName and I wanted to call it on an object, obj1, then I could do so by doing obj1[funcName]() instead of using a potentially dangerous call to eval. Eval allows for arbitrary code to be executed. Allowing this on a page means that an attacker may be able to enter malicious scripts on other people's browsers.

When an object is created, its definition is inherited from a prototype. Weirdly each prototype is also an object so even prototypes have prototypes. Well, except for the object which is the top-level prototype. The advantage to attaching functions to the prototype is that only a single copy of the function is created; saving on memory. There are some complexities to prototypes but you can certainly survive without knowing about them. To make use of a prototype you need to simply assign functions to it as is shown here:

```
let Castle = function(name){
  this.name = name;
}
Castle.prototype.build = function(){ console.log(this.name);}
let instance1 = new Castle("Winterfell");
instance1.build();
```

One thing to note is that only the functions are assigned to the prototype. Instance variables such as name are still assigned to the instance. As these are unique to each instance there is no real impact on the memory usage.

In many ways a prototypical language is more powerful than a class-based inheritance model.

If you make a change to the prototype of an object at a later date then all the objects which share that prototype are updated with the new function. This removes some of the concerns expressed about monkey typing. An example of this behavior is shown here:

```
let Castle = function(name){
  this.name = name;
}
Castle.prototype.build = function(){
  console.log(this.name);
}
let instance1 = new Castle("Winterfell");
Castle.prototype.build = function(){
  console.log(this.name.replace("Winterfell", "Moat Cailin"));
}
instance1.build();//prints "Moat Cailin" to the console
```

When building up objects you should be sure to take advantage of the prototype object whenever possible.

Now we know about prototypes there is an alternative approach to building objects in JavaScript and that is to use the Object.create function. This is a new syntax introduced in ECMAScript 5. The syntax is as follows:

```
Object.create(prototype [, propertiesObject ] )
```

The create syntax will build a new object based on the given prototype. You can also pass in a propertiesObject object that describes additional fields on the created object. These descriptors consist of a number of optional fields:

- writable: This dictates whether the field should be writable
- configurable: This dictates whether the files should be removable from the object or support further configuration after creation
- enumerable: This dictates whether the property can be listed during an enumeration of the object's properties
- value: This dictates the default value of the field

It is also possible to assign a `get` and `set` functions within the descriptor that act as getters and setters for some other internal property.

Using `object.create` for our castle we can build an instance using `Object.create` like so:

```
let instance3 = Object.create(Castle.prototype, {name: { value:
"Winterfell", writable: false}});
instance3.build();
instance3.name="Highgarden";
instance3.build();
```

You'll notice that we explicitly define the `name` field. `Object.create` bypasses the constructor so the initial assignment we described in the preceding code won't be called. You might also notice that writeable is set to `false`. The result of this is that the reassignment of `name` to `Highgarden` has no effect. The output is as follows:

```
Winterfell
Winterfell
```

# Inheritance

One of the niceties of objects is that they can be built upon to create increasingly complex objects. This is a common pattern, which is used for any number of things. There is no inheritance in JavaScript because of its prototypical nature. However, you can combine functions from one prototype into another.

Let's say that we have a base class called `Castle` and we want to customize it into a more specific class called `Winterfell`. We can do so by first copying all of the properties from the `Castle` prototype onto the `Winterfell` prototype. This can be done like so:

```
let Castle = function(){};
Castle.prototype.build = function(){console.log("Castle built");}

let Winterfell = function(){};
Winterfell.prototype.build = Castle.prototype.build;
Winterfell.prototype.addGodsWood = function(){}
let winterfell = new Winterfell();
winterfell.build(); //prints "Castle built" to the console
```

Of course this is a very painful way to build objects. You're forced to know exactly which functions the base class has to copy them. It can be abstracted in a rather naïve fashion like this:

```
function clone(source, destination) {
```

```
    for(var attr in source.prototype){ destination.prototype[attr] =
        source.prototype[attr];}
}
```

If you are into object diagrams this shows how **Winterfell** extends **Castle** in this diagram:

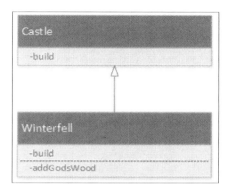

This can be used quite simply as follows:

```
let Castle = function(){};
Castle.prototype.build = function(){console.log("Castle built");}

let Winterfell = function(){};
clone(Castle, Winterfell);
let winterfell = new Winterfell();
winterfell.build();
```

We say that this is naïve because it fails to take into account a number of potential failure conditions. A fully-fledged implementation is quite extensive. The jQuery library provides a function called extend which implements prototype inheritance in a robust fashion. It is about 50 lines long and deals with deep copies and null values. The function is used extensively, internally in jQuery but it can be a very useful function in your own code. We mentioned that prototype inheritance is more powerful than the traditional methods of inheritance. This is because it is possible to mix and match bits from many base classes to create a new class. Most modern languages only support single inheritance: a class can have only one direct parent. There are some languages with multiple inheritance however, it is a practice that adds a great deal of complexity when attempting to decide which version of a method to call at runtime. Prototype inheritance avoids many of these issues by forcing selection of a method at assembly time.

Composing objects in this fashion permits taking properties from two or more different bases. There are many times when this can be useful. For example a class representing a wolf might take some of its properties from a class describing a dog and some from another class describing a quadruped.

By using classes built in this way we can meet pretty much all of the requirements for constructing a system of classes including inheritance. However inheritance is a very strong form of coupling. In almost all cases it is better to avoid inheritance in favor of a looser form of coupling. This will allow for classes to be replaced or altered with a minimum impact on the rest of the system.

# Modules

Now that we have a complete class system it would be good to address the global namespace discussed earlier. Again there is no first class support for namespaces but we can easily isolate functionality to the equivalent of a namespace. There are a number of different approaches to creating modules in JavaScript. We'll start with the simplest and add some functionality as we go along.

To start we simply need to attach an object to the global namespace. This object will contain our root namespace. We'll name our namespace Westeros; the code simply looks like:

```
Westeros = {}
```

This object is, by default, attached to the top level object so we need not do anything more than that. A typical usage is to first check if the object already exists and use that version instead of reassigning the variable. This allows you to spread your definitions over a number of files. In theory you could define a single class in each file and then bring them all together as part of the build process before delivering them to the client or using them in an application. The short form of this is:

```
Westeros = Westeros || {}
```

Once we have the object, it is simply a question of assigning our classes as properties of that object. If we continue to use the Castle object then it would look like:

```
let Westeros = Westeros || {};
Westeros.Castle = function(name){this.name = name}; //constructor
Westeros.Castle.prototype.Build = function(){console.log("Castle
  built: " +  this.name)};
```

If we want to build a hierarchy of namespaces that is more than a single level deep, that too is easily accomplished, as seen in this code:

```
let Westeros = Westeros || {};
Westeros.Structures = Westeros.Structures || {};
Westeros.Structures.Castle = function(name){ this.name = name};
//constructor
Westeros.Structures.Castle.prototype.Build =
    function(){console.log("Castle built: " +  this.name)};
```

This class can be instantiated and used in a similar way to previous examples:

```
let winterfell = new Westeros.Structures.Castle("Winterfell");
winterfell.Build();
```

Of course with JavaScript there is more than one way to build the same code structure. An easy way to structure the preceding code is to make use of the ability to create and immediately execute a function:

```
let Castle = (function () {
  function Castle(name) {
    this.name = name;
  }
  Castle.prototype.Build = function () {
    console.log("Castle built: " + this.name);
  };
  return Castle;
})();
Westros.Structures.Castle = Castle;
```

This code seems to be a bit longer than the previous code sample but I find it easier to follow due to its hierarchical nature. We can create a new castle using them in the same structure as shown in the preceding code:

```
let winterfell = new Westeros.Structures.Castle("Winterfell");
winterfell.Build();
```

Inheritance using this structure is also relatively easily done. If we were to define a BaseStructure class which was to be in the ancestor of all structures, then making use of it would look like this:

```
let BaseStructure = (function () {
  function BaseStructure() {
  }
  return BaseStructure;
})();
Structures.BaseStructure = BaseStructure;
```

```
let Castle = (function (_super) {
  __extends(Castle, _super);
  function Castle(name) {
    this.name = name;
    _super.call(this);
  }
  Castle.prototype.Build = function () {
    console.log("Castle built: " + this.name);
  };
  return Castle;
})(BaseStructure);
```

You'll note that the base structure is passed into the Castle object when the closure is evaluated. The highlighted line of code makes use of a helper method called __extends. This method is responsible for copying the functions over from the base prototype to the derived class. This particular piece of code was generated from a TypeScript compiler which also, helpfully, generated an extends method which looks like:

```
let __extends = this.__extends || function (d, b) {
  for (var p in b) if (b.hasOwnProperty(p)) d[p] = b[p];
  function __() { this.constructor = d; }
  __.prototype = b.prototype;
  d.prototype = new __();
};
```

We can continue the rather nifty closure syntax we've adopted for a class to implement an entire module. This is shown here:

```
var Westeros;
(function (Westeros) {
  (function (Structures) {
    let Castle = (function () {
      function Castle(name) {
        this.name = name;
      }
      Castle.prototype.Build = function () {
        console.log("Castle built " + this.name);
      };
      return Castle;
    })();
    Structures.Castle = Castle;
  })(Westeros.Structures || (Westeros.Structures = {}));
  var Structures = Westeros.Structures;
})(Westeros || (Westeros = {}));
```

Within this structure you can see the same code for creating modules that we explored earlier. It is also relatively easy to define multiple classes inside a single module. This can be seen in this code:

```
var Westeros;
(function (Westeros) {
  (function (Structures) {
    let Castle = (function () {
      function Castle(name) {
        this.name = name;
      }
      Castle.prototype.Build = function () {
        console.log("Castle built: " + this.name);
        var w = new Wall();
      };
      return Castle;
    })();
    Structures.Castle = Castle;
    var Wall = (function () {
      function Wall() {
        console.log("Wall constructed");
      }
      return Wall;
    })();
    Structures.Wall = Wall;
  })(Westeros.Structures || (Westeros.Structures = {}));
  var Structures = Westeros.Structures;
})(Westeros || (Westeros = {}));
```

The highlighted code creates a second class inside of the module. It is also perfectly permissible to define one class in each file. Because the code checks to get the current value of westeros before blindly reassigning it, we can safely split the module definition across multiple files.

The last line of the highlighted section shows exposing the class outside of the closure. If we want to make private classes that are only available within the module then we only need to exclude that line. This is actually known as the revealing module pattern. We only reveal the classes that need to be globally available. It is a good practice to keep as much functionality out of the global namespace as possible.

# ECMAScript 2015 classes and modules

We've seen so far that it is perfectly possible to build classes and even modules in pre ECMAScript -2015 JavaScript. The syntax is, obviously, a bit more involved than in a language such as C# or Java. Fortunately ECMAScript-2015, brings support for some syntactic sugar for making classes:

```
class Castle extends Westeros.Structures.BaseStructure {
  constructor(name, allegience) {
    super(name);
    ...
  }
  Build() {
    ...
    super.Build();
  }
}
```

ECMAScript-2015 also brings a well thought out module system for JavaScript. There's also syntactic sugar for creating modules which looks like this:

```
module 'Westeros' {
  export function Rule(rulerName, house) {
    ...
    return "Long live " + rulerName + " of house " + house;
  }
}
```

As modules can contain functions they can, of course, contain classes. ECMAScript-2015 also defines a module import syntax and support for retrieving modules from remote locations. Importing a module looks like this:

```
import westeros from 'Westeros';
module JSON from 'http://json.org/modules/json2.js';
westeros.Rule("Rob Stark", "Stark");
```

Some of this syntactic sugar is available in any environment which has full ECMAScript-2015 support. At the time of writing, all major browser vendors have very good support for the class portion of ECMAScript-2015 so there is almost no reason not to use it if you don't have to support ancient browsers.

# Best practices and troubleshooting

In an ideal world everybody would get to work on greenfield projects where they can put in standards right from the get go. However that isn't the case. Frequently you may find yourself in a situation where you have a bunch of non-modular JavaScript code as part of a legacy system.

In these situations it may be advantageous to simply ignore the non-modular code until there is an actual need to upgrade it. Despite the popularity of JavaScript, much of the tooling for JavaScript is still immature making it difficult to rely on a compiler to find errors introduced by JavaScript refactoring. Automatic refactoring tools are also complicated by the dynamic nature of JavaScript. However, for new code, proper use of modular JavaScript can be very helpful to avoid namespace conflicts and improve testability.

How to arrange JavaScript is an interesting question. From a web perspective I have taken the approach of arranging my JavaScript in line with the web pages. So each page has an associated JavaScript file, which is responsible for the functionality of that page. In addition, components which are common between pages, say a grid control, are placed into a separate file. At compile time all the files are combined into a single JavaScript file. This helps strike a balance between having a small code file with which to work and reducing the number of requests to the server from the browser.

# Summary

It has been said that there are only two really hard things in computing science. What those issues are varies depending on who is speaking. Frequently it is some variation of cache invalidation and naming. How to organize your code is a large part of that naming problem.

As a group we seem to have settled quite firmly on the idea of namespaces and classes. As we've seen, there is no direct support for either of these two concepts in JavaScript. However there are myriad ways to work around the problem, some of which actually provide more power than one would get through a traditional namespace/class system.

The primary concern with JavaScript is to avoid polluting the global namespace with a large number of similarly named, unconnected objects. Encapsulating JavaScript into modules is a key step on the road toward writing maintainable and reusable code.

As we move forward we'll see that many of the patterns which are quite complex arrangements of interfaces become far simpler in the land of JavaScript. Prototype-based inheritance, which seems difficult at the outset, is a tremendous tool for aiding in the simplification of design patterns.

# 3
# Creational Patterns

In the last chapter we took a long look at how to fashion a class. In this chapter we'll look at how to create instances of classes. On the surface it seems like a simple concern but how we create instances of a class can be of great importance.

We take great pains in creating our code so that it be as decoupled as possible. Ensuring that classes have minimal dependence on other classes is the key to building a system that can change fluently with the changing needs of those using the software. Allowing classes to be too closely related means that changes ripple through them like, well, ripples.

One ripple isn't a huge problem but, as you throw more and more changes into the mix, the ripples add up and create interference patterns. Soon the once placid surface is an unrecognizable mess of additive and destructive nodes. This same problem occurs in our applications: the changes magnify and interact in unexpected ways. One place where we tend to forget about coupling is in the creation of objects:

```
let Westeros;
(function (Westeros) {
  let Ruler = (function () {
    function Ruler() {
      this.house = new Westeros.Houses.Targaryen();
    }
    return Ruler;
  })();
  Westeros.Ruler = Ruler;
})(Westeros || (Westeros = {}));
```

You can see in this class that the Ruler's house is strongly coupled to the class `Targaryen`. If this were ever to change then this tight coupling would have to change in a great number of places. This chapter discusses a number of patterns, which were originally presented in the gang of four book, *Design Patterns: Elements of Reusable Object-Oriented Software*. The goal of these patterns is to improve the degree of coupling in applications and increase the opportunities for code reuse. The patterns are as follows:

- Abstract factory
- Builder
- Factory method
- Singleton
- Prototype

Of course not all of these are applicable to JavaScript, but we'll see all about that as we work through the creational patterns.

# Abstract factory

The first pattern presented here is a method for creating kits of objects without knowing the concrete types of the objects. Let's continue with the system presented in the preceding section for ruling a kingdom.

For the kingdom in question the ruling house changes with some degree of frequency. In all likelihood there is a degree of battling and fighting during the change of house but we'll ignore that for the moment. Each house will rule the kingdom differently. Some value peace and tranquility and rule as benevolent leaders, while others rule with an iron fist. The rule of a kingdom is too large for a single individual so the king defers some of his decisions to a second in command known as the hand of the king. The king is also advised on matters by a council, which consists of some of the more savvy lords and ladies of the land.

A diagram of the classes in our description look like this:

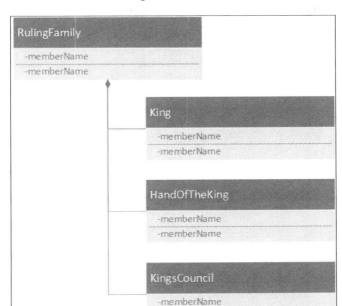

**Unified Modeling Language (UML)** is a standardized language developed by the Object Management Group, which describes computer systems. There is vocabulary in the language for creating user interaction diagrams, sequence diagrams, and state machines, amongst others. For the purposes of this book we're most interested in class diagrams, which describe the relationship between a set of classes.

The entire UML class diagram vocabulary is extensive and is beyond the scope of this book. However, the Wikipedia article available at `https://en.wikipedia.org/wiki/Class_diagram` acts as a great introduction as does Derek Banas' excellent video tutorial on class diagrams available at `https://www.youtube.com/watch?v=3cmzqZzwNDM`.

An issue is that, with the ruling family, and even the member of the ruling family on the throne, changing so frequently, coupling to a concrete family such as Targaryen or Lannister makes our application brittle. Brittle applications do not fare well in an ever-changing world.

An approach to fixing this is to make use of the abstract factory pattern. The abstract factory declares an interface for creating each of the various classes related to the ruling family.

The class diagram of this pattern is rather daunting:

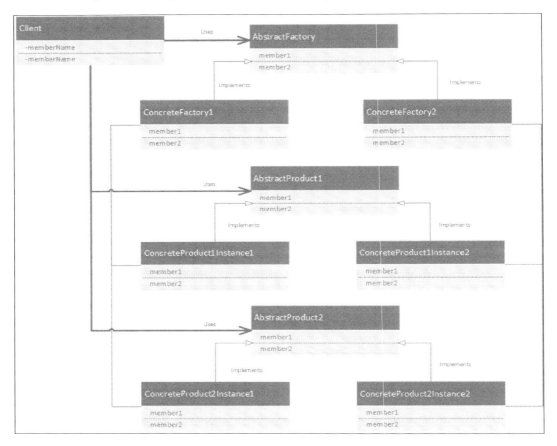

The abstract factory class may have multiple implementations for each of the various ruling families. These are known as concrete factories and each of them will implement the interface provided by the abstract factory. The concrete factories, in return, will return concrete implementations of the various ruling classes. These concrete classes are known as products.

Let's start by looking at the code for the interface for the abstract factory.

No code? Well, actually that is exactly the case. JavaScript's dynamic nature precludes the need for interfaces to describe classes. Instead of having interfaces we'll just create the classes right off the bat:

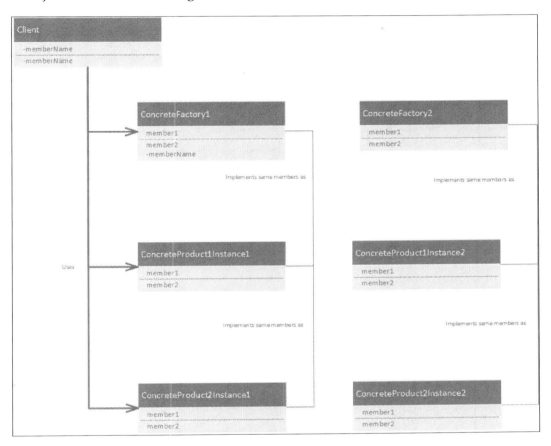

Instead of interfaces, JavaScript trusts that the class you provide implements all the appropriate methods. At runtime the interpreter will attempt to call the method you request and, if it is found, call it. The interpreter simply assumes that if your class implements the method then it is that class. This is known as **duck typing**.

**Duck typing**

The name duck typing comes from a 2000 post to the *comp.lang.python* news group by Alex Martelli in which he wrote:

*In other words, don't check whether it IS-a duck: check whether it QUACKS-like-a duck, WALKS-like-a duck, and so on, depending on exactly what subset of duck-like behavior you need to play your language-games with.*

I enjoy the possibility that Martelli took the term from the witch-hunt sketch from *Monty Python and the Holy Grail*. Although I can find no evidence of that, I think it quite likely as the Python programming language takes its name from Monty Python.

Duck typing is a powerful tool in dynamic languages allowing for much less overhead in implementing a class hierarchy. It does, however, introduce some uncertainty. If two classes implement an identically named method which have radically different meanings then there is no way to know if the one being called is the correct one. Consider for example this code:

```
class Boxer{
  function punch(){}
}
class TicketMachine{
  function punch(){}
}
```

Both classes have a punch() method but they clearly have different meanings. The JavaScript interpreter has no idea that they are different classes and will happily call punch on either class, even when one doesn't make sense.

Some dynamic languages support a generic method, which is called whenever an undefined method is called. Ruby, for instance, has missing_method, which has proven to be very useful in a number of scenarios. As of writing, there is currently no support for missing_method in JavaScript. However, ECMAScript 2016, the follow up to ECMAScript 2015, defines a new construct called Proxy which will support dynamically wrapping objects, with this one could implement an equivalent of missing_method.

# Implementation

To demonstrate an implementation of the Abstract Factory the first thing we'll need is an implementation of the King class. This code provides that implementation:

```
let KingJoffery= (function () {
  function KingJoffery() {
```

```
  }
  KingJoffery.prototype.makeDecision = function () {
    ...
  };
  KingJoffery.prototype.marry = function () {
    ...
  };
  return KingJoffery;
})();
```

This code does not include the module structure suggested in *Chapter 2, Organizing Code*. Including the boiler-plate module code in every example is tedious and you're all smart cookies so you know to put this in modules if you're going to actually use it. The fully modularized code is available in the distributed source code.

This is just a regular concrete class and could really contain any implementation details. We'll also need an implementation of the HandOfTheKing class which is equally unexciting:

```
let LordTywin = (function () {
  function LordTywin() {
  }
  LordTywin.prototype.makeDecision = function () {
  };
  return LordTywin;
})();
```

The concrete factory method looks like this:

```
let LannisterFactory = (function () {
  function LannisterFactory() {
  }
  LannisterFactory.prototype.getKing = function () {
    return new KingJoffery();
  };
  LannisterFactory.prototype.getHandOfTheKing = function ()
  {
    return new LordTywin();
  };
  return LannisterFactory;
})();
```

This code simply instantiates new instances of each of the required classes and returns them. An alternative implementation for a different ruling family would follow the same general form and might look like:

```
let TargaryenFactory = (function () {
  function TargaryenFactory() {
  }
  TargaryenFactory.prototype.getKing = function () {
    return new KingAerys();
  };
  TargaryenFactory.prototype.getHandOfTheKing = function () {
    return new LordConnington();
  };
  return TargaryenFactory;
})();
```

The implementation of the Abstract Factory in JavaScript is much easier than in other languages. However the penalty for this is that you lose the compiler checks, which force a full implementation of either the factory or the products. As we proceed through the rest of the patterns, you'll notice that this is a common theme. Patterns that have a great deal of plumbing in statically typed languages are far simpler but create a greater risk of runtime failure. Appropriate unit tests or a JavaScript compiler can ameliorate this situation.

To make use of the Abstract Factory we'll first need a class that requires the use of some ruling family:

```
let CourtSession = (function () {
  function CourtSession(abstractFactory) {
    this.abstractFactory = abstractFactory;
    this.COMPLAINT_THRESHOLD = 10;
  }
  CourtSession.prototype.complaintPresented = function (complaint)
  {
    if (complaint.severity < this.COMPLAINT_THRESHOLD) {
      this.abstractFactory.getHandOfTheKing().makeDecision();
    } else
    this.abstractFactory.getKing().makeDecision();
  };
  return CourtSession;
})();
```

We can now call this `CourtSession` class and inject different functionality depending on which factory we pass in:

```
let courtSession1 = new CourtSession(new TargaryenFactory());
courtSession1.complaintPresented({ severity: 8 });
courtSession1.complaintPresented({ severity: 12 });

let courtSession2 = new CourtSession(new LannisterFactory());
courtSession2.complaintPresented({ severity: 8 });
courtSession2.complaintPresented({ severity: 12 });
```

Despite the differences between a static language and JavaScript, this pattern remains applicable and useful in JavaScript applications. Creating a kit of objects, which work together, is useful in a number of situations; any time a group of objects need to collaborate to provide functionality but may need to be replaced wholesale. It may also be a useful pattern when attempting to ensure that a set of objects be used together without substitutions.

# Builder

In our fictional world we sometimes have some rather complicated classes, which need to be constructed. The classes contain different implementations of an interface depending on how they are constructed. In order to simplify the building of these classes and encapsulate the knowledge about building the class away from the consumers, a builder may be used. Multiple concrete builders reduce the complexity of the constructor in the implementation. When new builders are required, a constructor does not need to be added, a new builder just needs to be plugged in.

Tournaments are an example of a complicated class. Each tournament has a complicated setup involving the events, the attendees, and the prizes. Much of the setup for these tournaments is similar: each one has a joust, archery, and a melee. Creating a tournament from multiple places in the code means that the responsibility for knowing how to construct a tournament is distributed. If there is a need to change the initiation code then it must be done in a lot of different places.

Employing a builder pattern avoids this issue by centralizing the logic necessary to build the object. Different concrete builders can be plugged into the builder to construct different complicated objects. The relationship between the various classes in the builder pattern is shown here:

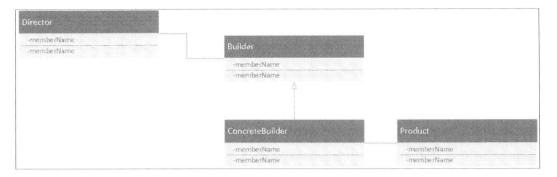

# Implementation

Let's drop in and look at some of the code. To start with, we'll create a number of utility classes, which will represent the parts of a tournament as shown in the following code:

```
let Event = (function () {
  function Event(name) {
    this.name = name;
  }
  return Event;
})();
Westeros.Event = Event;

let Prize = (function () {
  function Prize(name) {
    this.name = name;
  }
  return Prize;
})();
Westeros.Prize = Prize;

let Attendee = (function () {
  function Attendee(name) {
    this.name = name;
  }
  return Attendee;
})();
Westeros.Attendee = Attendee;
```

The tournament itself is a very simple class as we don't need to assign any of the public properties explicitly:

```
let Tournament = (function () {
  this.Events = [];
  function Tournament() {
  }
  return Tournament;
})();
Westeros.Tournament = Tournament;
```

We'll implement two builders which create different tournaments. This can be seen in the following code:

```
let LannisterTournamentBuilder = (function () {
  function LannisterTournamentBuilder() {
  }
  LannisterTournamentBuilder.prototype.build = function () {
    var tournament = new Tournament();
    tournament.events.push(new Event("Joust"));
    tournament.events.push(new Event("Melee"));
    tournament.attendees.push(new Attendee("Jamie"));
    tournament.prizes.push(new Prize("Gold"));
    tournament.prizes.push(new Prize("More Gold"));
    return tournament;
  };
  return LannisterTournamentBuilder;
})();
Westeros.LannisterTournamentBuilder = LannisterTournamentBuilder;

let BaratheonTournamentBuilder = (function () {
  function BaratheonTournamentBuilder() {
  }
  BaratheonTournamentBuilder.prototype.build = function () {
    let tournament = new Tournament();
    tournament.events.push(new Event("Joust"));
    tournament.events.push(new Event("Melee"));
    tournament.attendees.push(new Attendee("Stannis"));
    tournament.attendees.push(new Attendee("Robert"));
    return tournament;
  };
  return BaratheonTournamentBuilder;
})();
Westeros.BaratheonTournamentBuilder = BaratheonTournamentBuilder;
```

Finally the director, or as we're calling it `TournamentBuilder`, simply takes a builder and executes it:

```
let TournamentBuilder = (function () {
  function TournamentBuilder() {
  }
  TournamentBuilder.prototype.build = function (builder) {
    return builder.build();
  };
  return TournamentBuilder;
})();
Westeros.TournamentBuilder = TournamentBuilder;
```

Again you'll see that the JavaScript implementation is far simpler than the traditional implementation due to there being no need for interfaces.

Builders need not return a fully realized object. This means that you can create a builder which partially hydrates an object then allows the object to be passed on to another builder for it to finish. A good real world analogy might be the manufacturing process for a car. Each station along the assembly line builds just a part of the car before passing it onto the next station to build another part. This approach allows for dividing the work of building an object amongst several classes with limited responsibility. In our example above we could have a builder that is responsible for populating the events and another that is responsible for populating the attendees.

Does the builder pattern still make sense in view of JavaScript's prototype extension model? I believe so. There are still cases where a complicated object needs to be created according to different approaches.

# Factory method

We've already looked at the Abstract Factory and a builder. The Abstract Factory builds a family of related classes and the builder creates complicated objects using different strategies. The factory method pattern allows a class to request a new instance of an interface without the class making decisions about which implementation of the interface to use. The factory may use some strategy to select which implementation to return:

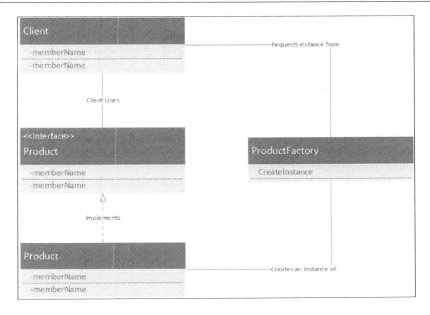

Sometimes this strategy is simply to take a string parameter or to examine some global setting to act as a switch.

# Implementation

In our example world of Westeros there are plenty of times when we would like to defer the choice of implementation to a factory. Just like the real world, Westeros has a vibrant religious culture with dozens of competing religions worshiping a wide variety of gods. When praying in each religion, different rules must be followed. Some religions demand sacrifices while others demand only that a gift be given. The prayer class doesn't want to know about all the different religions and how to construct them.

Let's start with creating a number of different gods to which prayers can be offered. This code creates three gods including a default god to whom prayers fall if no other god is specified:

```
let WateryGod = (function () {
  function WateryGod() {
  }
  WateryGod.prototype.prayTo = function () {
  };
  return WateryGod;
})();
```

```
    Religion.WateryGod = WateryGod;
    let AncientGods = (function () {
      function AncientGods() {
      }
      AncientGods.prototype.prayTo = function () {
      };
      return AncientGods;
    })();
    Religion.AncientGods = AncientGods;

    let DefaultGod = (function () {
      function DefaultGod() {
      }
      DefaultGod.prototype.prayTo = function () {
      };
      return DefaultGod;
    })();
    Religion.DefaultGod = DefaultGod;
```

I've avoided any sort of implementation details for each god. You may imagine whatever traditions you want to populate the prayTo methods. There is also no need to ensure that each of the gods implements an IGod interface. Next we'll need a factory, which is responsible for constructing each of the different gods:

```
    let GodFactory = (function () {
      function GodFactory() {
      }
      GodFactory.Build = function (godName) {
        if (godName === "watery")
          return new WateryGod();
        if (godName === "ancient")
          return new AncientGods();
        return new DefaultGod();
      };
      return GodFactory;
    })();
```

You can see that in this example we're taking in a simple string to decide how to create a god. It could be done via a global or via a more complicated object. In some polytheistic religions in Westeros, gods have defined roles as gods of courage, beauty, or some other aspect. The god to which one must pray is determined by not just the religion but the purpose of the prayer. We can represent this with a GodDeterminant class as is shown here:

```
    let GodDeterminant = (function () {
      function GodDeterminant(religionName, prayerPurpose) {
```

```
    this.religionName = religionName;
    this.prayerPurpose = prayerPurpose;
  }
  return GodDeterminant;
})();
```

The factory would be updated to take this class instead of the simple string.

Finally, the last step is to see how this factory would be used. It is quite simple, we just need to pass in a string that denotes which religion we wish to observe and the factory will construct the correct god and return it. This code demonstrates how to call the factory:

```
let Prayer = (function () {
  function Prayer() {
  }
  Prayer.prototype.pray = function (godName) {
  GodFactory.Build(godName).prayTo();
  };
  return Prayer;
})();
```

Once again there is certainly need for a pattern such as this in JavaScript. There are plenty of times where separating the instantiation from the use is useful. Testing the instantiation is also very simple thanks to the separation of concerns and the ability to inject a fake factory to allow testing of `Prayer` is also easy.

Continuing the trend of creating simpler patterns without interfaces, we can ignore the interface portion of the pattern and work directly with the types, thanks to duck typing.

Factory Method is a very useful pattern: it allows classes to defer the selection of the implementation of an instantiation to another class. This pattern is very useful when there are multiple similar implementations such as the strategy pattern (see *Chapter 5, Behavioral Patterns*) and is commonly used in conjunction with the Abstract Factory pattern. The Factory Method is used to build the concrete objects within a concrete implementation of the abstract factory. An Abstract Factory pattern may contain a number of Factory Methods. Factory Method is certainly a pattern that remains applicable in the land of JavaScript.

# Singleton

The Singleton pattern is perhaps the most overused pattern. It is also a pattern that has fallen out of favor in recent years. To see why people are starting to advise against using Singleton let's take a look at how the pattern works.

Singleton is used when a global variable is desirable, but Singleton provides protection against accidentally creating multiple copies of complex objects. It also allows for the deferral of object instantiation until the first use.

The UML diagram for Singleton looks like the following:

It is clearly a very simple pattern. The Singleton acts as a wrapper around an instance of the class and the singleton itself lives as a global variable. When accessing the instance we simply ask the Singleton for the current instance of the wrapped class. If the class does not yet exist within the Singleton it is common to create a new instance at that time.

# Implementation

Within our ongoing example in the world of Westeros, we need to find a case where there can only ever be one of something. Unfortunately, it is a land with frequent conflicts and rivalries, and so my first idea of using the king as the Singleton is simply not going to fly. This split also means that we cannot make use of any of the other obvious candidates (capital city, queen, general, and so on). However, in the far north of Westeros there is a giant wall constructed to keep an ancient enemy at bay. There is only one of these walls and it should pose no issue having it in the global scope.

Let's go ahead and create a singleton in JavaScript:

```javascript
let Westros;
(function (Westeros) {
  var Wall = (function () {
    function Wall() {
      this.height = 0;
      if (Wall._instance)
        return Wall._instance;
      Wall._instance = this;
    }
```

```
      Wall.prototype.setHeight = function (height) {
        this.height = height;
      };
      Wall.prototype.getStatus = function () {
        console.log("Wall is " + this.height + " meters tall");
      };
      Wall.getInstance = function () {
        if (!Wall._instance) {
          Wall._instance = new Wall();
        }
        return Wall._instance;
      };
      Wall._instance = null;
      return Wall;
    })();
    Westeros.Wall = Wall;
  })(Westeros || (Westeros = {}));
```

The code creates a lightweight representation of the Wall. The Singleton is demonstrated in the two highlighted sections. In a language like C# or Java we would normally just set the constructor to be private so that it could only be called by the static method getInstance. However, we don't have that ability in JavaScript: constructors cannot be private. Thus we do the best we can and return the current instance from the constructor. This may appear strange but in the way we've constructed our classes the constructor is no different from any other method so it is possible to return something from it.

In the second highlighted section we set a static variable, _instance, to be a new instance of the Wall when one is not already there. If that _instance already exists, we return that. In C# and Java, there would need to be some complicated locking logic in this function to avoid race conditions as two different threads attempted to access the instance at the same time. Fortunately, there is no need to worry about this in JavaScript where the multi-threading story is different.

# Disadvantages

Singletons have gained something of a bad reputation in the last few years. They are, in effect, glorified global variables. As we've discussed, global variables are ill conceived and the potential cause of numerous bugs. They are also difficult to test with unit tests as the creation of the instance cannot easily be overridden and any form of parallelism in the test runner can introduce difficult-to-diagnose race conditions. The single largest concern I have with them is that singletons have too much responsibility. They control not just themselves but also their instantiation. This is a clear violation of the single responsibility principle. Almost every problem that can be solved by using a Singleton is better solved using some other mechanism.

JavaScript makes the problem even worse. It isn't possible to create a clean implementation of the Singleton due to the restrictions on the constructor. This, coupled with the general problems around the Singleton, lead me to suggest that the Singleton pattern should be avoided in JavaScript.

# Prototype

The final creational pattern in this chapter is the Prototype pattern. Perhaps this name sounds familiar. It certainly should: it is the mechanism through which JavaScript inheritance is supported.

We looked at prototypes for inheritance but the applicability of prototypes need not be limited to inheritance. Copying existing objects can be a very useful pattern. There are numerous cases where being able to duplicate a constructed object is handy. For instance, maintaining a history of the state of an object is easily done by saving previous instances created by leveraging some sort of cloning.

# Implementation

In Westeros, we find that members of a family are frequently very similar; as the adage goes: "like father, like son". As each generation is born it is easier to create the new generation through copying and modifying an existing family member than to build one from scratch.

In *Chapter 2, Organizing Code*, we looked at how to copy existing objects and presented a very simple piece of code for cloning:

```
function clone(source, destination) {
  for(var attr in source.prototype){
    destination.prototype[attr] = source.prototype[attr];}
}
```

This code can easily be altered to be used inside a class to return a copy of itself:

```
var Westeros;
(function (Westeros) {
  (function (Families) {
    var Lannister = (function () {
      function Lannister() {
      }
      Lannister.prototype.clone = function () {
        var clone = new Lannister();
        for (var attr in this) {
          clone[attr] = this[attr];
```

```
    }
    return clone;
  };
  return Lannister;
})();
Families.Lannister = Lannister;
})(Westeros.Families || (Westeros.Families = {}));
var Families = Westeros.Families;
})(Westeros || (Westeros = {}));
```

The highlighted section of code is the modified clone method. It can be used as such:

```
let jamie = new Westeros.Families.Lannister();
jamie.swordSkills = 9;
jamie.charm = 6;
jamie.wealth = 10;

let tyrion = jamie.clone();
tyrion.charm = 10;
//tyrion.wealth == 10
//tyrion.swordSkill == 9
```

The Prototype pattern allows for a complex object to be constructed only once and then cloned into any number of objects that vary only slightly. If the source object is not complicated there is little to be gained from taking a cloning approach. Care must be taken when using the prototype approach to think about dependent objects. Should the clone be a deep one?

Prototype is obviously a useful pattern and one that forms an integral part of JavaScript from the get go. As such it is certainly a pattern that will see some use in any JavaScript application of appreciable size.

# Tips and tricks

Creational patterns allow for specialized behavior in creating objects. In many cases, such as the factory, they provide extension points into which crosscutting logic can be placed. That is to say logic that applies to a number of different types of objects. If you're looking for a way to inject, say, logging throughout your application, then being able to hook into a factory is of great utility.

For all the utility of these creational patterns they should not be used very frequently. The vast majority of your object instantiations should still be just the normal method of improving the objects. Although it is tempting to treat everything as a nail when you've got a new hammer, the truth is that each situation needs to have a specific strategy. All these patterns are more complicated than simply using new and complicated code is more liable to have bugs than simple code. Use new whenever possible.

# Summary

This chapter presented a number of different strategies for creating objects. These methods provide abstractions over the top of typical methods for creating objects. The Abstract Factory provides a method for building interchangeable kits or collections of related objects. The Builder pattern provides a solution to telescoping parameters issues. It makes the construction of large complicated objects easier. The Factory Method, which is a useful complement to Abstract Factory, allows different implementations to be created though a static factory. Singleton is a pattern for providing a single copy of a class that is available to the entire solution. It is the only pattern we've seen so far which has presented some questions around applicability in modern software. The Prototype pattern is a commonly used pattern in JavaScript for building objects based on other existing objects.

We'll continue our examination of classical design patterns in the next chapter by looking at structural patterns.

# 4
# Structural Patterns

In the previous chapter, we looked at a number of ways to create objects in order to optimize for reuse. In this chapter, we'll take a look at structural patterns; these are patterns that are concerned with easing the design by describing simple ways in which objects can interact.

Again, we will limit ourselves to the patterns described in the GoF book. There are a number of other interesting structural patterns that have been identified since the publication of the GoF and we'll look at those in part 2 of the book.

The patterns we'll examine here are:

- Adapter
- Bridge
- Composite
- Decorator
- Façade
- Flyweight
- Proxy

Once again, we'll discuss whether the patterns that were described years ago are still relevant for a different language and a different time.

# Adapter

From time to time there is a need to fit a round peg in a square hole. If you've ever played with a child's shape sorting toy then you may have discovered that you can, in fact, put a round peg in a square hole. The hole is not completely filled and getting the peg in there can be difficult:

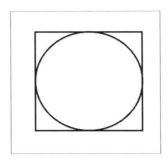

To improve the fit of the peg an adapter can be used. This adapter fills the hole in completely resulting in a perfect fit:

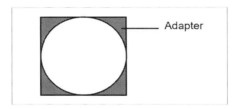

In software a similar approach is often needed. We may need to make use of a class that does not perfectly fit the required interface. The class may be missing methods or may have additional methods we would like to hide. This occurs frequently when dealing with third party code. In order to make it comply with the interface needed in your code, an adapter may be required.

The class diagram for an adapter is very simple as can be seen here:

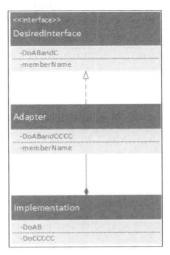

The interface of the implementation does not look the way we would like it to for use in our code. Normally the solution to this is to simply refactor the implementation so it looks the way we would like it to. However, there are a number of possible reasons that cannot be done. Perhaps the implementation exists inside third party code to which we have no access. It is also possible that the implementation is used elsewhere in the application where the interface is exactly as we would like it to be.

The adapter class is a thin piece of code that implements the required interface. It typically wraps a private copy of the implementation class and proxy calls through to it. The adapter pattern is frequently used to change the abstraction level of the code. Let's take a look at a quick example.

# Implementation

In the land of Westeros, much of the trade and travel is done by boat. It is not only more dangerous to travel by ship than to walk or travel by horse, but also riskier due to the constant presence of storms and pirates. These ships are not the sort which might be used by Royal Caribbean to cruise around the Caribbean; they are crude things which might look more at home captained by 15th century European explorers.

While I am aware that ships exist, I have very little knowledge of how they work or how I might go about navigating one. I imagine that many people are in the same (*cough!*) boat as me. If we look at the interface for a Ship in Westeros, it looks intimidating:

```
interface Ship{
  SetRudderAngleTo(angle: number);
  SetSailConfiguration(configuration: SailConfiguration);
  SetSailAngle(sailId: number, sailAngle: number);
  GetCurrentBearing(): number;
  GetCurrentSpeedEstimate(): number;
  ShiftCrewWeightTo(weightToShift: number, locationId: number);
}
```

I would really like a much simpler interface that abstracts away all the fiddly little details. Ideally something like the following:

```
interface SimpleShip{
  TurnLeft();
  TurnRight();
  GoForward();
}
```

This looks like something I could probably figure out even living in a city that is over 1000 kilometers from the nearest ocean. In short, what I'm looking for is a higher-level abstraction around the Ship. In order to transform a Ship into a SimpleShip we need an adapter.

The adapter will have the interface of SimpleShip but it will perform actions on a wrapped instance of Ship. The code might look something like this:

```
let ShipAdapter = (function () {
  function ShipAdapter() {
    this._ship = new Ship();
  }
  ShipAdapter.prototype.TurnLeft = function () {
    this._ship.SetRudderAngleTo(-30);
    this._ship.SetSailAngle(3, 12);
  };
  ShipAdapter.prototype.TurnRight = function () {
    this._ship.SetRudderAngleTo(30);
    this._ship.SetSailAngle(5, -9);
  };
  ShipAdapter.prototype.GoForward = function () {
```

```
    //do something else to the _ship
  };
  return ShipAdapter;
})();
```

In reality these functions would be far more complex, but it should not matter much because we've got a nice simple interface to present to the world. The presented interface can also be set up so as to restrict access to certain methods on the underlying type. When building library code, adapters can be used to mask the internal method and only present the limited functions needed to the end user.

To use this pattern, the code might look like:

```
var ship = new ShipAdapter();
ship.GoForward();
ship.TurnLeft();
```

You would likely not want to use adapter in the name of your client class as it leaks some information about the underlying implementation. Clients should be unaware they are talking to an adapter.

The adapter itself can grow to be quite complex to adjust one interface to another. In order to avoid creating very complex adapters, care must be taken. It is certainly not inconceivable to build several adapters, one atop another. If you find an adapter becoming too large then it is a good idea to stop and examine if the adapter is following the single responsibility principle. That is to say, ensure that each class has only one thing for which it has some responsibility. A class that looks up users from a database should not also contain functionality for sending e-mails to these users. That is too much responsibility. Complex adapters can be replaced with a composite object, which will be explored later in this chapter.

From the testing perspective, adapters can be used to totally wrap third party dependencies. In this scenario they provide a place into which to hook tests. Unit tests should avoid testing libraries but they can certainly test the adapters to ensure that they are proxying through the correct calls.

The adapter is a very powerful pattern for simplifying code interfaces. Massaging interfaces to better match a requirement is useful in countless places. The pattern is certainly useful in JavaScript. Applications written in JavaScript tend to make use of a large number of small libraries. By wrapping up these libraries in adapters I'm able to limit the number of places I interact with the libraries directly; this means that the libraries can easily be replaced.

The adapter pattern can be slightly modified to provide consistent interfaces over a number of different implementations. This is usually known as the bridge pattern.

# Bridge

The bridge pattern takes the adapter pattern to a new level. Given an interface, we can build multiple adapters, each one of which acts as an intermediary to a different implementation.

An excellent example that I've run across, is dealing with two different services that provide more or less the same functionality and are used in a failover configuration. Neither service provides exactly the interface required by the application and both services provide different APIs. In order to simplify the code, adapters are written to provide a consistent interface. The adapters implement a consistent interface and provide fills so that each API can be called consistently. To expand on the shape sorter metaphor a bit more, we can imagine that we have a variety of different pegs we would like to use to fill the square hole. Each adapter fills in the missing bits and helps us get a good fit:

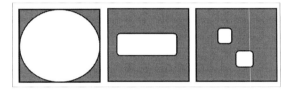

The bridge is a very useful pattern. Let's take a look at how to implement it:

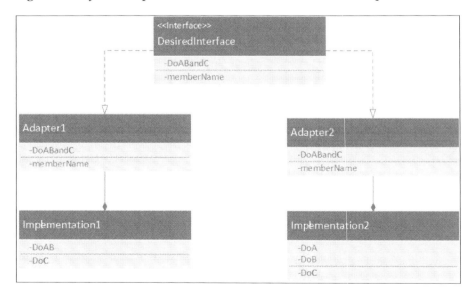

The adapters shown in the preceding diagram sit between the implementation and the desired interface. They modify the implementation to fit in with the desired interface.

# Implementation

We've already discussed that in the land of Westeros the people practice a number of disparate religions. Each one has a different way of praying and making offerings. There is a lot of complexity around making the correct prayers at the correct time and we would like to avoid exposing this complexity. Instead we'll write a series of adapters that can simplify prayers.

The first thing we need is a number of different gods to which we can pray:

```
class OldGods {
  prayTo(sacrifice) {
    console.log("We Old Gods hear your prayer");
  }
}
Religion.OldGods = OldGods;
class DrownedGod {
  prayTo(humanSacrifice) {
    console.log("*BUBBLE* GURGLE");
  }
}
Religion.DrownedGod = DrownedGod;
class SevenGods {
  prayTo(prayerPurpose) {
    console.log("Sorry there are a lot of us, it gets confusing
      here. Did you pray for something?");
  }
}
Religion.SevenGods = SevenGods;
```

These classes should look familiar as they are basically the same classes found in the previous chapter where they were used as examples for the factory method. You may notice, however, that the signature for the prayTo method for each religion is slightly different. This proves to be something of an issue when building a consistent interface like the one shown in pseudo code here:

```
interface God
{
  prayTo():void;
}
```

So let's slot in a few adapters to act as a bridge between the classes we have and the signature we would like the following:

```
class OldGodsAdapter {
  constructor() {
    this._oldGods = new OldGods();
  }
  prayTo() {
    let sacrifice = new Sacrifice();
    this._oldGods.prayTo(sacrifice);
  }
}
Religion.OldGodsAdapter = OldGodsAdapter;
class DrownedGodAdapter {
  constructor() {
    this._drownedGod = new DrownedGod();
  }
  prayTo() {
    let sacrifice = new HumanSacrifice();
    this._drownedGod.prayTo(sacrifice);
  }
}
Religion.DrownedGodAdapter = DrownedGodAdapter;
class SevenGodsAdapter {
  constructor() {
    this.prayerPurposeProvider = new PrayerPurposeProvider();
    this._sevenGods = new SevenGods();
  }
  prayTo() {
    this._sevenGods.prayTo(this.prayerPurposeProvider.GetPurpose());
  }
}
Religion.SevenGodsAdapter = SevenGodsAdapter;
class PrayerPurposeProvider {
  GetPurpose() { }
  }
Religion.PrayerPurposeProvider = PrayerPurposeProvider;
```

Each one of these adapters implements the God interface we wanted and abstracts away the complexity of dealing with three different interfaces, one for each god:

To use the Bridge pattern, we could write code like so:

```
let god1 = new Religion.SevenGodsAdapter();
let god2 = new Religion.DrownedGodAdapter();
```

```
let god3 = new Religion.OldGodsAdapter();

let gods = [god1, god2, god3];
for(let i =0; i<gods.length; i++){
  gods[i].praryTo();
}
```

This code uses the bridges to provide a consistent interface to the gods such that they can all be treated as equals.

In this case we are simply wrapping the individual gods and proxying method calls through to them. The adapters could each wrap a number of objects and this is another useful place in which to use the adapter. If a complex series of objects needs to be orchestrated, then an adapter can take some responsibility for that orchestration providing a simpler interface to other classes.

You can imagine how useful the bridge pattern is. It can be used well in conjunction with the factory method pattern presented in the previous chapter.

This pattern certainly remains a very useful one for use in JavaScript. As I mentioned at the start of this section, it is handy for dealing with different APIs in a consistent fashion. I have used it for swapping in different third party components such as different graphing libraries or phone system integration points. If you're building applications on a mobile platform using JavaScript, then the bridge pattern is going to be a great friend for you, allowing you to separate your common and platform specific code cleanly. Because there are no interfaces in JavaScript, the bridge pattern is far closer to the adapter in JavaScript than in other languages. In fact, it is basically exactly the same.

A bridge also makes testing easier. We are able to implement a fake bridge and use this to ensure that the calls into the bridge are correct.

# Composite

In the previous chapter I mentioned that we would like to avoid coupling our objects together tightly. Inheritance is a very strong form of coupling and I suggested that, instead, composites should be used. The composite pattern is a special case of this in which the composite is treated as interchangeable with the components. Let's explore how the composite pattern works.

The following class diagram contains two different ways to build a composite component:

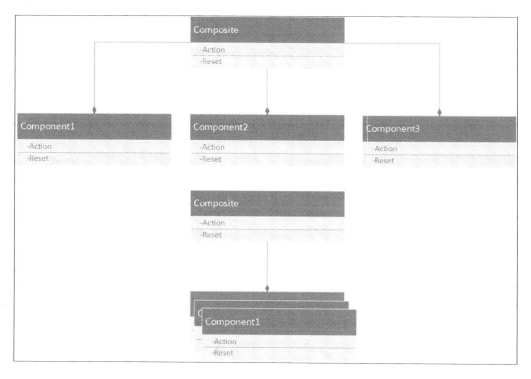

In the first one, the composite component is built from a fixed number of a variety of components. The second component is constructed from a collection of indeterminate length. In both cases the components contained within the parent composition could be of the same type as the composition. So a composition may contain instances of its own type.

The key feature of the composite pattern is the interchangeability of a component with its children. So, if we have a composite which implements IComponent, then all of the components of the composite will also implement IComponent. This is, perhaps, best illustrated with an example.

# Example

Tree structures are very useful in computing. It turns out that a hierarchical tree can represent many things. A tree is made up of a series of nodes and edges and is a cyclical. In a binary tree, each node contains a left and right child until we get down to the terminal nodes known as leaves.

While life is difficult in Westeros there is an opportunity for taking joy in things like religious holidays or weddings. At these events there is typically a great deal of feasting on delicious foods. The recipes for these foods is much as you would find in your own set of recipes. A simple dish like baked apples contains a list of ingredients:

- Baking apple
- Honey
- Butter
- Nuts

Each one of these ingredients implements an interface which we'll refer to as IIngredient. More complex recipes contain more ingredients, but in addition to that, more complex recipes may contain complex ingredients that are themselves made from other ingredients.

A popular dish in a southern part of Westeros is a dessert which is not at all unlike what we would call tiramisu. It is a complex recipe with ingredients such as:

- Custard
- Cake
- Whipped cream
- Coffee

Of course custard itself is made from:

- Milk
- Sugar
- Eggs
- Vanilla

Custard is a composite as is coffee and cake.

Operations on the composite object are typically proxied through to all of the contained objects.

# Implementation

A simple ingredient, one which would be a leaf node, is shown in this code:

```
class SimpleIngredient {
  constructor(name, calories, ironContent, vitaminCContent) {
    this.name = name;
    this.calories = calories;
```

```
      this.ironContent = ironContent;
      this.vitaminCContent = vitaminCContent;
    }
    GetName() {
      return this.name;
    }
    GetCalories() {
      return this.calories;
    }
    GetIronContent() {
      return this.ironContent;
    }
    GetVitaminCContent() {
      return this.vitaminCContent;
    }
  }
```

It can be used interchangeably with a compound ingredient which has a list of ingredients:

```
  class CompoundIngredient {
    constructor(name) {
      this.name = name;
      this.ingredients = new Array();
    }
    AddIngredient(ingredient) {
      this.ingredients.push(ingredient);
    }
    GetName() {
      return this.name;
    }
    GetCalories() {
      let total = 0;
      for (let i = 0; i < this.ingredients.length; i++) {
        total += this.ingredients[i].GetCalories();
      }
      return total;
    }
    GetIronContent() {
      let total = 0;
      for (let i = 0; i < this.ingredients.length; i++) {
        total += this.ingredients[i].GetIronContent();
      }
      return total;
    }
```

```
GetVitaminCContent() {
    let total = 0;
    for (let i = 0; i < this.ingredients.length; i++) {
        total += this.ingredients[i].GetVitaminCContent();
    }
    return total;
  }
}
```

The composite ingredient loops over its internal ingredients and performs the same operation on each of them. There is, of course, no need to define an interface due to the prototype model.

To make use of this compound ingredient we might do:

```
let egg = new SimpleIngredient("Egg", 155, 6, 0);
let milk = new SimpleIngredient("Milk", 42, 0, 0);
let sugar = new SimpleIngredient("Sugar", 387, 0,0);
let rice = new SimpleIngredient("Rice", 370, 8, 0);

let ricePudding = new CompoundIngredient("Rice Pudding");
ricePudding.AddIngredient(egg);
ricePudding.AddIngredient(rice);
ricePudding.AddIngredient(milk);
ricePudding.AddIngredient(sugar);

console.log("A serving of rice pudding contains:");
console.log(ricePudding.GetCalories() + " calories");
```

Of course this only shows part of the power of the pattern. We could use rice pudding as an ingredient in an even more complicated recipe: rice pudding stuffed buns (they have some strange foods in Westeros). As both the simple and compound version of the ingredient have the same interface, the caller does not need to know that there is any difference between the two ingredient types.

Composite is a heavily used pattern in JavaScript code that deals with HTML elements, as they are a tree structure. For example, the jQuery library provides a common interface if you have selected a single element or a collection of elements. When a function is called it is actually called on all the children, for instance:

```
$("a").hide()
```

This will hide all the links on a page regardless of how many elements are actually found by calling $("a"). The composite is a very useful pattern for JavaScript development.

# Decorator

The decorator pattern is used to wrap and augment an existing class. Using a decorator pattern is an alternative to subclassing an existing component. Subclassing is typically a compile time operation and is a tight coupling. This means that once subclassing is performed, there is no way to alter it at runtime. In cases where there are many possible subclassings that can act in combination, the number of combinations of subclassings explodes. Let's look at an example.

The armor worn by knights in Westeros can be quite configurable. Armor can be fabricated in a number of different styles: scale, lamellar, chainmail, and so on. In addition to the style of armor, there is also a variety of different face guards, knee, and elbow joints, and, of course, colors. The behavior of armor made from lamellar and a grille is different from chainmail with a face visor. You can see, however, that there is a large number of possible combinations; far too many combinations to explicitly code.

What we do instead is implement the different styles of armor using the decorator pattern. A decorator works using a similar theory to the adapter and bridge patterns, in that it wraps another instance and proxy calls through. The decorator pattern, however, performs the redirections at runtime by having the instance to wrap passed into it. Typically, a decorator will act as a simple pass through for some methods and for others it will make some modifications. These modifications could be limited to performing an additional action before passing the call off to the wrapped instance or could go so far as to change the parameters passed in. A UML representation of the decorator pattern looks like the following diagram:

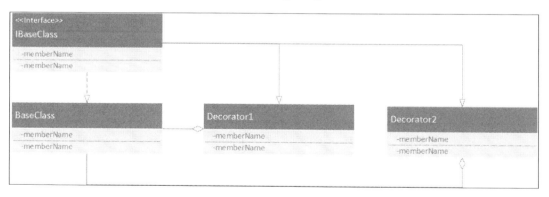

This allows for very granular control over which methods are altered by the decorator and which remain as mere pass-through. Let's take a look at an implementation of the pattern in JavaScript.

# Implementation

In this code we have a base class, BasicArmor, and it is then decorated by the
ChainMail class:

```
class BasicArmor {
  CalculateDamageFromHit(hit) {
    return hit.Strength * .2;
  }
  GetArmorIntegrity() {
    return 1;
  }
}

class ChainMail {
  constructor(decoratedArmor) {
    this.decoratedArmor = decoratedArmor;
  }
  CalculateDamageFromHit(hit) {
    hit.Strength = hit.Strength * .8;
    return this.decoratedArmor.CalculateDamageFromHit(hit);
  }
  GetArmorIntegrity() {
    return .9 * this.decoratedArmor.GetArmorIntegrity();
  }
}
```

The ChainMail armor takes in an instance of armor that complies with an interface,
such as:

```
export interface IArmor{
  CalculateDamageFromHit(hit: Hit):number;
  GetArmorIntegrity():number;
}
```

That instance is wrapped and calls proxied through. The method GetArmorIntegiry
modifies the result from the underlying class while CalculateDamageFromHit
modifies the arguments that are passed into the decorated class. This ChainMail
class could, itself, be decorated with several more layers of decorators until a long
chain of methods is actually called for each method call. This behavior, of course,
remains invisible to outside callers.

To make use of this armor decorator, look at the following code:

```
let armor = new ChainMail(new Westeros.Armor.BasicArmor());
console.log(armor.CalculateDamageFromHit({Location: "head", Weapon:
  "Sock filled with pennies", Strength: 12}));
```

It is tempting to make use of JavaScript's ability to rewrite individual methods on classes to implement this pattern. Indeed, in an earlier draft of this section I had intended to suggest just that. However, doing so is syntactically messy and not a common way of doing things. One of the most important things to keep in mind when programming is that code must be maintainable, not only by you but also by others. Complexity breeds confusion and confusion breeds bugs.

The decorator pattern is a valuable pattern for scenarios where inheritance is too limiting. These scenarios still exist in JavaScript, so the pattern remains useful.

# Façade

The façade pattern is a special case of the Adapter pattern that provides a simplified interface over a collection of classes. I mentioned such a scenario in the section on the adapter pattern but only within the context of a single class, SimpleShip. This same idea can be expanded to provide an abstraction around a group of classes or an entire subsystem. The façade pattern in UML form looks like the following diagram:

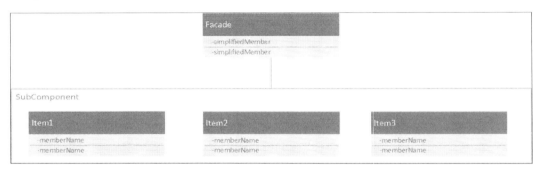

# Implementation

If we take the same SimpleShip as before and expand it to an entire fleet, we have a great example of a use for creating a façade. If it was difficult to sail a single ship it would be far more difficult to command an entire fleet of ships. There is a great deal of nuance required, commands to individual ships would have to be made. In addition to the individual ships there must also be a fleet Admiral and a degree of coordination between the ships in order to distribute supplies. All of this can be abstracted away. If we have a collection of classes representing the aspects of a fleet such as these:

```
let Ship = (function () {
  function Ship() {
```

```
  }
  Ship.prototype.TurnLeft = function () {
  };
  Ship.prototype.TurnRight = function () {
  };
  Ship.prototype.GoForward = function () {
  };
  return Ship;
})();
Transportation.Ship = Ship;

let Admiral = (function () {
  function Admiral() {
  }
  return Admiral;
})();
Transportation.Admiral = Admiral;

let SupplyCoordinator = (function () {
  function SupplyCoordinator() {
  }
  return SupplyCoordinator;
})();
Transportation.SupplyCoordinator = SupplyCoordinator;
```

Then we might build a façade as follows:

```
let Fleet = (function () {
  function Fleet() {
  }
  Fleet.prototype.setDestination = function (destination) {
    //pass commands to a series of ships, admirals and whoever else
    needs it
  };

  Fleet.prototype.resupply = function () {
  };

  Fleet.prototype.attack = function (destination) {
    //attack a city
  };
  return Fleet;
})();
```

Façades are very useful abstractions, especially in dealing with APIs. Using a façade around a granular API can create an easier interface. The level of abstraction at which the API works can be raised so that it is more in sync with how your application works. For instance, if you're interacting with the Azure blob storage API you could raise the level of abstraction from working with individual files to working with collections of files. Instead of writing the following:

```
$.ajax({method: "PUT",
url: "https://settings.blob.core.windows.net/container/set1",
data: "setting data 1"});

$.ajax({method: "PUT",
url: "https://settings.blob.core.windows.net/container/set2",
data: "setting data 2"});

$.ajax({method: "PUT",
url: "https://settings.blob.core.windows.net/container/set3",
data: "setting data 3"});
```

A façade could be written which encapsulates all of these calls and provides an interface, like:

```
public interface SettingSaver{
   Save(settings: Settings); //preceding code in this method
   Retrieve():Settings;
}
```

As you can see façades remain useful in JavaScript and should be a pattern that remains in your toolbox.

# Flyweight

In boxing there is a light weight division between 49-52 kg known as the flyweight division. It was one of the last divisions to be established and was named, I imagine, for the fact that the fighters in it were tiny, like flies.

The flyweight pattern is used in instances when there are a large number of instances of objects which vary only slightly. I should perhaps pause here to mention that a large number, in this situation, is probably in the order of 10,000 objects rather than 50 objects. However, the cutoff for the number of instances is highly dependent on how expensive the object is to create.

In some cases, the object may be so expensive that only a handful are required before they overload the system. In this case introducing flyweight at a smaller number would be beneficial. Maintaining a full object for each object consumes a lot of memory. It seems that the memory is largely consumed wastefully too, as most of the instances have the same value for their fields. Flyweight offers a way to compress this data by only keeping track of the values that differ from some prototype in each instance.

JavaScript's prototype model is ideal for this scenario. We can simply assign the most common value to the prototype and have individual instances override them as needed. Let's see how that looks with an example.

# Implementation

Returning once more to Westeros (aren't you glad I've opted for a single overarching problem domain?) we find that armies are full of ill-equipped fighting people. Within this set of people there is really very little difference from the perspective of the generals. Certainly each person has their own life, ambitions, and dreams but they have all been adapted into simple fighting automatons in the eyes of the general. The general is only concerned with how well the soldiers fight, if they're healthy, and if they're well fed. We can see the simple set of fields in this code:

```
let Soldier = (function () {
  function Soldier() {
    this.Health = 10;
    this.FightingAbility = 5;
    this.Hunger = 0;
  }
  return Soldier;
})();
```

Of course, with an army of 10,000 soldiers, keeping track of all of this requires quite some memory. Let's take a different approach and use a class:

```
class Soldier {
  constructor() {
    this.Health = 10;
    this.FightingAbility = 5;
    this.Hunger = 0;
  }
}
```

Using this approach, we are able to defer all requests for the soldier's health to the prototype. Setting the value is easy too:

```
let soldier1 = new Soldier();
let soldier2 = new Soldier();
console.log(soldier1.Health); //10
soldier1.Health = 7;
console.log(soldier1.Health); //7
console.log(soldier2.Health); //10
delete soldier1.Health;
console.log(soldier1.Health); //10
```

You'll note that we make a call to delete to remove the property override and return the value back to the parent value.

# Proxy

The final pattern presented in this chapter is the proxy. In the previous section I mentioned how it is expensive to create objects and how we would like to avoid creating too many of them. The proxy pattern provides a method of controlling the creation and use of expensive objects. The UML of the proxy pattern looks like the following diagram:

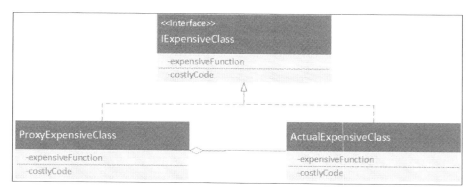

As you can see, the proxy mirrors the interface of the actual instance. It is substituted in for the instance in all the clients and, typically, wraps a private instance of the class. There are a number of places where the proxy pattern can be of use:

- Lazy instantiation of an expensive object
- Protection of secret data
- Stubbing for remote method invocation
- Interposing additional actions before or after method invocation

Often an object is expensive to instantiate and we don't want to have instances created before they're actually used. In this case the proxy can check its internal instance and, if not yet initiated, create it before passing on the method call. This is known as lazy instantiation.

If a class has been designed without any security in mind but now requires some, this can be provided through the use of a proxy. The proxy will check the call and only pass on the method call in cases where the security checks out.

The proxy may be used to simply provide an interface to methods that are invoked somewhere else. In fact, this is exactly how a number of web socket libraries function, proxying calls back to the web server.

Finally, there may be cases where it is useful to interpose some functionality into the method invocation. This could be logging of parameters, validating of parameters, altering results, or any number of things.

# Implementation

Let's take a look at a Westeros example where method interposition is needed. As tends to happen, the units of measurement for liquids vary greatly from one side of the land to the other. In the north, one might buy a pint of beer, while in the south, one would buy it by the dragon. This causes no end of confusion and code duplication, but can be solved by wrapping classes that care about measurement in proxies.

For example, this code is for a barrel calculator which estimates the number of barrels needed to ship a quantity of liquid:

```
class BarrelCalculator {
  calculateNumberNeeded(volume) {
    return Math.ceil(volume / 157);
  }
}
```

Although it is not well documented, here this version takes pints as a volume parameter. A proxy is created which deals with the transformation thusly:

```
class DragonBarrelCalculator {
  calculateNumberNeeded(volume) {
    if (this._barrelCalculator == null)
      this._barrelCalculator = new BarrelCalculator();
    return this._barrelCalculator.calculateNumberNeeded(volume *
      .77);
  }
}
```

Equally we might create another proxy for a pint-based barrel calculator:

```
class PintBarrelCalculator {
  calculateNumberNeeded(volume) {
    if (this._barrelCalculator == null)
      this._barrelCalculator = new BarrelCalculator();
    return this._barrelCalculator.calculateNumberNeeded(volume *
      1.2);
  }
}
```

This proxy class does the unit conversion for us and helps alleviate some confusion around units. Some languages, such as F#, support the concept of units of measure. In effect it is a typing system which is overlaid over simple data types such as integers, preventing programmers from making mistakes such as adding a number representing pints to one representing liters. Out of the box in JavaScript there is no such capability. Using a library such as JS-Quantities (http://gentooboontoo.github.io/js-quantities/) is an option however. If you look at it, you'll see the syntax is quite painful. This is because JavaScript doesn't permit operator overloading. Having seen how weird adding things such as an empty array to an empty array are (it results in an empty string), I think perhaps we can be thankful that operator overloading isn't supported.

If we wanted to protect against accidentally using the wrong sort of calculator when we have pints and think we have dragons, then we could stop with our primitive obsession and use a type for the quantity, a sort of poor person's units of measure:

```
class PintUnit {
  constructor(unit, quantity) {
    this.quanity = quantity;
  }
}
```

This can then be used as a guard in the proxy:

```
class PintBarrelCalculator {
  calculateNumberNeeded(volume) {
    if(PintUnit.prototype == Object.getPrototypeOf(volume))
      //throw some sort of error or compensate
    if (this._barrelCalculator == null)
      this._barrelCalculator = new BarrelCalculator();
    return this._barrelCalculator.calculateNumberNeeded(volume *
      1.2);
  }
}
```

As you can see, we end up with pretty much what JS-Quantities does but in a more ES6 form.

The proxy is absolutely a useful pattern within JavaScript. I already mentioned that it is used by web socket libraries when generating stubs but it finds itself useful in countless other locations.

# Hints and tips

Many of the patterns presented in this chapter provide methods of abstracting functionality and of molding interfaces to look the way you want. Keep in mind that with each layer of abstraction a cost is introduced. Function calls take longer but it is also much more confusing for people who need to understand your code. Tooling can help a little but tracking a function call through nine layers of abstraction is never fun.

Also be wary of doing too much in the façade pattern. It is very easy to turn the façade into a fully-fledged management class and that degrades easily into a God object that is responsible for coordinating and doing everything.

# Summary

In this chapter we've looked at a number of patterns used to structure the interaction between objects. Some of them are quite similar to each other but they are all useful in JavaScript, although the bridge is effectively reduced to an adapter. In the next chapter we'll finish our examination of the original GoF patterns by looking at behavioral patterns.

.

# 5
# Behavioral Patterns

In the last chapter we looked at structural patterns that describe ways in which objects can be constructed to ease interaction.

In this chapter we'll take a look at the final, and largest, grouping of GoF patterns: behavioral patterns. These patterns are ones that provide guidance on how objects share data or, from a different perspective, how data flows between objects.

The patterns we'll look at are as follows:

- Chain of responsibility
- Command
- Interpreter
- Iterator
- Mediator
- Memento
- Observer
- State
- Strategy
- Template method
- Visitor

Once again there are a number of more recently identified patterns that could well be classified as behavioral patterns. We'll defer looking at those until a later chapter, instead keeping to the GoF patterns.

# Chain of responsibility

We can think of a function call on an object as sending that object a message. Indeed this message passing mentality is one that dates back to the days of Smalltalk. The chain of responsibility pattern describes an approach in which a message tickles down from one class to another. A class can either act on the message or allow it to be passed on to the next member of the chain. Depending on the implementation there are a few different rules that can be applied to the message passing. In some situations only the first matching link in the chain is permitted to act. In others, every matching link acts on the message. Sometimes the links are permitted to stop processing or even to mutate the message as it continues down the chain:

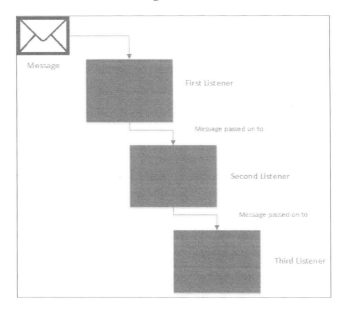

Let's see if we can find a good example of this pattern in our go-to example: the land of Westeros.

# Implementation

There is very little in the way of a legal system in Westeros. Certainly there are laws and even city guards who enforce them but the judicial system is scant. The law of the land is really decided by the king and his advisors. Those with the time and money can petition for an audience with the king who will listen to their complaint and pass a ruling. This ruling is law. Of course any king who spent his entire day listening to the complaints of peasants would go mad. For this reason many of the cases are caught and solved by his advisors before they reach his ears.

To represent this in code we'll need to start by thinking about how the chain of responsibility would work. A complaint comes in and it starts with the lowest possible person who can solve it. If that person cannot or will not solve the problem it tickles up to a more senior member of the ruling class. Eventually the problem reaches the king who is the final arbiter of disputes. We can think of him as the default dispute solver who is called upon when all else fails. The chain of responsibility is visible in the following diagram:

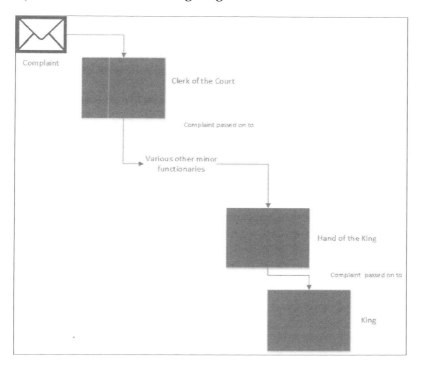

We'll start with an interface to describe those who might listen to complaints:

```
export interface ComplaintListener{
  IsAbleToResolveComplaint(complaint: Complaint): boolean;
  ListenToComplaint(complaint: Complaint): string;
}
```

The interface requires two methods. The first is a simple check to see if the class is able to resolve a given complaint. The second listens to and resolves the complaint. Next we'll need to describe what constitutes a complaint:

```
var Complaint = (function () {
  function Complaint() {
    this.ComplainingParty = "";
```

```
      this.ComplaintAbout = "";
      this.Complaint = "";
   }
   return Complaint;
})();
```

Next we need a couple of different classes which implement `ComplaintListener` and are able to solve complaints:

```
class ClerkOfTheCourt {
  IsInterestedInComplaint(complaint) {
    //decide if this is a complaint which can be solved by the clerk
    if(isInterested())
      return true;
    return false;
  }
  ListenToComplaint(complaint) {
    //perform some operation
    //return solution to the complaint
    return "";
  }
}
JudicialSystem.ClerkOfTheCourt = ClerkOfTheCourt;
class King {
  IsInterestedInComplaint(complaint) {
    return true;//king is the final member in the chain so must
      return true
  }
  ListenToComplaint(complaint) {
    //perform some operation
    //return solution to the complaint
    return "";
  }
}
JudicialSystem.King = King;
```

Each one of these classes implements a different approach to solving the complaint. We need to chain them together making sure that the king is in the default position. This can be seen in this code:

```
class ComplaintResolver {
  constructor() {
    this.complaintListeners = new Array();
     this.complaintListeners.push(new ClerkOfTheCourt());
     this.complaintListeners.push(new King());
```

```
        }
        ResolveComplaint(complaint) {
            for (var i = 0; i < this.complaintListeners.length; i++) {
                if
                    (this.complaintListeners[i].IsInterestedInComplaint(complaint))
                {
                    return
                        this.complaintListeners[i].ListenToComplaint(complaint);
                }
            }
        }
    }
```

This code will work its way through each of the listeners until it finds one that is interested in hearing the complaint. In this version the result is returned immediately, halting any further processing. There are variations of this pattern in which multiple listeners could fire, even allowing the listeners to mutate the parameters for the next listener. The following diagram shows multiple listeners configured:

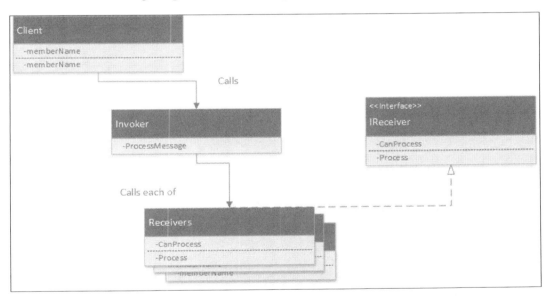

Chain of responsibility is a highly useful pattern in JavaScript. In browser-based JavaScript the events that fire fall through a chain of responsibility. For instance you can attach multiple listeners to the click event on a link and each of them will fire and then, finally, the default navigation listener. It is likely that you're using chain of responsibility in much of your code without even knowing it.

# Command

The command pattern is a method of encapsulating both the parameters to a method, as well as the current object state, and which method is to be called. In effect the command pattern packs up everything needed to call a method at a later date into a nice little package. Using this approach one can issue a command and wait until a later date to decide which piece of code will execute the command. This package can then be queued or even serialized for later execution. Having a single point of command execution also allows for easily adding functionality such as undo or command logging.

This pattern can be a bit difficult to imagine so let's break it down into its components:

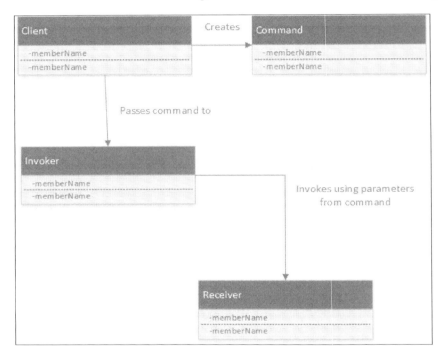

# Command message

The first component of the command pattern is, predictably, the command itself. As I mentioned, the command encapsulates everything needed to invoke a method. This includes the method name, the parameters, and any global state. As you can imagine keeping track of global state in each command is very difficult. What happens if the global state changes after the command has been created? This dilemma is yet another reason why using a global state is problematic and should be avoided.

There are a couple of options for setting up commands. At the simple end of the scale all that is needed is to track a function and a set of parameters. Because functions are first class objects in JavaScript, they can easily be saved into an object. We can also save the parameters to the function into a simple array. Let's build a command using this very simple approach.

The deferred nature of commands suggests an obvious metaphor in the land of Westeros. There are no methods of communicating quickly in Westeros. The best method is to attach small messages to birds and release them. The birds have a tendency to want to return to their homes, so each lord raises a number of birds in their home and, when they come of age, sends them to other lords who might wish to communicate with them. The lords keep an aviary of birds and retain records of which bird will travel to which other lord. The king of Westeros sends many of his commands to his loyal lords through this method.

The commands sent by the king contain all necessary instructions for the lords. The command may be something like bring your troops and the arguments to that command may be a number of troops, a location, and a date by which the command must be carried out.

In JavaScript the simplest way of representing this is through an array:

```
var simpleCommand = new Array();
simpleCommand.push(new LordInstructions().BringTroops);
simpleCommand.push("King's Landing");
simpleCommand.push(500);
simpleCommand.push(new Date());
```

This array can be passed around and invoked at will. To invoke it, a generic function can be used:

```
simpleCommand[0](simpleCommand[1], simpleCommand[2],
simpleCommand[3]);
```

As you can see, this function only works for commands with three arguments. You can, of course, expand this to any number:

```
simpleCommand[0](simpleCommand[1], simpleCommand[2],
simpleCommand[3], simpleCommand[4], simpleCommand[5],
simpleCommand[6]);
```

The additional parameters are undefined, but the function doesn't use them so there are no ill effects. Of course, this is not at all an elegant solution.

It is desirable to build a class for each sort of command. This allows you to ensure the correct arguments have been supplied and easily distinguish the different sorts of commands in a collection. Typically, commands are named using the imperative, as they are instructions. Examples of this are BringTroops, Surrender, SendSupplies, and so on.

Let's transform our ugly simple command into a proper class:

```
class BringTroopsCommand {
  constructor(location, numberOfTroops, when) {
    this._location = location;
    this._numberOfTroops = numberOfTroops;
    this._when = when;
  }
  Execute() {
    var receiver = new LordInstructions();
    receiver.BringTroops(this._location, this._numberOfTroops,
      this._when);
  }
}
```

We may wish to implement some logic to ensure that the parameters passed into the constructor are correct. This will ensure that the command fails on creation instead of on execution. It is easier to debug the issue during creation rather than during execution as execution could be delayed, even for days. The validation won't be perfect, but even if it catches only a small portion of the errors it is helpful.

As mentioned these commands can be saved for later use in memory or even written to disk.

# Invoker

The invoker is the part of the command pattern which instructs the command to execute its instructions. The invoker can really be anything: a timed event, a user interaction, or just the next step in the process may all trigger invocation. When we executed the `simpleCommand` command in the preceding section, we were playing at being the invoker. In a more rigorous command the invoker might look something like the following:

```
command.Execute()
```

As you can see, invoking a command is very easy. Commands may be invoked at once or at some later date. One popular approach is to defer the execution of the command to the end of the event loop. This can be done in a node with:

```
process.nextTick(function(){command.Execute();});
```

The function `process.nextTick` defers the execution of a command to the end of the event loop such that, if it is executed next time the process has nothing to do.

# Receiver

The final component in the command pattern is the receiver. This is the target of the command execution. In our example we created a receiver called `LordInstructions`:

```
class LordInstructions {
  BringTroops(location, numberOfTroops, when) {
    console.log(`You have been instructed to bring
      ${numberOfTroops} troops to ${location} by ${when}`);
  }
}
```

The receiver knows how to perform the action that the command has deferred. There need not be anything special about the receiver, in fact it may be any class at all.

Together these components make up the command pattern. A client will generate a command, pass it off to an invoker that may delay the command or execute it at once, and the command will act upon a receiver.

In the case of building an undo stack, the commands are special, in that they have both an `Execute` and an `Undo` method. One takes the application state forward and the other takes it backwards. To perform an undo, simply pop the command off the undo stack, execute the `Undo` function, and push it onto a redo stack. For redo, pop from redo, execute `Execute`, and push to the undo stack. Simple as that, although one must make sure all state mutations are performed through commands.

The GoF book outlines a slightly more complicated set of players for the command pattern. This is largely due to the reliance on interfaces that we've avoided in JavaScript. The pattern becomes much simpler thanks to the prototype inheritance model in JavaScript.

The command pattern is a very useful one for deferring the execution of some piece of code. We'll actually explore the command pattern and some useful companion patterns in *Chapter 10, Messaging Patterns*.

# Interpreter

The interpreter pattern is an interesting pattern as it allows for the creation of your own language. This might sound like something of a crazy idea, we're already writing JavaScript, why would we want to create a new language? Since the publication of the GoF book **Domain specific languages** (DSLs) have had something of a renaissance. There are situations where it is quite useful to create a language that is specific to one requirement. For instance the **Structured Query Language** (SQL) is very good at describing the querying of relational databases. Equally, regular expressions have proven themselves to be highly effective for the parsing and manipulation of text.

There are many scenarios in which being able to create a simple language is useful. That's really the key: a simple language. Once the language gets more complicated, the advantages are quickly lost to the difficulty of creating what is, in effect, a compiler.

This pattern is different from those we've seen to this point as there is no real class structure that is defined by the pattern. You can design your language interpreter however you wish.

# Example

For our example let us define a language which can be used to describe historical battles in the land of Westeros. The language must be simple for clerics to write and easy to read. We'll start by creating a simple grammar:

```
(aggressor -> battle ground <- defender) -> victor
```

Here you can see that we're just writing out a rather nice syntax that will let people describe battles. A battle between Robert Baratheon and RhaegarTargaryen at the river Trident would look like the following:

```
(Robert Baratheon -> River Trident <- RhaegarTargaryen) -> Robert
    Baratheon
```

Using this grammar we would like to build some code which is able to query a list of battles for answers. In order to do this we're going to rely on regular expressions. For most languages this wouldn't be a good approach as the grammar is too complicated. In those cases one might wish to create a lexor and a parser and build up syntax trees, however, by that point you may wish to re-examine if creating a DSL is really a good idea. For our language the syntax is very simple so we can get away with regular expressions.

# Implementation

The first thing we establish is a JavaScript data model for the battle like so:

```
class Battle {
  constructor(battleGround, agressor, defender, victor) {
    this.battleGround = battleGround;
    this.agressor = agressor;
    this.defender = defender;
    this.victor = victor;
  }
}
```

Next we need a parser:

```
class Parser {
  constructor(battleText) {
    this.battleText = battleText;
    this.currentIndex = 0;
    this.battleList = battleText.split("\n");
  }
  nextBattle() {
   if (!this.battleList[0])
     return null;
     var segments = this.battleList[0].match(/\((.+?)\s?-
       >\s?(.+?)\s?<-\s?(.+?)\s?->\s?(.+)/);
     return new Battle(segments[2], segments[1], segments[3],
       segments[4]);
  }
}
```

It is likely best that you don't think too much about that regular expression.
However, the class does take in a list of battles (one per line) and using `next Battle`,
allows one to parse them. To use the class we simply need to do the following:

```
var text = "(Robert Baratheon -> River Trident <-
  RhaegarTargaryen) -> Robert Baratheon";
var p = new Parser(text);
p.nextBattle()
```

This will be the output:

```
{
  battleGround: 'River Trident',
  agressor: 'Robert Baratheon',
  defender: 'RhaegarTargaryen)',
  victor: 'Robert Baratheon'
}
```

This data structure can now be queried like one would for any other structure in JavaScript.

As I mentioned earlier there is no fixed way to implement this pattern, so the implementation done in the preceding code is provided simply as an example. Your implementation will very likely look very different and that is just fine.

Interpreter can be a useful pattern in JavaScript. It is, however, a pretty infrequently used pattern in most situations. The best example of a language interpreted in JavaScript is the less language that is compiled, by JavaScript, to CSS.

# Iterator

Traversing collections of objects is an amazingly common problem. So much so that many languages provide for special constructs just for moving through collections. For example C# has a `foreach` loop and Python has `for x in`. These looping constructs are frequently built on top of an iterator. An iterator is a pattern that provides a simple method for selecting, sequentially, the next item in a collection.

The interface for an iterator looks like this:

```
interface Iterator{
  next();
}
```

# Implementation

In the land of Westeros there is a well-known sequence of people in line for the throne in the very unlikely event that the king was to die. We can set up a handy iterator over the top of this collection and simply call `next` on it should the ruler die:

```
class KingSuccession {
  constructor(inLineForThrone) {
    this.inLineForThrone = inLineForThrone;
    this.pointer = 0;
  }
  next() {
    return this.inLineForThrone[this.pointer++];
  }
}
```

This is primed with an array and then we can call it:

```
var king = new KingSuccession(["Robert Baratheon"
  ,"JofferyBaratheon", "TommenBaratheon"]);
king.next() //'Robert Baratheon'
king.next() //'JofferyBaratheon'
king.next() //'TommenBaratheon'
```

An interesting application of iterators is to not iterate over a fixed collection. For instance an iterator can be used to generate sequential members of an infinite set like the fibonacci sequence:

```
class FibonacciIterator {
  constructor() {
    this.previous = 1;
    this.beforePrevious = 1;
  }
  next() {
    var current = this.previous + this.beforePrevious;
    this.beforePrevious = this.previous;
    this.previous = current;
    return current;
  }
}
```

This is used like so:

```
var fib = new FibonacciIterator()
fib.next() //2
fib.next() //3
fib.next() //5
fib.next() //8
fib.next() //13
fib.next() //21
```

Iterators are handy constructs allowing for exploring not just arrays but any collection or even any generated list. There are a ton of places where this can be used to great effect.

# ECMAScript 2015 iterators

Iterators are so useful that they are actually part of the next generation of JavaScript. The iterator pattern used in ECMAScript 2015 is a single method that returns an object that contains `done` and `value`. `done` is `true` when the iterator is at the end of the collection. What is nice about the ECMAScript 2015 iterators is that the array collection in JavaScript will support the iterator. This opens up a new syntax which can largely replace the `for` loop:

```
var kings = new KingSuccession(["Robert Baratheon"
  ,"JofferyBaratheon", "TommenBaratheon"]);
for(var king of kings){
  //act on members of kings
}
```

Iterators are a syntactic nicety that has long been missing from JavaScript. Another great feature of ECMAScript-2015 are generators. This is, in effect, a built in iterator factory. Our fibonacci sequence could be rewritten like the following:

```
function* FibonacciGenerator (){
  var previous = 1;
  var beforePrevious = 1;
  while(true){
    var current = previous + beforePrevious;
    beforePrevious = previous;
    previous = current;
    yield current;
  }
}
```

This is used like so:

```
var fib = new FibonacciGenerator()
fib.next().value //2
fib.next().value //3
fib.next().value //5
fib.next().value //8
fib.next().value //13
fib.next().value //21
```

# Mediator

Managing many-to-many relationships in classes can be a complicated prospect. Let's consider a form that contains a number of controls, each of which wants to know if other controls on the page are valid before performing their action. Unfortunately, having each control know about each other control creates a maintenance nightmare. Each time a new control is added, each other control needs to be modified.

A mediator will sit between the various components and act as a single place in which message routing changes can be made. By doing so the mediator simplifies the otherwise complex work needed to maintain the code. In the case of controls on a form, the mediator is likely to be the form itself. The mediator acts much like a real life mediator would, clarifying and routing information exchange between a number of parties:

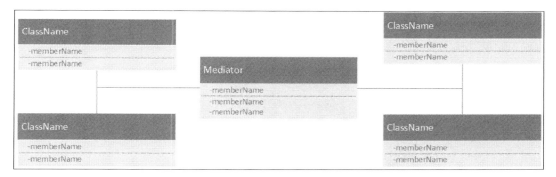

# Implementation

In the land of Westeros there are many times when a mediator is needed. Frequently the mediator ends up deceased, but I'm sure that won't be the case with our example.

There are a number of great families in Westeros who own large castles and vast tracts of land. Lesser lords swear themselves to the great houses forming an alliance, frequently supported through marriage.

When coordinating the various houses sworn to them, the great lord will act as a mediator, communicating information back and forth between the lesser lords and resolving any disputes they may have amongst themselves.

In this example we'll greatly simplify the communication between the houses and say that all messages pass through the great lord. In this case we'll use the house of Stark as our great lord. They have a number of other houses which talk with them. Each of the houses looks roughly like the following:

```
class Karstark {
  constructor(greatLord) {
    this.greatLord = greatLord;
  }
  receiveMessage(message) {
  }
  sendMessage(message) {
    this.greatLord.routeMessage(message);
  }
}
```

They have two functions, one of which receives messages from a third party and one of which sends messages out to their great lord, which is set upon instantiation. The `HouseStark` class looks like the following:

```
class HouseStark {
  constructor() {
    this.karstark = new Karstark(this);
    this.bolton = new Bolton(this);
    this.frey = new Frey(this);
    this.umber = new Umber(this);
  }
  routeMessage(message) {
  }
}
```

By passing all messages through the `HouseStark` class the various other houses do not need to concern themselves with how their messages are routed. This responsibility is handed off to `HouseStark` which acts as the mediator.

Mediators are best used when the communication is both complex and well defined. If the communication is not complex then the mediator adds extra complexity. If the communication is ill defined then it becomes difficult to codify the communication rules in a single place.

Simplifying communication between many-to-many objects is certainly useful in JavaScript. I would actually argue that in many ways jQuery acts as a mediator. When acting on a set of items on the page, it serves to simplify communication by abstracting away code's need to know exactly which objects on the page are being changed. For instance:

```
$(".error").slideToggle();
```

Is jQuery shorthand for toggling the visibility of all the elements on the page which have the `error` class?

# Memento

In the section on the command pattern we talked briefly about the ability to undo operations. Creating reversible commands is not always possible. For many operations there is no apparent reversing operation which can restore the original state. For instance, imagine code which squares a number:

```
class SquareCommand {
  constructor(numberToSquare) {
    this.numberToSquare = numberToSquare;
  }
  Execute() {
    this.numberToSquare *= this.numberToSquare;
  }
}
```

Giving this code -9 will result in 81 but giving it 9 will also result in 81. There is no way to reverse this command without additional information.

The memento pattern provides an approach to restore the state of objects to a previous state. The memento keeps a record of the previous values of a variable and provides the functionality to restore them. Keeping a memento around for each command allows for easy restoration of non-reversible commands.

In addition to an undo-stack there are many instances where having the ability to roll back the state of an object is useful. For instance doing what-if analysis requires that you make some hypothetical changes to state and then observe how things change. The changes are generally not permanent so they could be rolled back using the memento pattern or, if the projects are desirable, left in place. A diagram of the memento pattern can be seen here:

A typical memento implementation involves three players:

- **Originator**: The originator holds some form of state and provides an interface for generating new mementos.
- **Caretaker**: This is the client of the pattern, it is what requests that new mementos be taken and governs when they are to be restored.

- **Memento**: This is a representation of the saved state of the originator. This is what can be persisted to storage to allow for rolling back.

It can help to think of the members of the memento pattern as a boss and a secretary taking notes. The boss (caretaker) dictates some memo to the secretary (originator) who writes notes in a notepad (memento). From time to time the boss may request that the secretary cross out what he has just written.

The involvement of the caretaker can be varied slightly with the memento pattern. In some implementation the originator will generate a new memento each time a change is made to its state. This is commonly known as copy on write, as a new copy of the state is created and the change applied to it. The old version can be saved to a memento.

# Implementation

In the land of Westeros there are a number of soothsayers, foretellers of the future. They work by using magic to peer into the future and examine how certain changes in the present will play out in the future. Often there is need for numerous foretelling with slightly different starting conditions. When setting their starting conditions, a memento pattern is invaluable.

We start off with a world state which gives information on the state of the world for a certain starting point:

```
class WorldState {
  constructor(numberOfKings, currentKingInKingsLanding, season) {
    this.numberOfKings = numberOfKings;
    this.currentKingInKingsLanding = currentKingInKingsLanding;
    this.season = season;
  }
}
```

This `WorldState` class is responsible for tracking all the conditions that make up the world. It is what is altered by the application every time a change to the starting conditions is made. Because this world state encompasses all the states for the application, it can be used as a memento. We can serialize this object and save it to disk or send it back to some history server somewhere.

The next thing we need is a class which provides the same state as the memento and allows for the creation and restoration of mementos. In our example we've called this as `WorldStateProvider`:

```
class WorldStateProvider {
  saveMemento() {
    return new WorldState(this.numberOfKings,
```

```
        this.currentKingInKingsLanding, this.season);
  }
  restoreMemento(memento) {
    this.numberOfKings = memento.numberOfKings;
    this.currentKingInKingsLanding =
      memento.currentKingInKingsLanding;
    this.season = memento.season;
  }
}
```

Finally we need a client for the foretelling, which we'll call `Soothsayer`:

```
class Soothsayer {
  constructor() {
    this.startingPoints = [];
    this.currentState = new WorldStateProvider();
  }
  setInitialConditions(numberOfKings, currentKingInKingsLanding,
    season) {
    this.currentState.numberOfKings = numberOfKings;
    this.currentState.currentKingInKingsLanding =
      currentKingInKingsLanding;
    this.currentState.season = season;
  }
  alterNumberOfKingsAndForetell(numberOfKings) {
    this.startingPoints.push(this.currentState.saveMemento());
    this.currentState.numberOfKings = numberOfKings;
  }
  alterSeasonAndForetell(season) {
    this.startingPoints.push(this.currentState.saveMemento());
    this.currentState.season = season;
  }
  alterCurrentKingInKingsLandingAndForetell(currentKingInKingsLanding)
  {
    this.startingPoints.push(this.currentState.saveMemento());
    this.currentState.currentKingInKingsLanding =
      currentKingInKingsLanding;
    //run some sort of prediction
  }
  tryADifferentChange() {
    this.currentState.restoreMemento(this.startingPoints.pop());
  }
}
```

This class provides a number of convenience methods which alter the state of the world and then run a foretelling. Each of these methods pushes the previous state into the history array, startingPoints. There is also a method, tryADifferentChange, which undoes the previous state change ready to run another foretelling. The undo is performed by loading back the memento which is stored in an array.

Despite a great pedigree it is very rare that client side JavaScript applications provide an undo function. I'm sure there are various reasons for this, but for the most part it is likely that people do not expect such functionality. However in most desktop applications, having an undo function is expected. I imagine that, as client side applications continue to grow in their capabilities, undo functionality will become more important. When it does, the memento pattern is a fantastic way of implementing the undo stack.

# Observer

The observer pattern is perhaps the most used pattern in the JavaScript world. The pattern is used especially with modern single pages applications; it is a big part of the various libraries that provide **Model View View-Model** (**MVVM**) functionality. We'll explore those patterns in some detail in *Chapter 7, Reactive Programming*.

It is frequently useful to know when the value on an object has changed. In order to do so you could wrap up the property of interest with a getter and setter:

```
class GetterSetter {
  GetProperty() {
    return this._property;
  }
  SetProperty(value) {
    this._property = value;
  }
}
```

The setter function can now be augmented with a call to some other object which is interested in knowing that a value has changed:

```
SetProperty(value) {
  var temp = this._property;
  this._property = value;
  this._listener.Event(value, temp);
}
```

This setter will now notify the listener that a property change has occurred. In this case both the old and new value have been included. This is not necessary as the listener can be tasked with keeping track of the previous value.

The observer pattern generalizes and codifies this idea. Instead of having a single call to the listener, the observer pattern allows interested parties to subscribe to change notifications. Multiple subscribers can be seen in the following diagram:

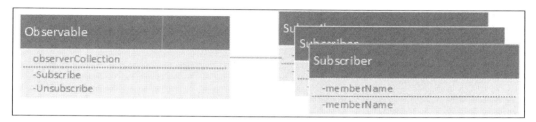

# Implementation

The court of Westeros is a place of great intrigue and trickery. Controlling who is on the throne and what moves they make is a complex game. Many of the players in the game of thrones employ numerous spies to discover what moves others are making. Frequently these spies are employed by more than one player and must report what they have found to all of the players.

The spy is a perfect place to employ the observer pattern. In our particular example, the spy being employed is the official doctor to the king and the players are very interested in how much painkiller is being prescribed to the ailing king. Knowing this can give a player advanced knowledge of when the king might die – a most useful piece of information.

The spy looks like the following:

```
class Spy {
  constructor() {
    this._partiesToNotify = [];
  }
  Subscribe(subscriber) {
    this._partiesToNotify.push(subscriber);
  }
  Unsubscribe(subscriber) {
    this._partiesToNotify.remove(subscriber);
  }
  SetPainKillers(painKillers) {
    this._painKillers = painKillers;
```

```
      for (var i = 0; i < this._partiesToNotify.length; i++) {
        this._partiesToNotify[i](painKillers);
      }
    }
  }
}
```

In other languages, the subscriber usually has to comply with a certain interface and the observer will call only the interface method. This encumbrance doesn't exist with JavaScript and, in fact, we just give the Spy class a function. This means that there is no strict interface required for the subscriber. This is an example:

```
class Player {
  OnKingPainKillerChange(newPainKillerAmount) {
    //perform some action
  }
}
```

This can be used like so:

```
let s = new Spy();
let p = new Player();
s.Subscribe(p.OnKingPainKillerChange); //p is now a subscriber
s.SetPainKillers(12); //s will notify all subscribers
```

This provides a very simple and highly effective way of building observers. Having subscribers decouples the subscriber from the observable object.

The observer pattern can also be applied to methods as well as properties. In so doing you can provide hooks for additional behavior to happen. This is a common method of providing a plugin infrastructure for JavaScript libraries.

In browsers all the event listeners on various items in the DOM are implemented using the observer pattern. For instance, using the popular jQuery library, one can subscribe to all the click events on buttons on a page by doing the following:

```
$("body").on("click", "button", function(){/*do something*/})
```

Even in vanilla JavaScript the same pattern applies:

```
let buttons = document.getElementsByTagName("button");
for(let i =0; i< buttons.length; i++)
{
  buttons[i].onclick = function(){/*do something*/}
}
```

Clearly the observer pattern is very useful when dealing with JavaScript. There is no need to change the pattern in any significant fashion.

# State

State machines are an amazingly useful device in computer programming. Unfortunately they are not used very frequently by most programmers. I'm sure that at least some of the objection to state machines is that many people implement them as a giant `if` statement like so:

```
function (action, amount) {
  if (this.state == "overdrawn" && action == "withdraw") {
    this.state = "on hold";
  }
  if (this.state == "on hold" && action != "deposit") {
    this.state = "on hold";
  }
  if (this.state == "good standing" && action == "withdraw" &&
    amount <= this.balance) {
    this.balance -= amount;
  }
  if (this.state == "good standing" && action == "withdraw" &&
    amount >this.balance) {
    this.balance -= amount;
    this.state = "overdrawn";
  }
};
```

This is just a sample of what could be much longer. The `if` statements of this length are painful to debug and highly error prone. Simply flipping a greater than sign is enough to drastically change how the `if` statement works.

Instead of using a single giant `if` statement block we can make use of the state pattern. The state pattern is characterized by having a state manager which abstracts away the internal state and proxies a message through to the appropriate state which is implemented as a class. All the logic within states and governing state transitions is governed by the individual state classes. The state manager pattern can be seen in the following diagram:

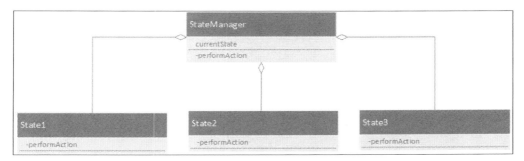

Splitting state into a class per state allows for much smaller blocks of code to debug and makes testing much easier.

The interface for the state manager is fairly simple and usually just provides the methods needed to communicate with the individual states. The manager may also contain some shared state variables.

# Implementation

As alluded to in the if statement example, Westeros has a banking system. Much of it is centered on the island of Braavos. Banking there runs in much the same way as banking here, with accounts, deposits, and withdrawals. Managing the state of a bank account involves keeping an eye on all of the transactions and changing the state of the bank account in accordance with the transactions.

Let's take a look at some of the code which is needed to manage a bank account at the Iron Bank of Braavos. First is the state manager:

```
class BankAccountManager {
  constructor() {
    this.currentState = new GoodStandingState(this);
  }
  Deposit(amount) {
    this.currentState.Deposit(amount);
  }
  Withdraw(amount) {
    this.currentState.Withdraw(amount);
  }
  addToBalance(amount) {
    this.balance += amount;
  }
  getBalance() {
    return this.balance;
  }
  moveToState(newState) {
    this.currentState = newState;
  }
}
```

The BankAccountManager class provides a state for the current balance and also the current state. To protect the balance, it provides an accessory for reading the balance and another for adding to the balance. In a real banking application, I would rather expect the function that sets the balance, have more protection than this. In this version of BankManager, the ability to manipulate the current state is accessible to the states. They have the responsibility to change states. This functionality can be centralized in the manager but that increases the complexity of adding new states.

We've identified three simple states for the bank account: `Overdrawn`, `OnHold`, and `GoodStanding`. Each one is responsible for dealing with withdrawals and deposits when in that state. The `GoodStandingstate` class looks like the following:

```
class GoodStandingState {
  constructor(manager) {
    this.manager = manager;
  }
  Deposit(amount) {
    this.manager.addToBalance(amount);
  }
  Withdraw(amount) {
    if (this.manager.getBalance() < amount) {
      this.manager.moveToState(new OverdrawnState(this.manager));
    }
    this.manager.addToBalance(-1 * amount);
  }
}
```

The `OverdrawnState` class looks like the following:

```
class OverdrawnState {
  constructor(manager) {
    this.manager = manager;
  }
  Deposit(amount) {
    this.manager.addToBalance(amount);
    if (this.manager.getBalance() > 0) {
      this.manager.moveToState(new
        GoodStandingState(this.manager));
    }
  }
  Withdraw(amount) {
    this.manager.moveToState(new OnHold(this.manager));
    throw "Cannot withdraw money from an already overdrawn bank
      account";
  }
}
```

Finally, the `OnHold` state looks like the following:

```
class OnHold {
  constructor(manager) {
    this.manager = manager;
  }
  Deposit(amount) {
```

```
      this.manager.addToBalance(amount);
      throw "Your account is on hold and you must attend the bank to
        resolve the issue";
    }
  Withdraw(amount) {
    throw "Your account is on hold and you must attend the bank to
      resolve the issue";
    }
  }
}
```

You can see that we've managed to reproduce all the logic of the confusing `if` statement in a number of simple classes. The amount of code here looks to be far more than the `if` statement but, in the long run, encapsulating the code into individual classes will pay off.

There is plenty of opportunity to make use of this pattern within JavaScript. Keeping track of state is a typical problem in most applications. When the transitions between the states are complex, then wrapping it up in a state pattern is one method of simplifying things. It is also possible to build up a simple workflow by registering events as sequential. A nice interface for this might be a fluent one so that you could register states like the following:

```
goodStandingState
.on("withdraw")
.when(function(manager){return manager.balance > 0;})
  .transitionTo("goodStanding")
.when(function(manager){return mangaer.balance <=0;})
  .transitionTo("overdrawn");
```

# Strategy

It has been said that there is more than one way to skin a cat. I have, wisely, never looked into how many ways there are. The same is frequently true for algorithms in computer programming. Frequently there are numerous versions of an algorithm that trades off memory usage for CPU usage. Sometimes there are different approaches that provide different levels of fidelity. For example, performing a geo-location on a smart phone typically uses one of three different sources of data:

- GPS chip
- Cell phone triangulation
- Nearby WiFi points

Using the GPS chip provides the highest level of fidelity however it is also the slowest and requires the most battery. Looking at the nearby WiFi points requires very little energy and is very quick, however it provides poor fidelity.

The strategy pattern provides a method of swapping these strategies out in a transparent fashion. In a traditional inheritance model each strategy would implement the same interface which would allow for any of the strategies to be swapped in. The following diagram shows multiple strategies that could be swapped in:

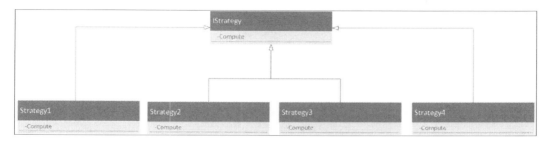

Selecting the correct strategy to use can be done in a number of different ways. The simplest method is to select the strategy statically. This can be done through a configuration variable or even hard coded. This approach is best for times when the strategy changes infrequently or is specific to a single customer or user.

Alternately an analysis can be run on the dataset on which the strategy is to be run and then a proper strategy selected. If it is known that strategy A works better than strategy B when the data passed in is clustered around a mean, then a fast algorithm for analyzing spread could be run first and then the appropriate strategy selected.

If a particular algorithm fails on data of a certain type, this too can be taken into consideration when choosing a strategy. In a web application this can be used to call a different API depending on the shape of data. It can also be used to provide a fallback mechanism should one of the API endpoints be down.

Another interesting approach is to use progressive enhancement. The fastest and least accurate algorithm is run first to provide rapid user feedback. At the same time a slower algorithm is also run and, when it is finished, the superior results are used to replace the existing results. This approach is frequently used in the GPS situation outlined above. You may notice when using a map on a mobile device your location is updated a moment after the map loads; this is an example of progressive enhancement.

Finally, the strategy can be chosen completely at random. It sounds like a strange approach but can be useful when comparing the performance of two different strategies. In this case, statistics would be gathered about how well each approach works and an analysis run to select the best strategy. The strategy pattern can be the foundation for A/B testing.

Selecting which strategy to use can be an excellent place to apply the factory pattern.

# Implementation

In the land of Westeros there are no planes, trains, or automobiles but there is still a wide variety of different ways to travel. One can walk, ride a horse, sail on a seagoing vessel, or even take a boat down the river. Each one has different advantages and drawbacks but in the end they still take a person from point A to point B. The interface might look something like the following:

```
export interface ITravelMethod{
  Travel(source: string, destination: string) : TravelResult;
}
```

The travel result communicates back to the caller some information about the method of travel. In our case we track how long the trip will take, what the risks are, and how much it will cost:

```
class TravelResult {
  constructor(durationInDays, probabilityOfDeath, cost) {
    this.durationInDays = durationInDays;
    this.probabilityOfDeath = probabilityOfDeath;
    this.cost = cost;
  }
}
```

In this scenario we might like to have an additional method which predicts some of the risks to allow for automating selection of a strategy.

Implementing the strategies is as simple as the following:

```
class SeaGoingVessel {
  Travel(source, destination) {
    return new TravelResult(15, .25, 500);
  }
}

class Horse {
  Travel(source, destination) {
    return new TravelResult(30, .25, 50);
```

```
    }
  }

  class Walk {
    Travel(source, destination) {
      return new TravelResult(150, .55, 0);
    }
  }
```

In a traditional implementation of the strategy pattern the method signature for each strategy should be the same. In JavaScript there is a bit more flexibility as excess parameters to a function are ignored and missing parameters can be given default values.

Obviously, the actual calculations around risk, cost, and duration would not be hard coded in an actual implementation. To make use of these one needs only to do the following:

```
var currentMoney = getCurrentMoney();
var strat;
if (currentMoney> 500)
  strat = new SeaGoingVessel();
else if (currentMoney> 50)
  strat = new Horse();
else
  strat = new Walk();
var travelResult = strat.Travel();
```

To improve the level of abstraction for this strategy we might replace the specific strategies with more generally named ones that describe what it is we're optimizing for:

```
var currentMoney = getCurrentMoney();
var strat;
if (currentMoney> 500)
  strat = new FavorFastestAndSafestStrategy();
else
  strat = new FavorCheapest();
var travelResult = strat.Travel();
```

Strategy is a very useful pattern in JavaScript. We're also able to make the approach much simpler than in a language which doesn't use prototype inheritance: there is no need for an interface. We don't need to return the same shaped object from each of the different strategies. So long as the caller is somewhat aware that the returned object may have additional fields, this is a perfectly reasonable, if difficult to maintain, approach.

# Template method

The strategy pattern allows for replacing an entire algorithm with a complimentary one. Frequently, replacing the entire algorithm is overkill: the vast majority of the algorithm remains the same in every strategy with only minor variations in specific sections.

The template method pattern is an approach which allows for some sections of an algorithm to be shared and other sections implemented using different approaches. These farmed out sections can be implemented by any one of a family of methods:

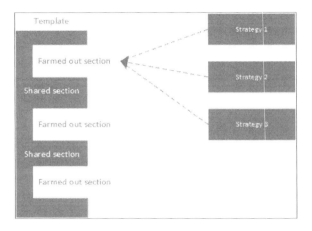

The template class implements parts of the algorithm and leaves other parts as abstract to later be overridden by classes which extend it. The inheritance hierarchy can be several layers deep, with each level implementing more and more of the template class.

An abstract class is one that contains abstract methods. Abstract methods are simply methods that have no body to them. The abstract class cannot be used directly and must, instead, be extended by another class that implements the abstract methods. An abstract class may extend another abstract class so that not all methods need to be implemented by the extending class.

This approach applies the principles of progressive enhancement to an algorithm. We move closer and closer to a fully implemented algorithm and, at the same time, build up an interesting inheritance tree. The template method helps keep identical code to a single location while still allowing for some deviation. A chain of partial implementations can be seen in the following diagram:

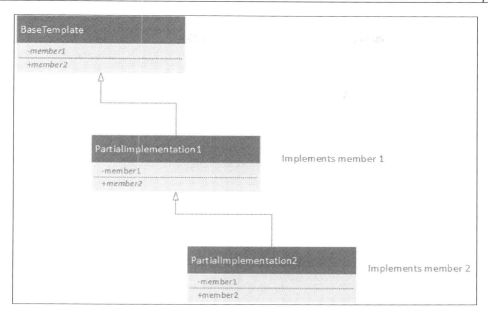

Overriding methods left as abstract is a quintessential part of object oriented programming. It is likely that this pattern is one which you've used frequently without even being aware that it had a name.

# Implementation

I have been told, by those in the know, that there are many different ways to produce beer. These beers differ in their choice of ingredients and in their method of production. In fact beer does not even need to contain hops – it can be made from any number of grains. However there are similarities between all beers. They are all created through the fermentation process and all proper beers contain some alcohol content.

In Westeros there are a great number of craftsmen who pride themselves on creating top notch beers. We would like to describe their processes as a set of classes, each one describing a different beer making methodology. We start with a simplified implementation of creating a beer:

```
class BasicBeer {
  Create() {
    this.AddIngredients();
    this.Stir();
    this.Ferment();
```

```
      this.Test();
      if (this.TestingPassed()) {
        this.Distribute();
      }
    }
    AddIngredients() {
      throw "Add ingredients needs to be implemented";
    }
    Stir() {
      //stir 15 times with a wooden spoon
    }
    Ferment() {
      //let stand for 30 days
    }
    Test() {
      //draw off a cup of beer and taste it
    }
    TestingPassed() {
      throw "Conditions to pass a test must be implemented";
    }
    Distribute() {
      //place beer in 50L casks
    }
  }
```

As there is no concept of abstract in JavaScript we've added exceptions to the various methods which must be overridden. The remaining methods can be changed but do not require it. An implementation of this for a raspberry beer would look like the following:

```
class RaspberryBeer extends BasicBeer {
  AddIngredients() {
    //add ingredients, probably including raspberries
  }
  TestingPassed() {
    //beer must be reddish and taste of raspberries
  }
}
```

Additional sub-classing may be performed at this stage for more specific raspberry beers.

The template method remains a fairly useful pattern in JavaScript. There is some added syntactic sugar around creating classes, but it isn't anything we haven't already seen in a previous chapter. The only warning I would give is that the template method uses inheritance and thus strongly couples the inherited classes with the parent class. This is generally not a desirable state of affairs.

# Visitor

The final pattern in this section is the visitor pattern. The visitor provides a method of decoupling an algorithm from the object structure on which it operates. If we wanted to perform some action over a collection of objects which differ in type and we want to perform a different action depending on the object type, we would typically need to make use of a large `if` statement.

Let's get right into an example of this in Westeros. An army is made up of a few different classes of fighting person (it is important that we be politically correct as there are many notable female fighters in Westeros). However, each member of the army implements a hypothetical interface called `IMemberOfArmy`:

```
interface IMemberOfArmy{
  printName();
}
```

A simple implementation of this might be the following:

```
class Knight {
  constructor() {
    this._type = "Westeros.Army.Knight";
  }
  printName() {
    console.log("Knight");
  }
  visit(visitor) {
    visitor.visit(this);
  }
}
```

Now we have a collection of these different types, we can use an `if` statement to only call the `printName` function on the knights:

```
var collection = [];
collection.push(new Knight());
collection.push(new FootSoldier());
collection.push(new Lord());
collection.push(new Archer());
```

```
    for (let i = 0; i<collection.length; i++) {
      if (typeof (collection[i]) == 'Knight')
        collection[i].printName();
      else
        console.log("Not a knight");
    }
```

Except, if you run this code, you'll actually find that all we get is the following:

```
Not a knight
Not a knight
Not a knight
Not a knight
```

This is because, despite an object being a knight, it is still an object and typeof will return object in all cases.

An alternative approach is to use instanceof instead of typeof:

```
    var collection = [];
    collection.push(new Knight());
    collection.push(new FootSoldier());
    collection.push(new Lord());
    collection.push(new Archer());

    for (var i = 0; i < collection.length; i++) {
      if (collection[i] instanceof Knight)
        collection[i].printName();
      else
        console.log("No match");
    }
```

The instance of approach works great until we run into somebody who makes use of the Object.create syntax:

```
    collection.push(Object.create(Knight));
```

Despite being a knight this will return false when asked if it is an instance of Knight.

This poses something of a problem for us. The problem is exacerbated by the visitor pattern as it requires that the language supports method overloading. JavaScript does not really support this. There are various hacks which can be used to make JavaScript somewhat aware of overloaded methods but the usual advice is to simply not bother and create methods with different names.

Let's not abandon this pattern just yet, though; it is a useful pattern. What we need is a way to reliably distinguish one type from another. The simplest approach is to just define a variable on the class which denotes its type:

```
var Knight = (function () {
  function Knight() {
    this._type = "Knight";
  }
  Knight.prototype.printName = function () {
    console.log("Knight");
  };
  return Knight;
})();
```

Given the new _type variable we can now fake having real method overrides:

```
var collection = [];
collection.push(new Knight());
collection.push(new FootSoldier());
collection.push(new Lord());
collection.push(new Archer());

for (vari = 0; i<collection.length; i++) {
  if (collection[i]._type == 'Knight')
    collection[i].printName();
  else
    console.log("No match");
}
```

Given this approach we can now implement a visitor. The first step is to expand our various members of the army to have a generic method on them which takes a visitor and applies it:

```
var Knight = (function () {
  function Knight() {
    this._type = "Knight";
  }
  Knight.prototype.printName = function () {
    console.log("Knight");
  };
  Knight.prototype.visit = function (visitor) {
    visitor.visit(this);
  };
  return Knight;
})();
```

Now we need to build a visitor. This code approximates the `if` statements we had in the preceding code:

```
varSelectiveNamePrinterVisitor = (function () {
  function SelectiveNamePrinterVisitor() {
  }
  SelectiveNamePrinterVisitor.prototype.Visit = function
    (memberOfArmy) {
    if (memberOfArmy._type == "Knight") {
      this.VisitKnight(memberOfArmy);
    } else {
      console.log("Not a knight");
    }
  };

  SelectiveNamePrinterVisitor.prototype.VisitKnight = function
    (memberOfArmy) {
    memberOfArmy.printName();
  };
  return SelectiveNamePrinterVisitor;
})();
```

This visitor would be used as such:

```
var collection = [];
collection.push(new Knight());
collection.push(new FootSoldier());
collection.push(new Lord());
collection.push(new Archer());
var visitor = new SelectiveNamePrinterVisitor();
for (vari = 0; i<collection.length; i++) {
  collection[i].visit(visitor);
}
```

As you can see we've pushed the decisions about the type of the item in the collection down to the visitor. This decouples the items themselves from the visitor as can be seen in the following diagram:

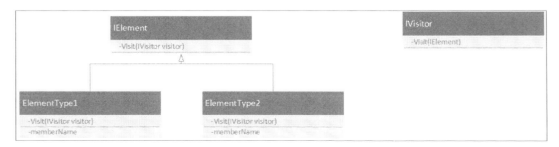

If we allow the visitor to make decisions about what methods are called on the visited objects there is a fair bit of trickery required. If we can provide a constant interface for the visited objects then all the visitor needs do is call the interface method. This does, however, move logic from the visitor into the objects that are visited, which is contrary to the idea that the objects shouldn't know they are part of a visitor.

Whether suffering through the trickery is worthwhile is really an exercise for you. Personally I would tend to avoid using the visitor pattern in JavaScript as the requirements to get it working are complicated and non-obvious.

# Hints and tips

Here are a couple of brief tips to keep in mind about some of the patterns we've seen in this chapter:

- When implementing the interpreter pattern you may be tempted to use JavaScript proper as your DSL and then use the `eval` function to execute the code. This is actually a very dangerous idea as `eval` opens up an entire world of security issues. It is generally considered to be very bad form to use `eval` in JavaScript.

- If you find yourself in the position to audit the changes to data in your project, then the memento pattern can easily be modified to suit. Instead of keeping track of just the state changes, you can also track when the change was made and who changed it. Saving these mementos to disk somewhere allows you to go back and rapidly build an audit log pointing to precisely what happened to change the object.

- The observer pattern is notorious for causing memory leaks when listeners aren't properly unregistered. This can happen even in a memory managed environment such as JavaScript. Be wary of failing to unhook observers.

# Summary

In this chapter we've looked at a bunch of behavioral patterns. Some of these patterns such as observer and iterator will be ones you'll use almost every day, while others such as interpreter you might use no more than a handful of times in your entire career. Learning about these patterns should help you identify well-defined solutions to common problems.

Most of the patterns are directly applicable to JavaScript and some of them, such as the strategy pattern, become more powerful in a dynamic language. The only pattern we found that has some limitations is the visitor pattern. The lack of static classes and polymorphism makes this pattern difficult to implement without breaking proper separation of concerns.

These aren't, by any means, all of the behavioral patterns in existence. The programming community has spent the past two decades building on the ideas of the GoF book and identifying new patterns. The remainder of this book is dedicated to these newly identified patterns. The solutions may be very old ones but not generally recognized as common solutions until more recently. As far as I'm concerned this is the point where the book starts to get very interesting as we start looking at less well known and more JavaScript-specific patterns.

# Part 2

## Other Patterns

Functional Programming

Reactive Programming

Application Patterns

Web Patterns

Messaging Patterns

Microservices

Patterns for Testing

Advanced Patterns

ECMAScript-2015/2016 Solutions Today

In Part 1 we focused on patterns originally identified in the GoF book that were the original impetus behind patterns in software design. In this part of the book we'll expand beyond those patterns to look at patterns that are related to functional programming, large-scale patterns for structuring an entire application, patterns which are specific to the Web, and messaging patterns. In addition, we'll look at patterns for testing and some rather interesting advanced patterns. Finally, we'll look at how we can get many of the features of the next version of JavaScript today.

# Functional Programming

**6**

Functional programming is a different approach to development than the heavily object oriented approach that we have focused on so far. Object oriented programming is a fantastic tool for solving a great number of problems but it has some issues. Parallel programming within an object oriented context is difficult as the state can be changed by various different threads with unknown side effects. Functional programming does not permit state or mutable variables. Functions act as primary building blocks in functional programming. Places where you might have used a variable in the past will now use a function.

Even in a single threaded program, functions can have side-effects that change global state. This means that, when calling an unknown function, it can alter the whole flow of the program. This makes debugging a program quite difficult.

JavaScript is not a functional programming language but we can still apply some functional principles to our code. We'll look at a number of patterns in the functional space:

- Function passing
- Filters and pipes
- Accumulators
- Memoization
- Immutability
- Lazy instantiation

# Functional functions are side-effect-free

A core tenant of functional programming is that functions should not change state. Values local to the function may be set but nothing outside the function may change. This approach is very useful for making code more maintainable. There need no longer be any concern that passing an array into a function is going to play havoc with its contents. This is especially a concern when using libraries that are not under your control.

There is no mechanism within JavaScript to prevent you from changing global state. Instead you must rely on developers to write side-effect-free functions. This may be difficult or not, depending on the maturity of the team.

It may not be desirable to put all the code from your application into functions, but separating as much as possible is desirable. There is a pattern called command query separation that suggests that methods should fall into two categories. Either they are a function that reads a value or they are a command that sets a value. Never the twain should meet. Keeping methods categorized like this eases in debugging and in code reuse.

One of the consequences of side effect-free functions is that they can be called any number of times with the same inputs and the result will be the same. Furthermore, because there are no changes to state, calling the function many times will not cause any ill side effects, other than making it run slower.

# Function passing

In functional programming languages, functions are first class citizens. Functions can be assigned to variables and passed around just like you would with any other variable. This is not entirely a foreign concept. Even languages such as C had function pointers that could be treated just like other variables. C# has delegates and, in more recent versions, lambdas. The latest release of Java has also added support for lambdas as they have proven to be so useful.

JavaScript allows for functions to be treated as variables and even as objects and strings. In this way JavaScript is functional in nature.

Because of JavaScript's single threaded nature, callbacks are a common convention and you can find them pretty much everywhere. Consider calling a function at a later date on a web page. This is done by setting a timeout on the window object like so:

```
setTimeout(function(){alert("Hello from the past")}, 5 * 1000);
```

The arguments for the set timeout function are a function to call and a time to delay in milliseconds.

Irrespective of the JavaScript environment in which you're working, it is almost impossible to avoid functions in the shape of callbacks. Node.js' asynchronous processing model is highly dependent on being able to call a function and pass in something to be completed at a later date. Making calls to external resources in a browser is also dependent on a callback to notify the caller that some asynchronous operation has completed. In basic JavaScript this looks like the following:

```
let xmlhttp = new XMLHttpRequest()
xmlhttp.onreadystatechange = function()
if (xmlhttp.readyState==4 && xmlhttp.status==200){
  //process returned data
}
};
xmlhttp.open("GET", http://some.external.resource, true);
xmlhttp.send();
```

You may notice that we assign the onreadystatechange function before we even send the request. This is because assigning it later may result in a race condition in which the server responds before the function is attached to the ready state change. In this case, we've used an inline function to process the returned data. Because functions are first class citizens we can change this to look like the following:

```
let xmlhttp;
function requestData(){
  xmlhttp = new XMLHttpRequest()
  xmlhttp.onreadystatechange=processData;
  xmlhttp.open("GET", http://some.external.resource, true);
  xmlhttp.send();
}

function processData(){
  if (xmlhttp.readyState==4 &&xmlhttp.status==200){
    //process returned data
  }
}
```

This is typically a cleaner approach and avoids performing complex processing in line with another function.

However, you might be more familiar with the jQuery version of this, which looks something like the following:

```
$.getJSON('http://some.external.resource', function(json){
  //process returned data
});
```

In this case the boiler plate of dealing with ready state changes is handled for you. There is even convenience provided for you if the request for data fails:

```
$.ajax('http://some.external.resource',
  { success: function(json){
      //process returned data
    },
    error: function(){
      //process failure
    },
    dataType: "json"
});
```

In this case, we've passed an object into the `ajax` call which defines a number of properties. Amongst these properties are function callbacks for success and failure. This method of passing numerous functions into another suggests a great way of providing expansion points for classes.

Likely you've seen this pattern in use before without even realizing it. Passing functions into constructors as part of an options object is a commonly used approach to providing extension hooks in JavaScript libraries. We saw some treatment of functions in the previous chapter, *Chapter 5*, *Behavioral Patterns*, when passing function into the observer.

# Implementation

In Westeros the tourism industry is almost non-extant. There are great difficulties with bandits killing tourists and tourists becoming entangled in regional conflicts. Nonetheless, some enterprising folks have started to advertise a grant tour of Westeros in which they will take those with the means on a tour of all the major attractions. From King's Landing to Eyrie, to the great mountains of Dorne - the tour will cover it all. In fact, a rather mathematically inclined member of the tourism board has taken to calling it a Hamiltonian tour as it visits everywhere once.

The `HamiltonianTour` class provides an options object which allows the definition of an options object. This object contains the various places to which a callback can be attached. In our case the interface for it would look something like the following:

```
export class HamiltonianTourOptions{
  onTourStart: Function;
  onEntryToAttraction: Function;
  onExitFromAttraction: Function;
  onTourCompletion: Function;
}
```

The full `HamiltonianTour` class looks like the following:

```
class HamiltonianTour {
  constructor(options) {
    this.options = options;
  }
  StartTour() {
    if (this.options.onTourStart && typeof
      (this.options.onTourStart) === "function")
      this.options.onTourStart();
      this.VisitAttraction("King's Landing");
      this.VisitAttraction("Winterfell");
      this.VisitAttraction("Mountains of Dorne");
      this.VisitAttraction("Eyrie");
    if (this.options.onTourCompletion && typeof
      (this.options.onTourCompletion) === "function")
      this.options.onTourCompletion();
  }
  VisitAttraction(AttractionName) {
    if (this.options.onEntryToAttraction && typeof
      (this.options.onEntryToAttraction) === "function")
      this.options.onEntryToAttraction(AttractionName);
      //do whatever one does in a Attraction
    if (this.options.onExitFromAttraction && typeof
      (this.options.onExitFromAttraction) === "function")
      this.options.onExitFromAttraction(AttractionName);
  }
}
```

You can see in the highlighted code how we check the options and then execute the callback as needed. This can be used by simply doing the following:

```
var tour = new HamiltonianTour({
  onEntryToAttraction: function(cityname){console.log("I'm
    delighted to be in " + cityname)}});
    tour.StartTour();
```

The output from running this code would be the following:

```
I'm delighted to be in King's Landing
I'm delighted to be in Winterfell
I'm delighted to be in Mountains of Dorne
I'm delighted to be in Eyrie
```

Passing functions is a great approach to solving a number of problems in JavaScript and tends to be used extensively by libraries such as jQuery and frameworks such as express. It is so commonly adopted that using it provides added barriers to your code's readability.

# Filters and pipes

If you're at all familiar with the Unix command line or, to a lesser extent, the Windows command line, then you'll have probably made use of pipes. A pipe, which is represented by the | character is shorthand for "take the output of program A and put it into program B". This relatively simple idea makes the Unix command line incredibly powerful. For instance, if you wanted to list all the files in a directory and then sort them and filter for any which start with either the letters b or g and end with an f then the command might look like the following:

```
ls|sort|grep "^[gb].*f$"
```

The ls command lists all files and directories, the sort command sorts them, and the grep command matches file names against a regular expression. Running this command in the etc directory on an Ubuntu box in /etc would give a result which looks something like the following:

```
stimms@ubuntu1:/etc$ ls|sort|grep "^[gb].*f$"
blkid.conf
bogofilter.cf
brltty.conf
gai.conf
gconf
groff
gssapi_mech.conf
```

Some functional programming languages such as F# offer a special syntax for piping between functions. In F#, filtering a list for even numbers can be done in the following way:

```
[1..10] |>List.filter (fun n -> n% 2 = 0);;
```

This syntax is very nice-looking, especially when used for long chains of functions. As an example, taking a number, casting it to a float, square rooting it, and then rounding it would look like the following:

```
10.5 |> float |>Math.Sqrt |>Math.Round
```

This is a clearer syntax than the C-style syntax that would look more like the following:

```
Math.Round(Math.Sqrt((float)10.5))
```

Unfortunately, there is no ability to write pipes in JavaScript using a nifty F# style syntax, but we can still improve upon the normal method shown in the preceding code by using method chaining.

Everything in JavaScript is an object, which means that we can have some real fun adding functionality to existing objects to improve their look. Operating on collections of objects is a space in which functional programming provides some powerful features. Let's start by adding a simple filtering method to the array object. You can think of these queries as being like SQL database queries written in a functional fashion.

# Implementation

We would like to provide a function that performs a match against each member of the array and returns a set of results:

```
Array.prototype.where = function (inclusionTest) {
  let results = [];
  for (let i = 0; i<this.length; i++) {
    if (inclusionTest(this[i]))
      results.push(this[i]);
  }
  return results;
};
```

The rather simple looking function allows us to quickly filter an array:

```
var items = [1,2,3,4,5,6,7,8,9,10];
items.where(function(thing){ return thing % 2 ==0;});
```

What we return is also an object, an array object in this case. We can continue to chain methods onto it like the following:

```
items.where(function(thing){ return thing % 2 ==0;})
  .where(function(thing){ return thing % 3 == 0;});
```

The result of this is an array containing only the number 6, as it is the only number between 1 and 10 which is both even and divisible by three. This method of returning a modified version of the original object without changing the original is known as a fluent interface. By not changing the original item array, we've introduced a small degree of immutability into our variables.

If we add another function to our library of array extensions, we can start to see how useful these pipes can be:

```
Array.prototype.select=function(projection){
  let results = [];
  for(let i = 0; i<this.length;i++){
    results.push(projection(this[i]));
  }
  return results;
};
```

This extension allows for projections of the original items based on an arbitrary projection function. Given a set of objects which contain IDs and names, we can use our fluent extensions to array to perform complex operations:

```
let children = [{ id: 1, Name: "Rob" },
{ id: 2, Name: "Sansa" },
{ id: 3, Name: "Arya" },
{ id: 4, Name: "Brandon" },
{ id: 5, Name: "Rickon" }];
let filteredChildren = children.where(function (x) {
  return x.id % 2 == 0;
}).select(function (x) {
  return x.Name;
});
```

This code will build a new array which contains only children with even IDs and instead of full objects, the array will contain only their names: Sansa and Brandon. For those familiar with .Net these functions may look very familiar. The **Language Integrated Queries (LINQ)** library on .Net provides similarly named functional inspired functions for the manipulation of collections.

Chaining functions in this manner can be both easier to understand and easier to build than alternatives: temporary variables are avoided and the code made terser. Consider the preceding example re-implemented using loops and temporary variables:

```
let children = [{ id: 1, Name: "Rob" },
{ id: 2, Name: "Sansa" },
{ id: 3, Name: "Arya" },
{ id: 4, Name: "Brandon" },
```

```
  { id: 5, Name: "Rickon" }];
  let evenIds = [];
  for(let i=0; i<children.length;i++)
  {
    if(children[i].id%2==0)
      evenIds.push(children[i]);
  }
  let names = [];
  for(let i=0; i< evenIds.length;i++)
  {
    names.push(evenIds[i].name);
  }
```

A number of JavaScript libraries such as d3 are constructed to encourage this sort of programming. At first it seems like the code created following this convention is bad due to very long line length. I would argue that this is a function of line length not being a very good tool to measure complexity rather than an actual problem with the approach.

# Accumulators

We've looked at some simple array functions which add filtering and pipes to arrays. Another useful tool is the accumulator. Accumulators aid in building up a single result by iterating over a collection. Many common operations such as summing up the elements of an array can be implemented using an accumulator instead of a loop.

Recursion is popular within functional programming languages and many of them actually offer an optimization called "tail call optimization". A language that supports this provides optimizations for functions using recursion in which the stack frame is reused. This is very efficient and can easily replace most loops. Details on whether tail call optimization is supported in any JavaScript interpreter are sketchy. For the most part it doesn't seem like it is but we can still make use of recursion.

The problem with `for` loops is that the control flow through the loop is mutable. Consider this rather easy-to-make mistake:

```
  let result = "";
  let multiArray = [[1,2,3], ["a", "b", "c"]];
  for(vari=0; i<multiArray.length; i++)
    for(var j=0; i<multiArray[i].length; j++)
      result += multiArray[i][j];
```

Did you spot the error? It took me several attempts to get a working version of this code I could break. The problem is in the loop counter in the second loop, it should read as follows:

```
let result = "";
let multiArray = [[1,2,3], ["a", "b", "c"]];
for(let i=0; i<multiArray.length; i++)
  for(let j=0; j<multiArray[i].length; j++)
    result +=multiArray[i][j];
```

Obviously this could be somewhat mitigated through better variable naming but we would like to avoid the problem altogether.

Instead we can make use of an accumulator, a tool for combining multiple values from a collection into a single value. We've rather missed Westeros for a couple of patterns so let's get back to our mythical example land. Wars cost a great deal of money but fortunately there are a great number of peasants to pay taxes and finance the lords in their games for the throne.

# Implementation

Our peasants are represented by a simple model which looks like the following:

```
let peasants = [
  {name: "Jory Cassel", taxesOwed: 11, bankBalance: 50},
  {name: "VardisEgen", taxesOwed: 15, bankBalance: 20}];
```

Over this set of peasants we have an accumulator which looks like the following:

```
TaxCollector.prototype.collect = function (items, value, projection) {
  if (items.length> 1)
    return projection(items[0]) + this.collect(items.slice(1), value,
      projection);
  return projection(items[0]);
};
```

This code takes a list of items, an accumulator value, and a function that projects the value to be integrated into the accumulation.

The projection function looks something like the following:

```
function (item) {
  return Math.min(item.moneyOwed, item.bankBalance);
}
```

In order to prime this function, we simply need to pass in an initial value for the accumulator along with the array and projection. The priming value will vary but more often than not it will be an identity; an empty string in the case of a string accumulator and a 0 or 1 in the case of mathematical ones.

Each pass through the accumulator shrinks the size of the array over which we are operating. All this is done without a single mutable variable.

The inner accumulation can really be any function you like: string appending, addition, or something more complicated. The accumulator is somewhat like the visitor pattern except that modifying values in the collection inside an accumulator is frowned upon. Remember that functional programming is side-effect-free.

# Memoization

Not to be confused with memorization, memoization is a specific term for retaining a number of previously calculated values from a function.

As we saw earlier, side-effect-free functions can be called multiple times without causing problems. The corollary to this is that a function can also be called fewer times than needed. Consider an expensive function which does some complex or, at least, time-consuming math. We know that the result of the function is entirely predicated on the inputs to the function. So the same inputs will always produce the same outputs. Why, then, would we need to call the function multiple times? If we saved the output of the function, we could retrieve that instead of redoing the time-consuming math.

Trading off space for time is a classic computing science problem. By caching the result, we make the application faster but we will consume more memory. Deciding when to perform caching and when to simply recalculate the result is a difficult problem.

# Implementation

In the land of Westeros, learned men, known as Maesters, have long had a fascination with a sequence of numbers which seems to reappear a great deal in the natural world. In a strange coincidence they call this sequence the Fibonacci sequence. It is defined by adding the two previous terms in the sequence to get the next one. The sequence is bootstrapped by defining the first few terms as 0, 1, 1. So to get the next term we would simply add 1 and 1 to get 2. The next term would add 2 and 1 to get 3 and so forth. Finding an arbitrary member of the sequence requires finding the two previous members, so it can end up being a bit of calculation.

In our world we have discovered a closed form that avoids much of this calculation but in Westeros no such discovery has been made.

A naïve approach is to simply calculate every term like so:

```
let Fibonacci = (function () {
  function Fibonacci() {
  }
  Fibonacci.prototype.NaieveFib = function (n) {
    if (n == 0)
      return 0;
    if (n <= 2)
      return 1;
    return this.NaieveFib(n - 1) + this.NaieveFib(n - 2);
  };
  return Fibonacci;
})();
```

This solution works very quickly for small numbers such as 10. However, for larger numbers, say greater than 40, there is a substantial slow-down. This is because the base case is called 102,334,155 times.

Let's see if we can improve things by memoizing some values:

```
let Fibonacci = (function () {
  function Fibonacci() {
    this.memoizedValues = [];
  }

  Fibonacci.prototype.MemetoFib = function (n) {
    if (n == 0)
      return 0;
    if (n <= 2)
      return 1;
    if (!this. memoizedValues[n])
      this. memoizedValues[n] = this.MemetoFib(n - 1) +
        this.MemetoFib(n - 2);
    return this. memoizedValues[n];
  };
  return Fibonacci;
})();
```

We have just memoized every item we encounter. As it turns out for this algorithm we store *n+1* items, which is a pretty good trade-off. Without memoization, calculating the 40th fibonacci number took 963ms while the memoization version took only 11ms. The difference is far more pronounced when the functions become more complex to calculate. Fibonacci of 140 took 12 ms for the memoization version while the naïve version took… well, it is has been a day and it is still running.

The best part of this memoization is that subsequent calls to the function with the same parameter will be lightning-fast as the result is already computed.

In our example only a very small cache was needed. In more complex examples it is difficult to know how large a cache should be or how frequently a value will need to be recomputed. Ideally your cache will be large enough that there will always be room to put more results in. However, this may not be realistic and tough decisions will need to be made about which members of the cache should be removed to save space. There is a plethora of methods for performing cache invalidation. It has been said that cache invalidation is one of the toughest problems in computing science, the reason being that we're effectively trying to predict the future. If anybody has perfected a method of telling the future, it is likely they are applying their skills in a more important domain than cache invalidation. Two options are to prey on the least recently used member of the cache or the least frequently used member. It is possible that the shape of the problem may dictate a better strategy.

Memoization is a fantastic tool for speeding up calculations which need to be performed multiple times or even calculations which have common sub-calculations. One can consider memoization as just a special case of caching, which is a commonly used technique when building web servers or browsers. It is certainly worthwhile exploring in more complex JavaScript applications.

# Immutability

One of the cornerstones of functional programming is that so called variables can be assigned only once. This is known as immutability. ECMAScript 2015 supports a new keyword, const. The const keyword can be used in the same way as var except that variables assigned with const will be immutable. For instance, the following code shows a variable and a constant that are both manipulated in the same way:

```
let numberOfQueens = 1;
const numberOfKings = 1;
numberOfQueens++;
numberOfKings++;
console.log(numberOfQueens);
console.log(numberOfKings);
```

The output of running this is the following:

```
2
1
```

As you can see, the results for the constant and variable are different.

If you're using an older browser without support, then `const` won't be available to you. A possible workaround is to make use of the `Object.freeze` functionality which is more widely adopted:

```
let consts = Object.freeze({ pi : 3.141});
consts.pi = 7;
console.log(consts.pi);//outputs 3.141
```

As you can see, the syntax here is not very user-friendly. Also an issue is that attempting to assign to an already assigned `const` simply fails silently instead of throwing an error. Failing silently in this fashion is not at all a desirable behavior; a full exception should be thrown. If you enable strict mode, a more rigorous parsing mode is added in ECMAScript 5, and an exception is actually thrown:

```
"use strict";
var consts = Object.freeze({ pi : 3.141});
consts.pi = 7;
```

The preceding code will throw the following error:

```
consts.pi = 7;
         ^

TypeError: Cannot assign to read only property 'pi' of #<Object>
```

An alternative is the `object.Create` syntax we spoke about earlier. When creating properties on the object, one can specify `writable: false` to make the property immutable:

```
var t = Object.create(Object.prototype,
{ value: { writable: false,
  value: 10}
});
t.value = 7;
console.log(t.value);//prints 10
```

However, even in strict mode no exception is thrown when attempting to write to a non-writable property. Thus I would claim that the `const` keyword is not perfect for implementing immutable objects. You're better off using freeze.

# Lazy instantiation

If you go into a higher-end coffee shop and place an order for some overly complex beverage (Grande Chai Tea Latte, 3 Pump, Skim Milk, Lite Water, No Foam, Extra Hot anybody?) then that beverage is going to be made on-the-fly and not in advance. Even if the coffee shop knew which orders were going to come in that day, they would still not make all the beverages up front. First, because it would result in a large number of ruined, cold beverages, and second, it would be a very long time for the first customer to get their order if they had to wait for all the orders of the day to be completed.

Instead coffee shops follow a just-in-time approach to crafting beverages. They make them when they're ordered. We can apply a similar approach to our code through the use of a technique known as lazy instantiation or lazy initialization.

Consider an object which is expensive to create; that is to say that it takes a great deal of time to create the object. If we are unsure if the object's value will be needed, we can defer its full creation until later.

# Implementation

Let's jump into an example of this. Westeros isn't really big on expensive coffee shops but they do love a good bakery. This bakery takes requests for different bread types in advance and then bakes them all at once should they get an order. However, creating the bread object is an expensive operation so we would like to defer that until somebody actually comes to pick up the bread:

```
class Bakery {
  constructor() {
    this.requiredBreads = [];
  }
  orderBreadType(breadType) {
    this.requiredBreads.push(breadType);
  }
}
```

We start by creating a list of bread types to be created as needed. This list is appended to by ordering a bread type:

```
var Bakery = (function () {
  function Bakery() {
    this.requiredBreads = [];
  }
  Bakery.prototype.orderBreadType = function (breadType) {
    this.requiredBreads.push(breadType);
  };
```

This allows for breads to be rapidly added to the required bread list without paying the price for each bread to be created.

Now when `pickUpBread` is called we'll actually create the breads:

```
pickUpBread(breadType) {
  console.log("Picup of bread " + breadType + " requested");
  if (!this.breads) {
    this.createBreads();
  }
  for (var i = 0; i < this.breads.length; i++) {
    if (this.breads[i].breadType == breadType)
      return this.breads[i];
  }
}
createBreads() {
  this.breads = [];
  for (var i = 0; i < this.requiredBreads.length; i++) {
    this.breads.push(new Bread(this.requiredBreads[i]));
  }
}
```

Here we call a series of operations:

```
let bakery = new Westeros.FoodSuppliers.Bakery();
bakery.orderBreadType("Brioche");
bakery.orderBreadType("Anadama bread");
bakery.orderBreadType("Chapati");
bakery.orderBreadType("Focaccia");

console.log(bakery.pickUpBread("Brioche").breadType + "picked up");
```

This will result in the following:

```
Pickup of bread Brioche requested.
Bread Brioche created.
Bread Anadama bread created.
Bread Chapati created.
Bread Focaccia created.
Brioche picked up
```

You can see that the collection of actual breads is left until after the pickup has been requested.

Lazy instantiation can be used to simplify asynchronous programming. Promises are an approach to simplifying callbacks which are common in JavaScript. Instead of building up complicated callbacks, a promise is an object which contains a state and a result. When first called, the promise is in an unresolved state; once the `async` operation completes, the state is updated to complete and the result is filled in. You can think of the result as being lazily instantiated. We'll look at promises and promise libraries in more detail in *Chapter 9, Web Patterns*.

Being lazy can save you quite a bit of time in creating expensive objects that end up never being used.

# Hints and tips

Although callbacks are the standard way of dealing with asynchronous methods in JavaScript they can get out of hand easily. There are a number of approaches to solving this spaghetti code: promise libraries provide a more fluent way of handling callbacks and future versions of JavaScript may adopt an approach similar to the C# `async`/`await` syntax.

I really like accumulators but they can be inefficient in terms of memory use. The lack of tail recursion means that each pass through adds another stack frame, so this approach may result in memory pressure. All things are a trade-off in this case between memory and code maintainability.

# Summary

JavaScript is not a functional programming language. That is not to say that it isn't possible to apply some of the ideas from functional programming to it. These approaches enable cleaner, easier to debug code. Some might even argue that the number of issues will be reduced although I have never seen any convincing studies on that.

In this chapter we looked at six different patterns. Lazy instantiation, memoization, and immutability are all creational patterns. Function passing is a structural pattern as well as a behavioral one. Accumulators are also behavioral in nature. Filters and pipes don't really fall into any of the GoF categories so one might think of them as a style pattern.

In the next chapter we'll look at a number of patterns for dividing the logic and presentation in applications. These patterns have become more important as JavaScript applications have grown.

# Reactive Programming

7

I once read a book that suggested that Newton came up with the idea for calculus when he was observing the flow of a river around a reed. I've never been able to find any other source which supports that assertion. It is, however, a nice picture to hold in your mind. Calculus deals with understanding how the state of a system changes over time. Most developers will rarely have to deal with calculus in their day to day work. They will, however, have to deal with systems changing. After all, having a system which doesn't change at all is pretty boring.

Over the last few years a number of different ideas have arisen in the area of treating change as a stream of events – just like the stream that Newton supposedly observed. Given a starting position and a stream of events it should be possible to figure out the state of the system. Indeed, this is the idea behind using an event store. Instead of keeping the final state of an aggregate in a database we instead keep track of all the events which have been applied to that aggregate. By replaying this series of events we can recreate the current state of the aggregate. This seems like a roundabout way of storing the state of an object but it is actually very useful for a number of situations. For example, a disconnected system, like a cell phone application when the phone isn't connected to the network, which uses an event store can be merged with other events much more easily than simply keeping the end state. It is also stunningly useful for audit scenarios as it is possible to pull the system back to the state it was in at any point in time by simply halting the replay at a time index. How frequently have you been asked, "why is the system in this state?", and you've been unable to reply? With an event store the answer should be easy to ascertain.

In this chapter we'll cover the following topics:

- Application state changes
- Streams
- Filtering streams
- Merging streams
- Streams for multiplexing

# Application state changes

Within an application we can think of all the events happening as a similar stream of events. The user clicks on a button? Event. The user's mouse enters some region? Event. A clock ticks? Event. In both front and backend applications, events are the things which trigger changes in state. You're likely already using events for event listeners. Consider attaching a click handler to a button:

```
var item = document.getElementById("item1");
item. addEventListener("click", function(event){ /*do something */ });
```

In this code we have attached a handler to the `click` event. This is fairly simple code but think about how rapidly the complexity of this code increases when we add conditions like "ignore additional click for 500ms once a click is fired to prevent people double-clicking" and "Fire a different event if the *Ctrl* key is being held when the button is clicked". Reactive programming or functional reactive programming provides a simple solution to these complex interaction scenarios through use of streams. Let's explore how your code can benefit from leveraging reactive programming.

# Streams

The easiest way to think of an event stream is not to think of the streams you've probably used before in programming, input reader streams, but to think of arrays. Let's say that you have an array with a series of numbers in it:

```
[1, 4, 6, 9, 34, 56, 77, 1, 2, 3, 6, 10]
```

Now you want to filter this array to only show you even numbers. In modern JavaScript this is easily done through the use of the `filter` function on the array:

```
[1, 4, 6, 9, 34, 56, 77, 1, 2, 3, 6, 10].filter((x)=>x%2==0) =>
[4, 6, 34, 56, 2, 6, 10]
```

A graphical representation can be seen here:

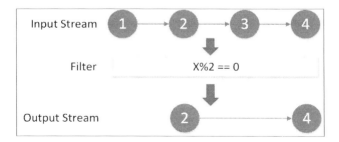

The filtering function here remains the same should we have ten items in the array or ten thousand items in the array. Now, what if the source array had new items being appended to it all the time? We would like to keep our dependent array up-to-date by inserting any new items which are even, into it. To do this we could hook into the add function on the array using a pattern-like decorator. Using a decorator we could call the filter method and, if a match was found, we would add it to the filtered array.

Streams are, in effect, an observable on a collection of future events. There are a number of interesting problems which can be solved using operations on streams. Let's start with a simple problem: handling clicks. This problem is so simple that, on the surface, it doesn't seem like there is any advantage to using streams. Don't worry we'll make it more difficult as we go along.

For the most part this book avoids making use of any specific JavaScript libraries. The idea is that patterns should be able to be implemented with ease without a great deal of ceremony. However, in this case we're actually going to make use of a library because streams have a few nuances to their implementation for which we'd like some syntactic niceties. If you're looking to see how to implement a basic stream, then you can base it on the observer pattern outlined in *Chapter 5, Behavioral Patterns*.

There are a number of stream libraries in JavaScript Reactive.js, Bacon.js, and RxJS to name a few. Each one has various advantages and disadvantages but the specifics are outside the purview of this book. In this book we'll make use of Reactive Extensions for JavaScript, the source code for which can be found on GitHub at `https://github.com/Reactive-Extensions/RxJS`.

Let's start with a brief piece of HTML:

```html
<body>
  <button id="button"> Click Me!</button>
  <span id="output"></span>
</body>
```

To this, let's add a quick click counter:

```html
<script>
  var counter = 0;
  var button = document.getElementById('button');
  var source = Rx.Observable.fromEvent(button, 'click');
  var subscription = source.subscribe(function (e) {
    counter++;
    output.innerHTML = "Clicked " + counter + " time" +
      (counter > 1 ? "s" : "");
  });
</script>
```

Here you can see we're creating a new stream of events from the `click` event on the button. The newly created stream is commonly referred to as a metastream. Whenever an event is emitted from the source stream it is automatically manipulated and published, as needed, to the metastream. We subscribe to this stream and increment a counter. If we wanted to react to only the even numbered events, we could do so by subscribing a second function to the stream:

```
var incrementSubscription = source.subscribe(() => counter++);
var subscription = source.filter(x=>counter%2==0).subscribe(function
(e) {
  output.innerHTML = "Clicked " + counter + " time" +
    (counter > 1 ? "s" : "");
});
```

Here you can see that we're applying a filter to the stream such that the counter is distinct from the function which updates the screen. Keeping a counter outside of the streams like this feels dirty, though, doesn't it? Chances are that incrementing every other click isn't the goal of this function anyway. It is much more likely that we would like to run a function only on double click.

This is difficult to do with traditional methods, however these sorts of complex interactions are easy to achieve using streams. You can see how we might approach the problem in this code:

```
source.buffer(() => source.debounce(250))
.map((list) => list.length)
.filter((x) => x >= 2)
.subscribe((x)=> {
  counter++;
  output.innerHTML = "Clicked " + counter + " time" + (counter > 1 ?
    "s" : "");
});
```

Here we take the click stream and buffer the stream using a debounce to generate the boundaries of the buffer. Debouncing is a term from the hardware world which means that we clean up a noisy signal into a single event. When a physical button is pushed, there are often a couple of additional high or low signals instead of the single point signal we would like. In effect we eliminate repeated signals which occur within a window. In this case we wait 250ms before firing an event to move to a new buffer. The buffer contains all the events fired during the debouncing and passes on a list of them to the next function in the chain. The map function generates a new stream with the list length as the contents. Next, we filter the stream to show only events with a value of 2 or more, that's two clicks or more. The stream of events look like the following diagram:

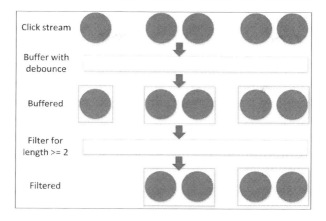

Performing the same logic as this using traditional event listeners and call-backs would be quite difficult. One could easily imagine a far more complex workflow that would spiral out of control. FRP allows for a more streamlined approach to handling events.

# Filtering streams

As we saw in the preceding section, it is possible to filter a stream of events and, from it produce a new stream of events. You might be familiar with being able to filter items in an array. ES5 introduced a number of new operators for arrays such as **filter** and **some**. The first of these produces a new array containing only elements which match the rule in the filter. some is a similar function which simply returns true if any element of the array matches. These same sorts of functions are also supported on streams as well as functions you might be familiar with from functional languages such as First and Last. In addition to the functions which would make sense for arrays, there are a number of time series based functions which make much more sense when you consider that streams exist in time.

We've already seen debounce which is an example of a time based filter. Another very simple application of debounce is to prevent the annoying bug of users double-clicking a submit button. Consider how much simpler the code for that is using a stream:

```
Rx.Observable.FromEvent(button, "click")
.debounce(1000).subscribe((x)=>doSomething());
```

You might also find it that functions like Sample – which generates a set of events from a time window. This is a very handy function when we're dealing with observables which may produce a large number of events. Consider an example from our example world of Westeros.

Unfortunately, Westeros is quite a violent place where people seem to die in unpleasant ways. So many people die that we can't possibly keep an eye on each one so we'd like to just sample the data and gather a few causes of death.

To simulate this incoming stream, we will start with an array, something like the following:

```
var deaths = [
  {
    Name:"Stannis",
    Cause: "Cold"
  },
  {
    Name: "Tyrion",
    Cause: "Stabbing"
  },
  ...
}
```

> You can see we're using an array to simulate a stream of events. This can be done with any stream and is a remarkably easy way to perform testing on complex code. You can build a stream of events in an array and then publish them with appropriate delays giving an accurate representation of anything from a stream of events from the filesystem to user interactions.

Now we need to make our array into a stream of events. Fortunately, there are some shortcuts for doing that using the `from` method. This will simply return a stream which is immediately executed. What we'd like is to pretend we have a regularly distributed stream of events or, in our rather morbid case, deaths. This can be done by using two methods from RxJS: `interval` and `zip`. `interval` creates a stream of events at a regular interval. `zip` matches up pairs of events from two streams. Together these two methods will emit a new stream of events at a regular interval:

```
function generateDeathsStream(deaths) {
  return
    Rx.Observable.from(deaths).zip(Rx.Observable.interval(500),
      (death,_)=>death);
}
```

In this code we zip together the deaths array with an interval stream which fires every `500`ms. Because we're not super interested in the interval event we simply discard it and project the item from the array onwards.

Now we can sample this stream by simply taking a sample and then subscribing to it. Here we're sampling every 1500ms:

```
generateDeathsStream(deaths).sample(1500).subscribe((item) => { /*do
    something */ });
```

You can have as many subscribers to a stream as you like so if you wanted to perform some sampling, as well as perhaps some aggregate functions like simply counting the events, you could do so by having several subscribers:

```
Var counter = 0;
generateDeathsStream(deaths).subscribe((item) => { counter++ });
```

# Merging streams

We've already seen the `zip` function that merges events one-to-one to create a new stream but there are numerous other ways of combining streams. A very simple example might be a page which has several code paths which all want to perform a similar action. Perhaps we have several actions all of which result in a status message being updated:

```
var button1 = document.getElementById("button1");
var button2 = document.getElementById("button2");
var button3 = document.getElementById("button3");
var button1Stream = Rx.Observable.fromEvent(button1, 'click');
var button2Stream = Rx.Observable.fromEvent(button2, 'click');
var button3Stream = Rx.Observable.fromEvent(button3, 'click');
var messageStream = Rx.Observable.merge(button1Stream, button2Stream,
    button3Stream);
messageStream.subscribe(function (x) { return console.log(x.type + "
    on " + x.srcElement.id); });
```

Here you can see how the various streams are passed into the merge function and the resulting merged stream:

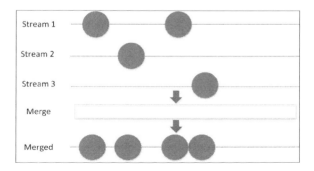

While useful, this code doesn't seem to be particularly better than simply calling the event handler directly, in fact it is longer than necessary. However, consider that there are more sources of status messages than just button pushes. We might want to have asynchronous events also write out information. For instance, sending a request to the server might also want to add status information. Another fantastic application may be with web workers which run in the background and communicate with the main thread using messaging. For web based JavaScript applications this is how we implement multithreaded applications. Let's see how that would look.

First we can create a stream from a worker role. In our example the worker simply calculates the fibonacci sequence. We've added a fourth button to our page and have it trigger the worker process:

```
var worker = Rx.DOM.fromWorker("worker.js");
button4Stream.subscribe(function (_) {
  worker.onNext({ cmd: "start", number: 35 });
});
```

Now we can subscribe to the merged stream and combine it with all the previous streams:

```
var messageStream = Rx.Observable.merge(button1Stream,
  button2Stream, button3Stream, worker);
messageStream.subscribe(function (x) {
  appendToOutput(x.type + (x.srcElement.id === undefined ? " with " +
    x.data : " on " + x.srcElement.id));
},
function (err) { return appendToOutput(err, true); }
);
```

This all looks really nice but we don't want to clobber the users with dozens of notifications at a time. We can throttle the stream of events so that only a single toast shows up at a time by using the same interval zip pattern we saw earlier. In this code we've replaced our appendToOutput method with a call to a toast display library:

```
var messageStream = Rx.Observable.merge(button1Stream,
  button2Stream, button3Stream, worker);
var intervalStream = Rx.Observable.interval(5000);
messageStream.zip(intervalStream, function (x, _) {
  return x;})
.subscribe(function (x) {
  toastr.info(x.type + (x.srcElement.id === undefined ? " with " +
    x.data : " on " + x.srcElement.id));
},
function (err) { return toastr.error(err); }
);
```

As you can see the code for this functionality is short and easy to understand yet it contains a great deal of functionality.

# Streams for multiplexing

One does not rise to a position of power on the King's council in Westeros without being a master at building networks of spies. Often the best spy is one who can respond the quickest. Similarly, we may have some code which has the option of calling one of many different services which can fulfill the same task. A great example would be a credit card processor: it doesn't really matter which processor we use as they're pretty much all the same.

To achieve this, we can kick off a number of HTTP requests to each of the services. If we take each of the requests and put them into a stream, we can use it to select the fastest to respond processor and then perform the rest of the actions using that processor.

With RxJS this looks like the following:

```
var processors = Rx.Observable.amb(processorStream1,
    processorStream2);
```

You could even include a timeout in the `amb` call which would be called to handle the eventuality that none of the processors responded in time.

# Hints and tips

There are a large number of different functions that can be applied to streams. If you happen to decide on the RxJS library for your FRP needs in JavaScript, many of the most common functions have been implemented for you. More complex functions can often be written as a chain of the included functions so try to think of a way to create the functionality you want by chaining before writing your own functions.

Frequently, asynchronous calls across the network in JavaScript fail. Networks are unreliable, mobile networks doubly so. For the most part when the network fails, our application fails. Streams provide an easy fix to this by allowing you to easily retry failed subscriptions. In RxJS this method is called `Retry`. Slotting it into any observable chain makes it more resilient to network failures.

# Summary

Functional reactive programming has many uses in different applications both on the server and on the client. On the client side it can be used to wrangle a large number of events together into a data flow enabling complex interactions. It can also be used for the simplest of things such as preventing a user from double-clicking a button. There is no huge cost to simply using streams for all of your data changes. They are highly testable and have a minimal impact on performance.

Perhaps the nicest thing about FRP is that it raises the level of abstraction. You have to deal with less finicky process flow code and can, instead, focus on the logical flow of the application.

# 8

# Application Patterns

Thus far we have spent a great deal of time examining patterns that are used to solve local problems, that is; problems that span only a handful of classes and not the whole application. These patterns have been narrow in scope. They frequently only relate to two or three classes and might be used but a single time in any given application. As you can imagine there are also larger scale patterns that are applicable to the application as a whole. You might think of "toolbar" as a general pattern that is used in many places in an application. What's more, it is a pattern that is used in a great number of applications to give them a similar look and feel. Patterns can help guide how the whole application is assembled.

In this chapter we're going to look at a family of patterns which I've taken to calling the MV* family. This family includes MVC, MVVM, MVP, and even PAC. Just like their names, the patterns themselves are pretty similar. The chapter will cover each of these patterns and show how, or if, we can apply them to JavaScript. We'll also pay special attention to how the patterns differ from one another. By the end of the chapter you should be able to thrill guests at a cocktail party with an explanation of the nuances of MVP versus MVC.

The topics covered will be as follows:

- History of Model View patterns
- Model View Controller
- Model View Presenter
- Model View ViewModel

# First, some history

Separating concerns inside an application is a very important idea. We live in a complex and ever-changing world. This means that not only is it nearly impossible to formulate a computer program which works in exactly the way users want, but that what users want is an ever-shifting maze. Couple this with the fact that an ideal program for user A is totally different from an ideal program for user B and we're guaranteed to end up in a mess. Our applications need to change as frequently as we change our socks: at least once a year.

Layering an application and maintaining modularity reduces the impact of a change. The less each layer knows about the other layers the better. Maintaining simple interfaces between the layers reduces the chances that a change to one layer will percolate to another layer.

If you've ever taken a close look at a high quality piece of nylon (from a hot air balloon, parachute, or expensive jacket) you may have noticed that that the fabric seems to form tiny squares. This is because, every few millimeters, a thick reinforcing thread is added to the weave to form a crosshatch pattern. If the fabric is ripped, then the rip will be stopped or at least slowed by the reinforcement. This limits the damage to a small area and prevents it from spreading.

Layers and modules in an application are exactly the same: they limit the spread of damage from a change.

In the early chapters of this book, we talked a bit about the seminal language, Smalltalk. It was the language which made classes famous. Like many of these patterns, the original MV* pattern, **Model View Controller** (**MVC**), was used long before it was ever identified. Although difficult to prove it seems that MVC was originally suggested in the late 1970s by Trygve Reenskaug, a Norwegian computer scientist, during a visit to the legendary Xerox PARC. Through the 1980s the pattern became heavily used in Smalltalk applications. However, it was not until 1988 that the pattern was more formally documented in an article entitled, *A Cookbook for Using the Model-View-Controller User Interface Paradigm* by Glenn E. Krasner and Stephen T. Pope.

# Model View Controller

MVC is a pattern that is useful for creating rich, interactive user interfaces: just the sort of interfaces which are becoming more and more popular on the web. The astute amongst you will have already figured out that the pattern is made up of three major components: model, view, and controller. You can see how information flows between the components in this illustration:

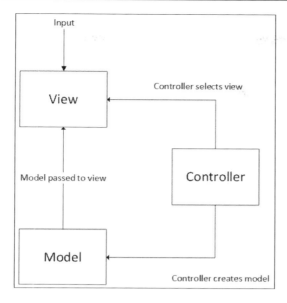

The preceding diagram shows the relationship between the three components in MVC.

The model contains the state of the program. In many applications this model is contained in some form, in a database. The model may be rehydrated from a persistent store such as the database or it can be transient. Ideally the model is the only mutable part of the pattern. Neither the view nor the controller has any state associated with them.

For a simple login screen the model might look like the following:

```
class LoginModel{
   UserName: string;
   Password: string;
   RememberMe: bool;
   LoginSuccessful: bool;
   LoginErrorMessage: string;
}
```

You'll notice that not only do we have fields for the inputs shown to the user but also for the state of the login. This would not be apparent to the user but it is still part of the application state.

The model is usually modeled as a simple container for information. Typically, there are no real functions in the model. It simply contains data fields and may also contain validation. In some implementations of the MVC pattern the model also contains meta-data about the fields such as validation rules.

The Naked Object pattern is a deviation from the typical MVC pattern. It augments the model with extensive business information as well as hits about the display and editing of data. It even contains methods for persisting the model to storage.

The views in the Naked Object pattern are generated from these models automatically. The controller is also automatically generated by examining the model. This centralizes the logic for displaying and manipulating application states and saves the developer from having to write their own views and controllers. So while the view and controller still exist, they are not actual objects but are dynamically created from the model.

Several systems have been successfully deployed using this pattern. Some criticism has emerged around the ability to generate an attractive user interface from just the models as well as how to properly coordinate multiple views.

In a foreword to the PhD thesis, *presenting Naked Objects* by Reenskaug, he suggests that the naked objects pattern is actually closer to his original vision for MVC than most of the derivations of MVC in the wild.

Updates to the model are communicated to the view whenever the state changes. This is typically done through the use of an observer pattern. The model does not typically know about either the controller or the view. The first is simply the thing telling it to change and the second is only updated through the observer pattern so the model doesn't have direct knowledge of it.

The view does pretty much what you would expect: communicate the model state to a target. I hesitate to suggest that the view must be a visual or graphical representation of the model as frequently the view is being communicated to another computer and may be in the form of XML, JSON, or some other data format. In most cases, especially those related to JavaScript, the view will be a graphical object. In a web context this will typically be HTML which is rendered by the browser. JavaScript is also gaining popularity on phones and on the desktop, so the view could also be a screen on a phone or on the desktop.

The view for the model presented in the preceding paragraph might look like the following figure:

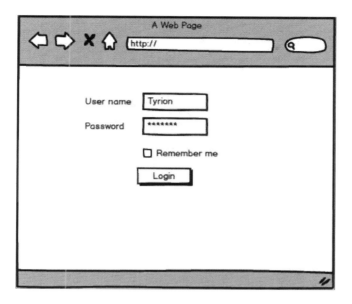

In cases, where the observer pattern is not used, then the view may poll the model at some interval looking for changes. In this case the view may have to keep a representation of the state itself or at least a version number. It is important that the view not unilaterally update this state without passing the updates to the controller, otherwise the model and the copy in the view will get out of sync.

Finally, the state of the model is updated by the controller. The controller usually contains all the logic and business rules for updating fields on the model. A simple controller for our login page might look like the following code:

```
class LoginController {
  constructor(model) {
    this.model = model;
  }
  Login(userName, password, rememberMe) {
    this.model.UserName = userName;
    this.model.Password = password;
    this.model.RememberMe = rememberMe;
    if (this.checkPassword(userName, password))
      this.model.LoginSuccessful;
    else {
```

```
            this.model.LoginSuccessful = false;
            this.model.LoginErrorMessage = "Incorrect username or password";
        }
    }
};
```

The controller knows about the existence of the model and is typically aware of the view's existence as well. It coordinates the two of them. A controller may be responsible for initializing more than one view. For instance, a single controller may provide a list view of all the instances of a model as well as a view that simply provides details. In many systems a controller will have create, read, update, and delete (CRUD) operations on it that work over a model. The controller is responsible for choosing the correct view and for wiring up the communication between the model and the view.

When there is a need for a change to the application then the location of the code should be immediately apparent. For example:

| Change | Location |
|---|---|
| Elements don't appear well spaced on the screen, change spacing. | View |
| No users are able to log in due to a logical error in password validation. | Controller |
| New field to be added. | All layers |

**Presentation-Abstraction-Control (PAC)** is another pattern that makes use of a triad of components. In this case its goal is to describe a hierarchy of encapsulated triples that more closely match how we think of the world. The control, similar to an MVC controller, passes interactions up in the hierarchy of encapsulated components allowing for information to flow between components. The abstraction is similar to a model but may represent only a few fields that are important for that specific PAC instead of the entire model. Finally, the presentation is effectively the same as a view.

The hierarchical nature of PAC allows for parallel processing of the components, meaning that it can be a powerful tool in today's multiprocessor systems.

You might notice that the last one there requires a change in all layers of the application. These multiple locations for responsibility are something that the Naked Objects pattern attempts to address by dynamically creating views and controllers. The MVC pattern splits code into locations by dividing the code by its role in user interaction. This means that a single data field lives in all the layers as is shown in this picture:

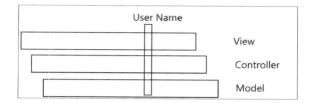

Some might call this a cross-cutting concern but really it doesn't span a sufficient amount of the application to be called such. Data access and logging are cross-cutting concerns as they are pervasive and difficult to centralize. This pervasion of a field through the different layers is really not a major problem. However, if it is bugging you then you might be an ideal candidate for using the Naked Objects pattern.

Let's step into building some code to represent a MVC in JavaScript.

# MVC code

Let's start with a simple scenario for which we can apply MVC. Unfortunately, Westeros has very few computers, likely due to the lack of electricity. Thus applying application structuring patterns using Westeros as an example is difficult. Sadly we'll have to take a step back and talk about an application which controls Westeros. Let's assume it to be a web application and implement the entirety of MVC on the client side.

It is possible to implement MVC by splitting the model, view and controller between client and server. Typically, the controller would sit on the server and provide an API which is known by the view. The model serves as a communication method both to the view which resides on the web browser and to the data store, likely a database of some form. It is also common that the controller be split between the server and the client in cases where some additional control is required on the client.

In our example we would like to create a screen that controls the properties of a castle. Fortunately, you're lucky that this is not a book on designing user interfaces with HTML as I would certainly fail. We'll stick to a picture in place of the HTML:

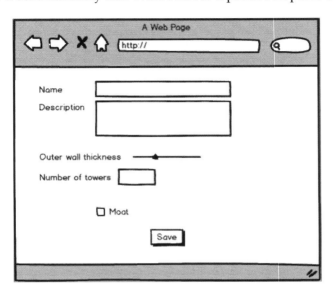

For the most part, the view simply provides a set of controls and data for the end user. In this example the view will need to know how to call the save function on the controller. Let's set that up:

```
class CreateCastleView {
  constructor(document, controller, model, validationResult) {
    this.document = document;
    this.controller = controller;
    this.model = model;
    this.validationResult = validationResult;
    this.document.getElementById("saveButton").
      addEventListener("click", () => this.saveCastle());
    this.document.getElementById("castleName").value = model.name;
    this.document.getElementById("description").value = model.
     description;
    this.document.getElementById("outerWallThickness").value = model.
     outerWallThickness;
    this.document.getElementById("numberOfTowers").value = model.
     numberOfTowers;
    this.document.getElementById("moat").value = model.moat;
  }
  saveCastle() {
```

```
    var data = {
      name: this.document.getElementById("castleName").value,
      description: this.document.getElementById("description").value,
      outerWallThickness: this.document.getElementById("outerWallThic
        kness").value,
      numberOfTowers: this.document.getElementById("numberOfTowers").
        value,
      moat: this.document.getElementById("moat").value
    };
    this.controller.saveCastle(data);
  }
}
```

You'll notice that the constructor for this view contains both a reference to the
document and to the controller. The document contains both HTML and styling,
provided by CSS. We can get away with not passing in a reference to the document
but injecting the document in this fashion allows for easier testability. We'll look at
testability more in a later chapter. It also permits reusing the view multiple times on
a single page without worrying about the two instances conflicting.

The constructor also contains a reference to the model which is used to add data to
fields on the page as needed. Finally, the constructor also references a collection of
errors. This allows for validation errors from the controller to be passed back to the
view to be handled. We have set the validation result to be a wrapped collection that
looks something like the following:

```
class ValidationResult{
  public IsValid: boolean;
  public Errors: Array<String>;
  public constructor(){
    this.Errors = new Array<String>();
  }
}
```

The only functionality here is that the button's onclick method is bound to calling
save on the controller. Instead of passing in a large number of parameters to the
saveCastle function on the controller, we build a lightweight object and pass
that in. This makes the code more readable, especially in cases where some of the
parameters are optional. No real work is done in the view and all the input goes
directly to the controller.

The controller contains the real functionality of the application:

```
class Controller {
  constructor(document) {
    this.document = document;
  }
  createCastle() {
    this.setView(new CreateCastleView(this.document, this));
  }
  saveCastle(data) {
    var validationResult = this.validate(data);
    if (validationResult.IsValid) {
      //save castle to storage
      this.saveCastleSuccess(data);
    }
    else {
      this.setView(new CreateCastleView(this.document, this, data,
        validationResult));
    }
  }
  saveCastleSuccess(data) {
    this.setView(new CreateCastleSuccess(this.document, this, data));
  }
  setView(view) {
    //send the view to the browser
  }
  validate(model) {
    var validationResult = new validationResult();
    if (!model.name || model.name === "") {
      validationResult.IsValid = false;
      validationResult.Errors.push("Name is required");
    }
    return;
  }
}
```

The controller here does a number of things. The first thing is that it has a `setView` function which instructs the browser to set the given view as the current one. This is likely done through the use of a template. The mechanics of how that works are not important to the pattern so I'll leave that up to your imagination.

Next, the controller implements a `validate` method. This method checks to make sure that the model is valid. Some validation may be performed on the client, such as testing the format of a postal code, but other validation requires a server trip. If a username must be unique then there is no reasonable way to test that on the client without communicating with the server. In some cases, the validation functionality may exist on the model rather than in the controller.

Methods for setting up various different views are also found in the controller. In this case we have a bit of a workflow with a view for creating a castle then views for both success and failure. The failure case just returns the same view with a collection of validation errors attached to it. The success case returns a whole new view.

The logic to save the model to some sort of persistent storage is also located in the controller. Again the implementation of this is less important than to see that the logic for communicating with the storage system is located in the controller.

The final letter in MVC is the model. In this case, it is a very light weight one:

```
class Model {
    constructor(name, description, outerWallThickness, numberOfTowers,
        moat) {
        this.name = name;
        this.description = description;
        this.outerWallThickness = outerWallThickness;
        this.numberOfTowers = numberOfTowers;
        this.moat = moat;
    }
}
```

As you can see, all it does is keep track of the variables that make up the state of the application.

Concerns are well separated in this pattern allowing for changes to be made with relative ease.

# Model View Presenter

The **Model View Presenter (MVP)** pattern is very similar to MVC. It is a fairly well known pattern in the Microsoft world and is generally used to structure WPF and Silverlight applications. It can be used in pure JavaScript as well. The key difference comes down to how the different parts of the system interact and where their responsibility ends.

The first difference is that, with the presenter, there is a one to one mapping between presenter and view. This means that the logic that existed in the controller in the MVC pattern, which selected the correct view to render, doesn't exist. Or rather it exists at a higher level outside the concern of the pattern. The selection of the correct presenter may be handled by a routing tool. Such a router will examine the parameters and provide the best choice for the presenter. The flow of information in the MVP pattern can be seen here:

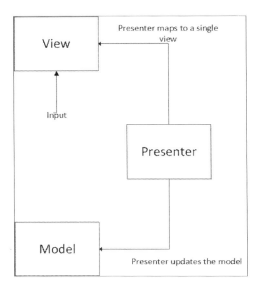

The presenter is aware of both the view and the model but the view is unaware of the model and the model unaware of the view. All communication is passed through the presenter.

The presenter pattern is often characterized by a great deal of two-way dispatch. A click will fire in the presenter and then the presenter will update the model with the change and then the view. The preceding diagram suggests that the input first passes through the view. In a passive version of the MVP pattern, the view has little to no interaction with the messages as they are passed onto the presenter. However, there is also a variation called active MVP that allows the view to contain some additional logic.

This active version of MVP can be more useful for web situations. It permits adding validation and other simple logic to the view. This reduces the number of requests that need to pass from the client back to the web server.

Let's update our existing code sample to use MVP instead of MVC.

# MVP code

Let's start again with the view:

```
class CreateCastleView {
  constructor(document, presenter) {
    this.document = document;
    this.presenter = presenter;
    this.document.getElementById("saveButton").
      addEventListener("click", this.saveCastle);
  }
  setCastleName(name) {
    this.document.getElementById("castleName").value = name;
  }
  getCastleName() {
    return this.document.getElementById("castleName").value;
  }
  setDescription(description) {
    this.document.getElementById("description").value = description;
  }
  getDescription() {
    return this.document.getElementById("description").value;
  }
  setOuterWallThickness(outerWallThickness) {
    this.document.getElementById("outerWallThickness").value =
      outerWallThickness;
  }
  getOuterWallThickness() {
    return this.document.getElementById("outerWallThickness").value;
  }
  setNumberOfTowers(numberOfTowers) {
    this.document.getElementById("numberOfTowers").value =
      numberOfTowers;
  }
  getNumberOfTowers() {
    return parseInt(this.document.getElementById("numberOfTowers").
      value);
  }
  setMoat(moat) {
    this.document.getElementById("moat").value = moat;
  }
  getMoat() {
    return this.document.getElementById("moat").value;
  }
  setValid(validationResult) {
  }
  saveCastle() {
```

```
      this.presenter.saveCastle();
    }
  }
```

As you can see the constructor for the view no longer takes a reference to the model. This is because the view in MVP doesn't have any idea about what model is being used. That information is abstracted away by the presenter. The reference to presenter remains in the constructor to allow sending messages back to the presenter.

Without the model there is an increase in the number of public setter and getter methods. These setters allow the presenter to make updates to the state of the view. The getters provide an abstraction over how the view stores the state and gives the presenter a way to get the information. The saveCastle function no longer passes any values to the presenter.

The presenter's code looks like the following:

```
class CreateCastlePresenter {
  constructor(document) {
    this.document = document;
    this.model = new CreateCastleModel();
    this.view = new CreateCastleView(document, this);
  }
  saveCastle() {
    var data = {
      name: this.view.getCastleName(),
      description: this.view.getDescription(),
      outerWallThickness: this.view.getOuterWallThickness(),
      numberOfTowers: this.view.getNumberOfTowers(),
      moat: this.view.getMoat()
    };
    var validationResult = this.validate(data);
    if (validationResult.IsValid) {
      //write to the model
      this.saveCastleSuccess(data);
    }
    else {
      this.view.setValid(validationResult);
    }
  }
  saveCastleSuccess(data) {
    //redirect to different presenter
  }
  validate(model) {
    var validationResult = new validationResult();
    if (!model.name || model.name === "") {
      validationResult.IsValid = false;
```

```
        validationResult.Errors.push("Name is required");
    }
    return;
    }
}
```

You can see that the view is now referenced in a persistent fashion in the presenter. The `saveCastle` method calls into the view to get its values. However, the presenter does make sure to use the public methods of the view instead of referencing the document directly. The `saveCastle` method updates the model. If there are validation errors, then it will call back into the view to update the `IsValid` flag. This is an example of the double dispatch I mentioned earlier.

Finally, the model remains unchanged from before. We've kept the validation logic in the presenter. At which level the validation is done, model or presenter, matters less than being consistent in where the validation is done through your application.

The MVP pattern is again a fairly useful pattern for building user interfaces. The larger separation between the view and the model creates a stricter API allowing for better adaptation to change. However, this comes at the expense of more code. With more code comes more opportunity for bugs.

# Model View ViewModel

The final pattern we'll look at in this chapter is the Model View ViewModel pattern, more commonly known as MVVM. By now this sort of pattern should be getting quite familiar. Again you can see the flow of information between components in this illustration:

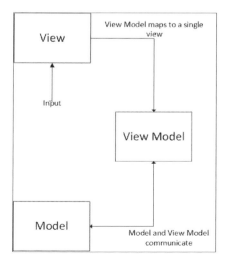

You can see here that many of the same constructs have returned but that the communication between them is somewhat different.

In this variation, what has previously been the controller and presenter is now the view model. Just like with MVC and MVP, the majority of the logic is held within the central component, in this case the view model. The model itself is actually very simple in MVVM. Typically, it acts as an envelope that just holds data. Validation is done within the view model.

Just like with MVP, the view is totally unaware of the existence of the model. The difference is that, with MVP, the view was aware that it was talking to some intermediate class. It called methods rather than simply setting values. In MVVM the view believes that the view model is its view. Instead of calling operations like saveCastle and passing in data or waiting for data to be requested, the view updates fields on the view model as they change. In effect, the fields on the view are bound to the view model. The view model may proxy these values through to the model or wait until a commit-like operation like save is called to pass the data along.

Equally, changes to the view model should be reflected at once in the view. A single view may have a number of view models. Each of these view models may push updates to the view or have changes pushed to it via the view.

Let's take a look at a really rudimentary implementation of this and then we'll discuss how to make it better.

# MVVM code

The naïve view implementation is, frankly, a huge mess:

```
var CreateCastleView = (function () {
  function CreateCastleView(document, viewModel) {
    this.document = document;
    this.viewModel = viewModel;
    var _this = this;
    this.document.getElementById("saveButton").
      addEventListener("click", function () {
      return _this.saveCastle();
    });
  this.document.getElementById("name").addEventListener("change",
    this.nameChangedInView);
  this.document.getElementById("description").
   addEventListener("change", this.descriptionChangedInView);
  this.document.getElementById("outerWallThickness").
   addEventListener("change", this.outerWallThicknessChangedInView);
```

```
      this.document.getElementById("numberOfTowers").
        addEventListener("change", this.numberOfTowersChangedInView);
      this.document.getElementById("moat").addEventListener("change",
        this.moatChangedInView);
    }
    CreateCastleView.prototype.nameChangedInView = function (name) {
      this.viewModel.nameChangedInView(name);
    };

    CreateCastleView.prototype.nameChangedInViewModel = function (name) {
      this.document.getElementById("name").value = name;
    };
    //snipped more of the same
    CreateCastleView.prototype.isValidChangedInViewModel = function
      (validationResult) {
      this.document.getElementById("validationWarning").innerHtml =
        validationResult.Errors;
      this.document.getElementById("validationWarning").className =
        "visible";
    };
    CreateCastleView.prototype.saveCastle = function () {
      this.viewModel.saveCastle();
    };
    return CreateCastleView;
})();
CastleDesign.CreateCastleView = CreateCastleView;
```

It is highly repetitive and each property must be proxied back to `ViewModel`. I've truncated most of this code but it adds up to a good 70 lines. The code inside the view model is equally terrible:

```
var CreateCastleViewModel = (function () {
  function CreateCastleViewModel(document) {
    this.document = document;
    this.model = new CreateCastleModel();
    this.view = new CreateCastleView(document, this);
  }
  CreateCastleViewModel.prototype.nameChangedInView = function (name)
  {
    this.name = name;
  };

  CreateCastleViewModel.prototype.nameChangedInViewModel = function
    (name) {
```

```
          this.view.nameChangedInViewModel(name);
      };
      //snip
      CreateCastleViewModel.prototype.saveCastle = function () {
        var validationResult = this.validate();
        if (validationResult.IsValid) {
          //write to the model
          this.saveCastleSuccess();
        } else {
          this.view.isValidChangedInViewModel(validationResult);
        }
      };

      CreateCastleViewModel.prototype.saveCastleSuccess = function () {
        //do whatever is needed when save is successful.
        //Possibly update the view model
      };

      CreateCastleViewModel.prototype.validate = function () {
        var validationResult = new validationResult();
        if (!this.name || this.name === "") {
          validationResult.IsValid = false;
            validationResult.Errors.push("Name is required");
        }
        return;
      };
    return CreateCastleViewModel;
})();
```

One look at this code should send you running for the hills. It is set up in a way that will encourage copy and paste programming: a fantastic way to introduce errors into a code base. I sure hope there is a better way to transfer changes between the model and the view.

# A better way to transfer changes between the model and the view

It may not have escaped your notice that there are a number of MVVM-style frameworks for JavaScript in the wild. Obviously they would not have been readily adopted if they followed the approach that we described in the preceding section. Instead they follow one of two different approaches.

The first approach is known as dirty checking. In this approach, after every interaction with the view model we loop over all of its properties looking for changes. When changes are found, the related value in the view is updated with the new value. For changes to values in the view change, actions are attached to all the controls. These then trigger updates to the view model.

This approach can be slow for large models as it is expensive to iterate over all the properties of a large model. The number of things which can cause a model to change is high and there is no real way to tell if a distant field in a model has been changed by changing another without going and validating it. On the upside, dirty checking allows you to use plain old JavaScript objects. There is no need to write your code any differently than before. The same is not true of the other approach: container objects.

With a container object a special interface is provided to wrap existing objects so that changes to the object may be directly observed. Basically this is an application of the observer pattern but applied dynamically so the underlying object has no idea it is being observed. The spy pattern, perhaps?

An example might be helpful here. Let us say that we have the model object we've been using up until now:

```
var CreateCastleModel = (function () {
  function CreateCastleModel(name, description, outerWallThickness,
    numberOfTowers, moat) {
    this.name = name;
    this.description = description;
    this.outerWallThickness = outerWallThickness;
    this.numberOfTowers = numberOfTowers;
    this.moat = moat;
  }
  return CreateCastleModel;
})();
```

Then, instead of `model.name` being a simple string, we would wrap some function around it. In the case of the Knockout library this would look like the following:

```
var CreateCastleModel = (function () {
  function CreateCastleModel(name, description, outerWallThickness,
    numberOfTowers, moat) {
    this.name = ko.observable(name);
    this.description = ko.observable(description);
    this.outerWallThickness = ko.observable(outerWallThickness);
    this.numberOfTowers = ko.observable(numberOfTowers);
```

```
        this.moat = ko.observable(moat);
    }
    return CreateCastleModel;
})();
```

In the highlighted code, the various properties of the model are being wrapped with an observable. This means that they must now be accessed differently:

```
var model = new CreateCastleModel();
model.name("Winterfell"); //set
model.name(); //get
```

This approach obviously adds some friction to your code and makes changing frameworks quite involved.

Current MVVM frameworks are split on their approach to container objects versus dirty checking. AngularJS uses dirty checking while Backbone, Ember, and Knockout all make use of container objects. There is currently no clear winner.

# Observing view changes

Fortunately, the pervasiveness of MV* patterns on the web and the difficulties with observing model changes has not gone unnoticed. You might be expecting me to say that this will be solved in ECMAScript-2015 as is my normal approach. Weirdly, the solution to all of this, `Object.observe`, is a feature under discussion for ECMAScript-2016. However, at the time of writing, at least one major browser already supports it.

It can be used like the following:

```
var model = { };
Object.observe(model, function(changes){
  changes.forEach(function(change) {
    console.log("A " + change.type + " occured on " + change.name +
      ".");
    if(change.type=="update")
      console.log("\tOld value was " + change.oldValue );
  });
});
model.item = 7;
model.item = 8;
delete model.item;
```

Having this simple interface to monitor changes to objects removes much of the logic provided by large MV* frameworks. It will be easier to roll your own functionality for MV* and there may, in fact, be no need to use external frameworks.

# Tips and tricks

The different layers of the various MV* patterns need not all be on the browser, nor do they all need to be written in JavaScript. Many popular frameworks allow for maintaining a model on the server and communicating with it using JSON.

`Object.observe` may not be available on all browsers yet, but there are polyfills that can be used to create a similar interface. The performance is not as good as the native implementation, but it is still usable.

# Summary

Separating concerns to a number of layers ensures that changes to the application are isolated like a ripstop. The various MV* patterns allow for separating the concerns in a graphical application. The differences between the various patterns come down to how the responsibilities are separated and how information is communicated.

In the next chapter we'll look at a number of patterns and techniques to improve the experience of developing and deploying JavaScript to the Web.

# 9
# Web Patterns

The rise of Node.js has proven that JavaScript has a place on web servers, even very high throughput servers. There is no denying that JavaScript's pedigree remains in the browser for client side programming.

In this chapter we're going to look at a number of patterns to improve the performance and usefulness of JavaScript on the client. I'm not sure that all of these can be thought of as patterns in the strictest sense. They are, however, important and worth mentioning.

The concepts we'll examine in this chapter are as follows:

- Sending JavaScript
- Plugins
- Multithreading
- Circuit breaker pattern
- Back-off
- Promises

## Sending JavaScript

Communicating JavaScript to the client seems to be a simple proposition: so long as you can get the code to the client it doesn't matter how that happens, right? Well not exactly. There are actually a number of things that need to be considered when sending JavaScript to the browser.

# Combining files

Way back in *Chapter 2, Organizing Code*, we looked at how to build objects using JavaScript, although opinions on this vary. I consider it to be good form to have a one-class-to-one-file organization of my JavaScript or really any of my object oriented code. By doing this, it makes finding code easy. Nobody needs to hunt through a 9000 line long JavaScript file to locate that one method. It also allows for a hierarchy to be established again allowing for good code organization. However, good organization for a developer is not necessarily good organization for a computer. In our case having a lot of small files is actually highly detrimental. To understand why, you need to know a little bit about how browsers ask for and receive content.

When you type a URL into the address bar of a browser and hit *Enter*, a cascading series of events happens. The first thing is that the browser will ask the operating system to resolve the website name to an IP address. On both Windows and Linux (and OSX) the standard C library function `gethostbyname` is used. This function will check the local DNS cache to see if the mapping from name to address is already known. If it is, then that information is returned. If not, then the computer makes a request to the DNS server one step up from it. Typically, this is the DNS server provided by the ISP but on a larger network it could also be a local DNS server. The path of a query between DNS servers can be seen here:

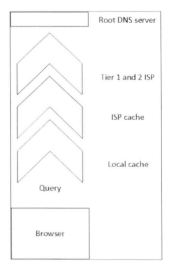

If a record doesn't exist on that server then the request is propagated up a chain of DNS servers in an attempt to find one that knows about the domain. Eventually the propagation stops at the root servers. These root servers are the stopping point for queries – if they don't know who is responsible for DNS information for a domain then the lookup is deemed to have failed.

Once the browser has an address for the site it opens up a connection and sends a request for the document. If no document is provided, then a / is sent. Should the connection be a secure one, then negotiation of SSL/TSL is performed at this time. There is some computational expense to setting up an encrypted connection but this is slowly being fixed.

The server will respond with a blob of HTML. As the browser receives this HTML it starts to process it; the browser does not wait for the entire HTML document to be downloaded before it goes to work. If the browser encounters a resource that is external to the HTML it will kick off a new request to open another connection to the web server and download that resource. The maximum number of connections to a single domain is limited so that the web server isn't flooded. It should also be mentioned that setting up a new connection to the web server carries overhead. The flow of data between a web client and server can be seen in this illustration:

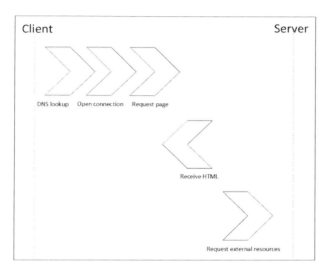

Connections to the web server should be limited to avoid paying the connection setup costs repeatedly. This brings us to our first concept: combining files.

If you've followed the advice to leverage namespaces and classes in your JavaScript, then putting all of your JavaScript together in a single file is a trivial step. One need only concatenate the files together and everything should continue to work as normal. Some minor care and attention may need to be paid to the order of inclusion, but not typically.

The previous code we've written has been pretty much one file per pattern. If there is a need for multiple patterns to be used, then we could simply concatenate the files together. For instance, the combined builder and factory method patterns might look like the following:

```
var Westeros;
(function (Westeros) {
  (function (Religion) {
     ...
  })(Westeros.Religion || (Westeros.Religion = {}));
  var Religion = Westeros.Religion;
})(Westeros || (Westeros = {}));
(function (Westeros) {
  var Tournament = (function () {
    function Tournament() {
    }
  return Tournament;
})();
Westeros.Tournament = Tournament;
  ...
})();
Westeros.Attendee = Attendee;
})(Westeros || (Westeros = {}));
```

The question may arise as to how much of your JavaScript should be combined and loaded at once. It is a surprisingly difficult question to answer. On one hand it is desirable to front load all the JavaScript for the entire site when users first arrive at the site. This means that users will pay a price initially but will not have to download any additional JavaScript as they travel about the site. This is because the browser will cache the script and reuse it instead of downloading it from the server again. However, if users only visit a small subset of the pages on the site then they will have loaded a great deal of JavaScript that was not needed.

On the other hand, splitting up the JavaScript means that additional page visits incur a penalty for retrieving additional JavaScript files. There is a sweet spot somewhere in the middle of these two approaches. Script can be organized into blocks that map to different sections of the website. This can be a place where using proper name spacing will come in handy once again. Each namespace can be combined into a single file and then loaded as users visit that part of the site.

In the end, the only approach that makes sense is to maintain statistics about how users move about the site. Based on this information an optimal strategy for finding the sweet spot can be established.

# Minification

Combining JavaScript into a single file solves the problem of limiting the number of requests. However, each request may still be large. Again we come to a schism between what makes code fast and readable by humans and what makes it fast and readable by computers.

We humans like descriptive variable names, bountiful whitespace, and proper indentation. Computers don't care about descriptive names, whitespace, or proper indentation. In fact, these things increase the size of the file and thus decrease the speed at which the code can be read.

Minification is a compile step that transforms the human readable code into smaller, but equivalent, code. External variables' names remain the same, as the minifier has no way to know what other code may be relying on the variable names remaining unchanged.

As an example, if we start with the composite code from *Chapter 4, Structural Patterns*, the minified code looks like the following:

```
var Westros;(function(Westros){(function(Food){var
SimpleIngredient=(function(){function SimpleIngredient(name
,calories,ironContent,vitaminCContent){this.name=name;this.
calories=calories;this.ironContent=ironContent;this.
vitaminCContent=vitaminCContent}SimpleIngredient.prototype.
GetName=function(){return this.name};SimpleIngredient.prototype.
GetCalories=function(){return this.calories};SimpleIngredient.
prototype.GetIronContent=function(){return this.
ironContent};SimpleIngredient.prototype.GetVitaminCContent=function()
{return this.vitaminCContent};return SimpleIngredient})();Food.Sim
pleIngredient=SimpleIngredient;var CompoundIngredient=(function()
{function CompoundIngredient(name){this.name=name;this.ingredients=new
Array()}CompoundIngredient.prototype.AddIngredient=function(ing
redient){this.ingredients.push(ingredient)};CompoundIngredient.
prototype.GetName=function(){return this.name};CompoundIngredient.
prototype.GetCalories=function(){var total=0;for(var i=0;i<this.
ingredients.length;i++){total+=this.ingredients[i].GetCalories()}
return total};CompoundIngredient.prototype.GetIronContent=function()
{var total=0;for(var i=0;i<this.ingredients.length;i++){total+=this.
ingredients[i].GetIronContent()}return total};CompoundIngredient.
prototype.GetVitaminCContent=function(){var total=0;for(var
i=0;i<this.ingredients.length;i++){total+=this.ingredients[i].
GetVitaminCContent()}return total};return CompoundIngredient})();Food.
CompoundIngredient=CompoundIngredient})(Westros.Food||(Westros.
Food={}));var Food=Westros.Food})(Westros||(Westros={}));
```

You'll notice that all the spacing has been removed and that any internal variables have been replaced with smaller versions. At the same time, you can spot some well-known variable names have remained unchanged.

Minification saved this particular piece of code 40%. Compressing the content stream from the server using gzip, a popular approach, is lossless compression. That means that there is a perfect bijection between compressed and uncompressed. Minification, on the other hand, is a lossy compression. There is no way to get back to the unminified code from just the minified code once it has been minified.

 You can read more about gzip compression at `http://betterexplained.com/articles/how-to-optimize-your-site-with-gzip-compression/`.

If there is a need to return to the original code, then source maps can be used. A source map is a file that provides a translation from one format of code to another. It can be loaded by the debugging tools in modern browsers to allow you to debug the original code instead of unintelligible minified code. Multiple source maps can be combine to allow for translation from, say, minified code to unminified JavaScript to TypeScript.

There are numerous tools which can be used to construct minified and combined JavaScript. Gulp and Grunt are JavaScript-based tools for building a pipeline which manages JavaScript assets. Both these tools call out to external tools such as Uglify to do the actual work. Gulp and Grunt are the equivalent to GNU Make or Ant.

# Content Delivery Networks

The final delivery trick is to make use of **Content Delivery Networks (CDNs)**. CDNs are distributed networks of hosts whose only purpose is to serve out static content. In much the same way that the browser will cache JavaScript between pages on the site, it will also cache JavaScript that is shared between multiple web servers. Thus, if your site makes use of jQuery, pulling jQuery from a well-known CDN such as `https://code.jquery.com/` or Microsoft's ASP.net CDN may be faster as it is already cached. Pulling from a CDN also means that the content is coming from a different domain and doesn't count against the limited connections to your server. Referencing a CDN is as simple as setting the source of the script tag to point at the CDN.

Once again, some metrics will need to be gathered to see whether it is better to use a CDN or simply roll libraries into the JavaScript bundle. Examples of such metrics may include the added time to perform additional DNS lookup and the difference in the download sizes. The best approach is to use the timing APIs in the browser.

The long and short of distributing JavaScript to the browser is that experimentation is required. Testing a number of approaches and measuring the results will give the best result for end users.

# Plugins

There are a great number of really impressive JavaScript libraries in the wild. For me the library that changed how I look at JavaScript was jQuery. For others it may have been one of the other popular libraries such as MooTool, Dojo, Prototype, or YUI. However, jQuery has exploded in popularity and has, at the time of writing, won the JavaScript library wars. 78.5% of the top ten thousand websites, by traffic, on the internet make use of some version of jQuery. None of the rest of the libraries even breaks 1%.

Many developers have seen fit to implement their own libraries on top of these foundational libraries in the form of plugins. A plugin typically modifies the prototype exposed by the library and adds additional functionality. The syntax is such that, to the end developer, it appears to be part of the core library.

How plugins are built varies depending on the library you're trying to extend. Nonetheless, let's take a look at how we can build a plugin for jQuery and then for one of my favourite libraries, d3. We'll see if we can extract some commonalities.

# jQuery

At jQuery's core is the CSS selector library called `sizzle.js`. It is sizzle that is responsible for all the really nifty ways jQuery can select items on a page using CSS3 selectors. Use jQuery to select elements on a page like so:

```
$(":input").css("background-color", "blue");
```

Here, a jQuery object is returned. The jQuery object acts a lot like, although not completely like, an array. This is achieved by creating a series of keys on the jQuery object numbered 0 through to n-1 where n is the number of elements matched by the selector. This is actually pretty smart as it enables array like accessors:

```
$($(":input")[2]).css("background-color", "blue");
```

While providing a bunch of additional functions, the items at the indices are plain HTML Elements and not wrapped with jQuery, hence the use of the second `$()`.

For jQuery plugins, we typically want to make our plugins extend this jQuery object. Because it is dynamically created every time the selector is fired we actually extend an object called `$.fn`. This object is used as the basis for creating all jQuery objects. Thus creating a plugin that transforms all the text in inputs on the page into uppercase is nominally as simple as the following:

```
$.fn.yeller = function(){
  this.each(function(_, item){
    $(item).val($(item).val().toUpperCase());
    return this;
  });
};
```

This plugin is particularly useful for posting to bulletin boards and for whenever my boss fills in a form. The plugin iterates over all the objects selected by the selector and converts their content to uppercase. It also returns this. By doing so we allow for chaining of additional functions. You can use the function like so:

```
$(function(){$("input").yeller();});
```

It does rather depend on the $ variable being assigned to jQuery. This isn't always the case as $ is a popular variable in JavaScript libraries, likely because it is the only character that isn't a letter or a number and doesn't already have special meaning.

To combat this, we can use an immediately evaluated function in much the same way we did way back in *Chapter 2, Organizing Code*:

```
(function($){
  $.fn.yeller2 = function(){
    this.each(function(_, item){
      $(item).val($(item).val().toUpperCase());
      return this;
    });
  };
})(jQuery);
```

The added advantage here is that, should our code require helper functions or private variables, they can be set inside the same function. You can also pass in any options required. jQuery provides a very helpful `$.extend` function that copies properties between objects, making it ideal for extending a set of default options with those passed in. We looked at this in some detail in a previous chapter.

The jQuery plugin documentation recommends that the jQuery object be polluted as little as possible with plugins. This is to avoid conflicts between multiple plugins that want to use the same names. Their solution is to have a single function that has different behaviours depending on the parameters passed in. For instance, the jQuery UI plugin uses this approach for dialog:

```
$(«.dialog»).dialog(«open»);
$(«.dialog»).dialog(«close»);
```

I would much rather call these like the following:

```
$(«.dialog»).dialog().open();
$(«.dialog»).dialog().close();
```

With dynamic languages there really isn't a great deal of difference but I would much rather have well named functions that can be discovered by tooling than magic strings.

# d3

d3 is a great JavaScript library that is used for creating and manipulating visualizations. For the most part, people use d3 in conjunction with scalable vector graphics to produce graphics such as this hexbin graph by Mike Bostock:

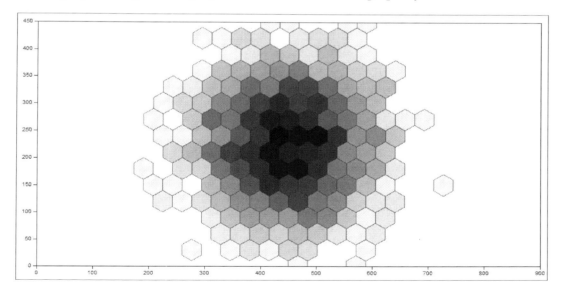

d3 attempts to be non-opinionated about the sorts of visualizations it creates. Thus there is no built-in support for creating such things as bar charts. There is, however, a collection of plugins that can be added to d3 to enable a wide variety of graphs including the hexbin one shown in the preceding figure.

Even more, the jQuery d3 places emphasis on creating chainable functions. For example, this code is a snippet that creates a column chart. You can see that all the attributes are being set through chaining:

```
var svg = d3.select(containerId).append("svg")
var bar = svg.selectAll("g").data(data).enter().append("g");
bar.append("rect")
.attr("height", yScale.rangeBand()).attr("fill", function (d, _) {
  return colorScale.getColor(d);
})
.attr("stroke", function (d, _) {
  return colorScale.getColor(d);
})
.attr("y", function (d, i) {
  return yScale(d.Id) + margins.height;
})
```

The core of d3 is the d3 object. Off that object hang a number of namespaces for layouts, scales, geometry, and numerous others. As well as whole namespaces, there are functions for doing array manipulation and loading data from external sources.

Creating a plugin for d3 starts with deciding where we're going to plug into the code. Let's build a plugin that creates a new color scale. A color scale is used to map a domain of values to a range of colors. For instance, we might wish to map the domain of the following four values onto a range of four colors:

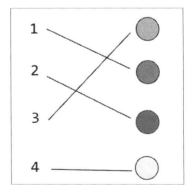

Let's plug in a function to provide a new color scale, in this case one that supports grouping elements. A scale is a function that maps a domain to a range. For a color scale, the range is a set of colors. An example might be a function that maps all even numbers to red and all odd to white. Using this scale on a table would result in zebra striping:

```
d3.scale.groupedColorScale = function () {
  var domain, range;

  function scale(x) {
    var rangeIndex = 0;
    domain.forEach(function (item, index) {
      if (item.indexOf(x) > 0)
        rangeIndex = index;
    });
    return range[rangeIndex];
  }

  scale.domain = function (x) {
    if (!arguments.length)
      return domain;
    domain = x;
    return scale;
  };

  scale.range = function (x) {
    if (!arguments.length)
      return range;
    range = x;
    return scale;
  };
  return scale;
};
```

We simply attach this plugin to the existing d3.scale object. This can be used by simply giving an array of arrays as a domain and an array as a range:

```
var s = d3.scale.groupedColorScale().domain([[1, 2, 3], [4, 5]]).
range(["#111111", "#222222"]);
s(3); //#111111
s(4); //#222222
```

This simple plugin extends the functionality of d3's scale. We could have replaced existing functionality or even wrapped it such that calls into existing functionality would be proxied through our plugin.

Plugins are generally not that difficult to build but they do vary from library to library. It is important to keep an eye on the existing variable names in libraries so we don't end up clobbering them or even clobbering functionality provided by other plugins. Some suggest prefixing functions with a string to avoid clobbering.

If the library has been designed with it in mind there may be additional places into which we can hook. A popular approach is to provide an options object that contains optional fields for hooking in our own functions as event handlers. If nothing is provided the function continues as normal.

# Doing two things at once – multithreading

Doing two things at once is hard. For many years the solution in the computer world was to use either multiple processes or multiple threads. The difference between the two is fuzzy due to implementation differences on different operating systems but threads are typically lighter-weight versions of processes. JavaScript on the browser supports neither of these approaches.

Historically, there has been no real need for multithreading on a browser. JavaScript was used to manipulate the user interface. When manipulating a UI, even in other languages and windowing environments, only one thread is permitted to act at a time. This avoids race conditions that would be very obvious to users.

However, as JavaScript grows in popularity, more and more complicated software is being written to run inside the browser. Sometimes that software could really benefit from performing complex calculations in the background.

Web workers provide a mechanism for doing two things at once in a browser. Although a fairly recent innovation, web workers now have good support in mainstream browsers. In effect a worker is a background thread that can communicate with the main thread using messages. Web workers must be self-contained in a single JavaScript file.

To make use of web workers is fairly easy. We'll revisit our example from a few chapters ago when we looked at the fibonacci sequence. The worker process listens for messages like so:

```
self.addEventListener('message', function(e) {
  var data = e.data;
  if(data.cmd == 'startCalculation'){
    self.postMessage({event: 'calculationStarted'});
    var result = fib(data.parameters.number);
    self.postMessage({event: 'calculationComplete', result: result});
  };
}, false);
```

Here we start a new instance of `fib` any time we get a `startCalculation` message. `fib` is simply the naive implementation from earlier.

The main thread loads the worker process from its external file and attaches a number of listeners:

```
function startThread(){
  worker =  new Worker("worker.js");
  worker.addEventListener('message', function(message) {
    logEvent(message.data.event);
    if(message.data.event == "calculationComplete"){
      writeResult(message.data.result);
    }
    if(message.data.event == "calculationStarted"){
      document.getElementById("result").innerHTML = "working";
    }
  });
};
```

In order to start the calculation, all that is needed is to send a command:

```
worker.postMessage({cmd: 'startCalculation',
  parameters: { number: 40}});
```

Here we pass the number of the term in the sequence we want to calculate. While the calculation is running in the background the main thread is free to do whatever it likes. When the message is received back from the worker it is placed in the normal event loop to be processed:

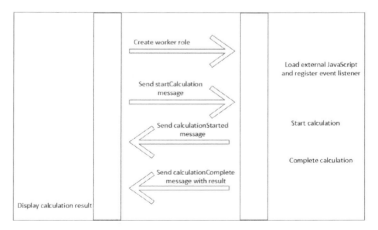

Web workers may be useful to you if you have to do any time consuming calculations in JavaScript.

If you're making use of server-side JavaScript through the use of Node.js then there is a different approach to doing more than one thing at a time. Node.js offers the ability to fork child processes and provides an interface not dissimilar to the web worker one to communicate between the child and parent processes. This method forks an entire process though, which is much more resource intensive than using lightweight threads.

Some other tools exist that create lighter-weight background workers in Node.js. These are probably a closer parallel to what exists on the web side than forking a child process.

# Circuit breaker pattern

Systems, even the best designed systems, fail. The larger and more distributed a system, the higher the probability of failure. Many large systems such as Netflix or Google have extensive built-in redundancies. The redundancies don't decrease the chance of a failure of a component but they do provide a backup. Switching to the backup is frequently transparent to the end user.

The circuit breaker pattern is a common component of a system that provides this sort of redundancy. Let's say that your application queries an external data source every five seconds, perhaps you're polling for some data that you're expecting to change. What happens when this polling fails? In many cases the failure is simply ignored and the polling continues. This is actually a pretty good behaviour on the client side as data updates are not always crucial. In some cases, a failure will cause the application to retry the request immediately. Retrying server requests in a tight loop can be problematic for both the client and the server. The client may become unresponsive as it spends more time in a loop requesting data.

On the server side, a system that is attempting to recover from a failure is being slammed every five seconds by what could be thousands of clients. If the failure is due to the system being overloaded, then continuing to query it will only make matters worse.

The circuit breaker pattern stops attempting to communicate with a system that is failing once a certain number of failures have been reached. Basically, repeated failures result in the circuit being broken and the application ceasing to query. You can see the general pattern of a circuit breaker in this illustration:

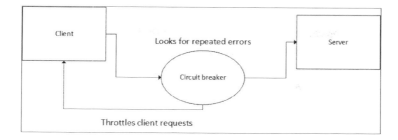

For the server, having the number of clients drop off as failures pile up allows for some breathing room to recover. The chances of a storm of requests coming in and keeping the system down is minimized.

Of course we would like the circuit breaker to reset at some point so that service can be restored. The two approaches for this are that, either the client polls periodically (less frequently than before) and resets the breaker, or that the external system communicates back to its clients that service has been restored.

# Back-off

A variation on the circuit breaker pattern is to use some form of back-off instead of cutting out communication to the server completely. This is an approach that is suggested by many database vendors and cloud providers. If our original polling was at five second intervals, then when a failure is detected change the interval to every 10 seconds. Repeat this process using longer and longer intervals.

When requests start to work again then the pattern of changing the time interval is reversed. Requests are sent closer and closer together until the original polling interval is resumed.

Monitoring the status of the external resource availability is a perfect place to use background worker roles. The work is not complex but it is totally detached from the main event loop.

Again this reduces the load on the external resource giving it more breathing room. It also keeps the clients unburdened by too much polling.

An example using jQuery's `ajax` function looks like the following:

```
$.ajax({
  url : 'someurl',
  type : 'POST',
  data :  ....,
  tryCount : 0,
```

```
  retryLimit : 3,
  success : function(json) {
    //do something
  },
  error : function(xhr, textStatus, errorThrown ) {
    if (textStatus == 'timeout') {
      this.tryCount++;
      if (this.tryCount <= this.retryLimit) {
        //try again
        $.ajax(this);
        return;
      }
      return;
    }
    if (xhr.status == 500) {
      //handle error
    } else {
      //handle error
    }
  }
});
```

You can see that the highlighted section retries the query.

This style of back-off is actually used in Ethernet to avoid repeated packet collisions.

# Degraded application behavior

There is likely a very good reason that your application is calling out to external resources. Backing off and not querying the data source is perfectly reasonable but it is still desirable that users have some ability to interact with the site. One solution to this problem is to degrade the behavior of the application.

For instance, if your application shows real-time stock quote information, but the system for delivering stock information is broken, then a less than real time service could be swapped in. Modern browsers have a whole raft of different technologies that allow for storing small quantities of data on the client computer. This storage space is ideal for caching old versions of some data should the latest versions be unavailable.

Even in cases where the application is sending data to the server, it is possible to degrade behaviour. Saving the data updates locally and then sending them altogether when the service is restored is generally acceptable. Of course, once a user leaves a page, then any background works will terminate. If the user never again returns to the site, then whatever updates they had queued to send to the server will be lost.

 A word of warning: if this is an approach you take it might be best to warn users that their data is old, especially if your application is a stock trading application.

# Promise pattern

I said earlier that JavaScript is single threaded. This is not entirely accurate. There is a single event loop in JavaScript. Blocking this event loop with a long running process is considered to be bad form. Nothing else can happen while your greedy algorithm is taking up all the CPU cycles.

When you launch an asynchronous function in JavaScript, such as fetching data from a remote server, then much of this activity happens in a different thread. The success or failure handler functions are executed in the main event thread. This is part of the reason that success handlers are written as functions: it allows them to be easily passed back and forth between contexts.

Thus there are activities which truly do happen in an asynchronous, parallel fashion. When the `async` method has completed then the result is passed into the handler we provided and the handler is put into the event queue to be picked up next time the event loop repeats. Typically, the event loop runs many hundreds or thousands of times a second, depending on how much work there is to do on each iteration.

Syntactically, we write the message handlers as functions and hook them up:

```
var xmlhttp = new XMLHttpRequest();
xmlhttp.onreadystatechange = function() {
  if (xmlhttp.readyState === 4){
    alert(xmlhttp.readyState);
  }
;};
```

This is reasonable if the situation is simple. However, if you would like to perform some additional asynchronous actions with the results of the callback then you end up with nested callbacks. If you need to add error handling that too is done using callbacks. The complexity of waiting for multiple callbacks to return and orchestrating your response rises quickly.

The promise pattern provides some syntactic help to clean up the asynchronous difficulties. If we take a common asynchronous operation such as retrieving data over XMLHttp Request using jQuery, then the code takes both an error and a success function. It might look something like the following:

```
$.ajax("/some/url",
{ success: function(data, status){},
  error: function(jqXHR, status){}
});
```

Using a promise instead would transform the code to look more like the following:

```
$.ajax("/some/url").then(successFunction, errorFunction);
```

In this case the `$.ajax` method returns a promise object that contains a value and a state. The value is populated when the async call completes. The status provides some information about the current state of the request: has it completed, was it successful?

The promise also has a number of functions called on it. The `then()` function takes a success and an error function and it returns an additional promise. Should the success function run synchronously, then the promise returns as already fulfilled. Otherwise it remains in a working state, known as pending, until the asynchronous success has fired.

In my mind, the method in which jQuery implements promises is not ideal. Their error handing doesn't properly distinguish between a promise that has failed to be fulfilled and a promise that has failed but has been handled. This renders jQuery promises incompatible with the general idea of promises. For instance, it is not possible to do the following:

```
$.ajax("/some/url").then(
  function(data, status){},
  function(jqXHR, status){
    //handle the error here and return a new promise
  }
).then(/*continue*/);
```

Even though the error has been handed and a new promise returned, processing will discontinue. It would be much better if the function could be written as the following:

```
$.ajax("/some/url").then(function(data, status){})
.catch(function(jqXHR, status){
  //handle the error here and return a new promise
})
.then(/*continue*/);
```

There has been much discussion about the implementation of promises in jQuery and other libraries. As a result of this discussion the current proposed promise specification is different from jQuery's promises and is incompatible. Promises/A+ are the certification that is met by numerous promise libraries such as `when.js` and Q. It also forms the foundation of the promises specification that came with ECMAScript-2015.

Promises provide a bridge between synchronous and asynchronous functions, in effect turning the asynchronous functions into something that can be manipulated as if it were synchronous.

If promise sounds a lot like the lazy evaluation pattern we saw some chapters ago then you're exactly correct. Promises are constructed using lazy evaluation, the actions called on them are queued inside the object rather than being evaluated at once. This is a wonderful application of a functional pattern and even enables scenarios like the following:

```
when(function(){return 2+2;})
.delay(1000)
.then(function(promise){ console.log(promise());})
```

Promises greatly simplify asynchronous programming in JavaScript and should certainly be considered for any project that is heavily asynchronous in nature.

# Hints and tips

ECMAScript 2015 promises are well supported on most browsers. Should you need to support an older browser then there are some great shims out there that can add the functionality with a minimum of overhead.

When examining the performance of retrieving JavaScript from a remote server, there are tools provided in most modern browsers for viewing a timeline of resource loading. This timeline will show when the browser is waiting for scripts to be downloaded and when it is parsing the scripts. Using this timeline allows for experimenting to find the best way to load a script or series of scripts.

# Summary

In this chapter we've looked at a number of patterns or approaches that improve the experience of developing JavaScript. We looked at a number of concerns around delivery to the browser. We also looked at how to implement plugins against a couple of libraries and extrapolated general practices. Next we took a look at how to work with background processes in JavaScript. Circuit breakers were suggested as a method of keeping remote resource-fetching sane. Finally, we examined how promises can improve the writing of asynchronous code.

In the next chapter we'll spend quite a bit more time looking at messaging patterns. We saw a little about messing with web workers but we'll expand quite heavily on them in the next section.

# 10
# Messaging Patterns

When Smalltalk, the first real object oriented programming language, was first developed, the communication between classes was envisioned as being messages. Somehow we've moved away from this pure idea of messages. We spoke a bit about how functional programming avoids side effects, well, much the same is true of messaging-based systems.

Messaging also allows for impressive scalability as messages can be fanned out to dozens, or even hundreds, of computers. Within a single application, messaging promotes low-coupling and eases testing.

In this chapter we're going to look at a number of patterns related to messaging. By the end of the chapter you should be aware of how messages work. When I first learned about messaging I wanted to rewrite everything using it.

We will be covering the following topics:

- What's a message anyway?
  - Commands
  - Events
- Request-reply
- Publish-subscribe
  - Fan out
- Dead letter queues
- Message replay
- Pipes and filters

# What's a message anyway?

In the simplest definition a message is a collection of related bits of data that have some meaning together. The message is named in a way that provides some additional meaning to it. For instance, both an `AddUser` and a `RenameUser` message might have the following fields:

- User ID
- Username

But the fact that the fields exist inside a named container gives them different meaning.

Messages are usually related to some action in the application or some action in the business. A message contains all the information needed for a receiver to act upon the action. In the case of the `RenameUser` message, the message contains enough information for any component that keeps track of a relationship between a user ID and a username to update its value for username.

Many messaging systems, especially those that communicate between application boundaries, also define an **envelope**. The envelope has metadata on it that could help with message auditing, routing, and security. The information on the envelope is not part of the business process but is part of the infrastructure. So having a security annotation on the envelope is fine, as security exists outside of the normal business workflow and is owned by a different part of the application. The contents on the envelope look like the one shown in the following diagram:

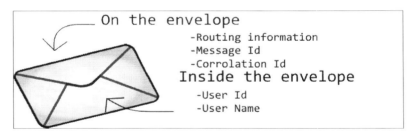

Messages should be sealed so that no changes can be made to them once they have been created. This makes certain operations like auditing and replaying much easier.

Messaging can be used to communicate inside a single process or it can be used between applications. For the most part there is no difference to sending a message within an application and between applications. One difference is the treatment of synchronicity. Within a single process, messages can be handled in a synchronous fashion. This means that the main processing effectively waits for the handling of the message to complete before continuing.

In an asynchronous scenario, the handling of the message may occur at a later date. Sometimes the later date is far in the future. When calling out to an external server, asynchronous will certainly be the correct approach – this is due to the inherit latency associated with network I/O. Even within a single process, the single threaded nature of JavaScript encourages using asynchronous messaging. While using asynchronous messaging, some additional care and attention needs to be taken as some of the assumptions made for synchronous messaging cease to be safe. For instance, assuming the messages will be replied to in the same order in which they were sent is no longer safe.

There are two different flavors of messages: commands and events. Commands instruct things to happen while events notify about something which has happened.

# Commands

A command is simply an instruction from one part of a system to another. It is a message so it is really just a simple data transfer object. If you think back to the command pattern introduced in *Chapter 5, Behavioral Patterns*, this is exactly what it uses.

As a matter of convention, commands are named using the imperative. The format is usually `<verb><object>`. Thus a command might be called `InvadeCity`. Typically, when naming a command, you want to avoid generic names and focus on exactly what is causing the command.

As an example, consider a command that changes the address of a user. You might be tempted to simply call the command `ChangeAddress` but doing so does not add any additional information. It would be better to dig deeper and see why the address is being changed. Did the person move or was the original address entered incorrectly? Intent is as important as the actual data changes. For instance, altering an address due to a mistake might trigger a different behavior from a person who has moved. Users that have moved could be sent a moving present, while those correcting their address would not.

Messages should have a component of business meaning to increase their utility. Defining messages and how they can be constructed within a complex business is a whole field of study on its own. Those interested might do well to investigate **domain driven design (DDD)**.

Commands are an instruction targeted at one specific component giving it instructions to perform a task.

Within the context of a browser you might consider that a command would be the click that is fired on a button. The command is transformed into an event and that event is what is passed to your event listeners.

Only one end point should receive a specific command. This means that only one component is responsible for an action taking place. As soon as a command is acted upon by more than one end point any number of race conditions are introduced. What if one of the end points accepts the command and another rejects it as invalid? Even in cases where several near identical commands are issued they should not be aggregated. For instance, sending a command from a king to all his generals should send one command to each general.

Because there is only one end point for a command it is possible for that end point to validate and even cancel the command. The cancellation of the command should have no impact on the rest of the application.

When a command is acted upon, then one or more events may be published.

# Events

An event is a special message that notifies that something has happened. There is no use in trying to change or cancel an event because it is simply a notification that something has happened. You cannot change the past unless you own a Delorian.

The naming convention for events is that they are written in the past tense. You might see a reversal of the ordering of the words in the command, so we could end up with `CityInvaded` once the `InvadeCity` command has succeeded.

Unlike commands, events may be received by any number of components. There are not real race conditions presented by this approach. As no message handler can change the message nor interfere with the delivery of other copies of the message, each handler is siloed away from all others.

You may be familiar with events from having done user interface work. When a user clicks a button then an event is "raised". In effect the event is broadcast to a series of listeners. You subscribe to a message by hooking into that event:

```
document.getElementById("button1").addEventListener("click",
    doSomething);
```

The events in browsers don't quite meet the definition of an event I gave in the preceding paragraph. This is because event handlers in the browser can cancel events and stop them from propagating to the next handler. That is to say, when there are a series of event handlers for the same message one of them can completely consume the message and not pass it on to subsequent handlers. There is certainly utility to an approach like this but it does introduce some confusion. Fortunately for UI messages, the number of handlers is typically quite small.

In some systems, events can be polymorphic in nature. That is to say that if I had an event called IsHiredSalary that is fired when somebody is hired in a salaried role, I could make it a descendant of the message IsHired. Doing so would allow for both handlers subscribed to IsHiredSalary and IsHired to be fired upon receipt of an IsHiredSalary event. JavaScript doesn't have polymorphism in the true sense, so such things aren't particularly useful. You can add a message field that takes the place of polymorphism but it looks somewhat messy:

```
var IsHiredSalary = { __name: "isHiredSalary",
  __alsoCall: ["isHired"],
  employeeId: 77,
  ...
}
```

In this case I've used __ to denote fields that are part of the envelope. You could also construct the message with separate fields for message and envelope, it really doesn't matter all that much.

Let's take a look at a simple operation like creating a user so we can see how commands and events interact:

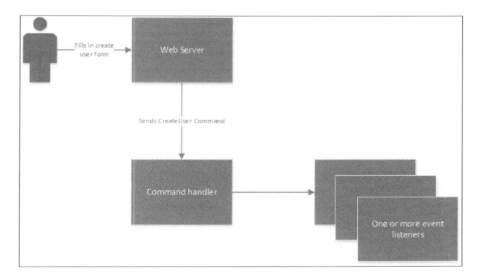

Here a user enters data into a form and submits it. The web server takes in the input, validates it and, if it is correct, creates a command. The command is now sent to the command handler. The command handler performs some action, perhaps writes to a database, it then publishes an event that is consumed by a number of event listeners. These event listeners might send confirmation e-mails, notify system administrators, or any number of things.

All of this looks familiar because systems already contain commands and events. The difference is that we are now modeling the commands and events explicitly.

# Request-reply

The simplest pattern you'll see with messaging is the request-reply pattern. Also known as request-response, this is a method of retrieving data that is owned by another part of the application.

In many cases the sending of a command is an asynchronous operation. A command is fired and the application flow continues on. Because of this, there is no easy way to do things like lookup a record by ID. Instead one needs to send a command to retrieve a record and then wait for the associated event to be returned. A normal workflow looks like the following diagram:

Most events can be subscribed to by any number listeners. While it is possible to have multiple event listeners for a request-response pattern, it is unlikely and is probably not advisable.

We can implement a very simple request-response pattern here. In Westeros there are some issues with sending messages in a timely fashion. Without electricity, sending messages over long distances rapidly can really only be accomplished by attaching tiny messages to the legs of crows. Thus we have a Crow Messaging System.

We'll start with building out what we'll call the **bus**. A bus is simply a distribution mechanism for messages. It can be implemented in process, as we've done here, or out of process. If implementing it out of process, there are many options from 0mq, a lightweight message queue, to RabbitMQ, a more fully featured messaging system, to a wide variety of systems built on top of databases and in the cloud. Each of these systems exhibit some different behaviors when it comes to message reliability and durability. It is important to do some research into the way that the message distribution systems work as they may dictate how the application is constructed. They also implement different approaches to dealing with the underlying unreliability of applications:

```
class CrowMailBus {
  constructor(requestor) {
    this.requestor = requestor;
    this.responder = new CrowMailResponder(this);
  }
  Send(message) {
    if (message.__from == "requestor") {
      this.responder.processMessage(message);
    }
    else {
      this.requestor.processMessage(message);
    }
  }
}
```

One thing which is a potential trip-up is that the order in which messages are received back on the client is not necessarily the order in which they were sent. To deal with this it is typical to include some sort of a correlation ID. When the event is raised it includes a known ID from the sender so that the correct event handler is used.

This bus is a highly naïve one as it has its routing hard coded. A real bus would probably allow the sender to specify the address of the end point for delivery. Alternately, the receivers could register themselves as interested in a specific sort of message. The bus would then be responsible for doing some limited routing to direct the message. Our bus is even named after the messages it deals with – certainly not a scalable approach.

Next we'll implement the requestor. The requestor contains only two methods: one to send a request and the other to receive a response from the bus:

```
class CrowMailRequestor {
  Request() {
    var message = { __messageDate: new Date(),
```

```
      __from: "requestor",
      __corrolationId: Math.random(),
      body: "Hello there. What is the square root of 9?" };
    var bus = new CrowMailBus(this);
    bus.Send(message);
    console.log("message sent!");
  }
  processMessage(message) {
    console.dir(message);
  }
}
```

The process message function currently just logs the response but it would likely do more in a real world scenario such as updating the UI or dispatching another message. The correlation ID is invaluable for understanding which sent message the reply is related to.

Finally, the responder simply takes in the message and replies to it with another message:

```
class CrowMailResponder {
  constructor(bus) {
    this.bus = bus;
  }
  processMessage(message) {
    var response = { __messageDate: new Date(),
    __from: "responder",
    __corrolationId: message.__corrolationId,
    body: "Okay invaded." };
    this.bus.Send(response);
    console.log("Reply sent");
  }
}
```

Everything in our example is synchronous but all it would take to make it asynchronous is to swap out the bus. If we're working in node then we can do this using process.nextTick which simply defers a function to the next time through the event loop. If we're in a web context, then web workers may be used to do the processing in another thread. In fact, when starting a web worker, the communication back and forth to it takes the form of a message:

```
class CrowMailBus {
  constructor(requestor) {
    this.requestor = requestor;
    this.responder = new CrowMailResponder(this);
```

```
    }
    Send(message) {
      if (message.__from == "requestor") {
        process.nextTick(() => this.responder.processMessage(message));
      }
      else {
        process.nextTick(() => this.requestor.processMessage(message));
      }
    }
  }
```

This approach now allows other code to run before the message is processed. If we weave in some print statements after each bus send, then we get output like the following:

```
Request sent!
Reply sent
{ __messageDate: Mon Aug 11 2014 22:43:07 GMT-0600 (MDT),
  __from: 'responder',
  __corrolationId: 0.5604551520664245,
  body: 'Okay, invaded.' }
```

You can see that the print statements are executed before the message processing as that processing happens on the next iteration.

# Publish-subscribe

I've alluded to the publish-subscribe model elsewhere in this chapter. Publish-subscribe is a powerful tool for decoupling events from processing code.

At the crux of the pattern is the idea that, as a message publisher, my responsibility for the message should end as soon as I send it. I should not know who is listening to messages or what they will do with the messages. So long as I am fulfilling a contract to produce correctly formatted messages, the rest shouldn't matter.

It is the responsibility of the listener to register its interest in the message type. You'll, of course, wish to register some sort of security to disallow registration of rogue services.

We can update our service bus to do more, to do a complete job of routing and sending multiple messages. Let's call our new method `Publish` instead of `Send`. We'll keep `Send` around to do the sending functionality:

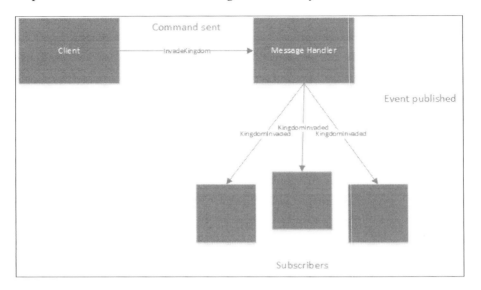

The crow mail analogy we used in the previous section starts to fall apart here as there is no way to broadcast a message using crows. Crows are too small to carry large banners and it is very difficult to train them to do sky writing. I'm unwilling to totally abandon the idea of crows so let's assume that there exists a sort of crow broadcast centre. Sending a message here allows for it to be fanned out to numerous interested parties who have signed up for updates. This centre will be more or less synonymous with a bus.

We'll write our router so that it works as a function of the name of the message. One could route a message using any of its attributes. For instance, a listener could subscribe to all the messages called `invoicePaid` where the `amount` field is greater than $10000. Adding this sort of logic to the bus will slow it down and make it far harder to debug. Really this is more the domain of business process orchestration engines than a bus. We'll continue on without that complexity.

The first thing to set up is the ability to subscribe to published messages:

```
CrowMailBus.prototype.Subscribe = function (messageName, subscriber) {
  this.responders.push({ messageName: messageName, subscriber:
    subscriber });
};
```

The Subscribe function just adds a message handler and the name of a message to consume. The responders array is simply an array of handlers.

When a message is published we loop over the array and fire each of the handlers that have registered for messages with that name:

```
Publish(message) {
  for (let i = 0; i < this.responders.length; i++) {
    if (this.responders[i].messageName == message.__messageName) {
      (function (b) {
        process.nextTick(() => b.subscriber.processMessage(message));
      })(this.responders[i]);
    }
  }
}
```

The execution here is deferred to the next tick. This is done using a closure to ensure that the correctly scoped variables are passed through. We can now change our CrowMailResponder to use the new Publish method instead of Send:

```
processMessage(message) {
  var response = { __messageDate: new Date(),
  __from: "responder",
  __corrolationId: message.__corrolationId,
  __messageName: "SquareRootFound",
  body: "Pretty sure it is 3." };
  this.bus.Publish(response);
  console.log("Reply published");
}
```

Instead of allowing the CrowMailRequestor object to create its own bus as earlier, we need to modify it to accept an instance of bus from outside. We simply assign it to a local variable in CrowMailRequestor. Similarly, CrowMailResponder should also take in an instance of bus.

In order to make use of this we simply need to create a new bus instance and pass it into the requestor:

```
var bus = new CrowMailBus();
bus.Subscribe("KingdomInvaded", new TestResponder1());
bus.Subscribe("KingdomInvaded", new TestResponder2());
var requestor = new CrowMailRequestor(bus);
requestor.Request();
```

Here we've also passed in two other responders that are interested in knowing about `KingdomInvaded` messages. They look like the following:

```
var TestResponder1 = (function () {
  function TestResponder1() {}
  TestResponder1.prototype.processMessage = function (message) {
    console.log("Test responder 1: got a message");
  };
  return TestResponder1;
})();
```

Running this code will now get the following:

```
Message sent!
Reply published
Test responder 1: got a message
Test responder 2: got a message
Crow mail responder: got a message
```

You can see that the messages are sent using `Send`. The responder or handler does its work and publishes a message that is passed onto each of the subscribers.

There are some great JavaScript libraries which make publish and subscribe even easier. One of my favorites is Radio.js. It has no external dependencies and its name is an excellent metaphor for publish subscribe. We could rewrite our preceding subscribe example like so:

```
radio("KingdomInvalid").subscribe(new TestResponder1().
  processMessage);
radio("KingdomInvalid").subscribe(new TestResponder2().
  processMessage);
```

Then publish a message using the following:

```
radio("KingdomInvalid").broadcast(message);
```

# Fan out and in

A fantastic use of the publish subscribe pattern is allowing you to fan out a problem to a number of different nodes. Moore's law has always been about the doubling of the number of transistors per square unit of measure. If you've been paying attention to processor clock speeds you may have noticed that there hasn't really been any significant change in clock speeds for a decade. In fact, clock speeds are now lower than they were in 2005.

This is not to say that processors are "slower" than they once were. The work that is performed in each clock tick has increased. The number of cores has also jumped up. It is now unusual to see a single core processor; even in cellular phones dual core processors are becoming common. It is the rule, rather than the exception, to have computers that are capable of doing more than one thing at a time.

At the same time, cloud computing is taking off. The computers you purchase outright are faster than the ones available to rent from the cloud. The advantage of cloud computing is that you can scale it out easily. It is nothing to provision a hundred or even a thousand computers to form a cloud provider.

Writing software that can take advantage of multiple cores is the great computing problem of our time. Dealing directly with threads is a recipe for disaster. Locking and contention is far too difficult a problem for most developers: me included! For a certain class of problems, they can easily be divided up into sub problems and distributed. Some call this class of problems "embarrassingly parallelizable".

Messaging provides a mechanism for communicating the inputs and outputs from a problem. If we had one of these easily parallelized problems, such as searching, then we would bundle up the inputs into one message. In this case it would contain our search terms. The message might also contain the set of documents to search. If we had 10,000 documents then we could divide the search space up into, say, four collections of 2500 documents. We would publish five messages with the search terms and the range of documents to search as can be seen here:

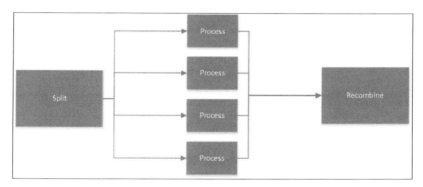

Different search nodes will pick up the messages and perform the search. The results will then be sent back to a node that will collect the messages and combine them into one. This is what will be returned to the client.

Of course this is a bit of an over simplification. It is likely that the receiving nodes themselves would maintain a list of documents over which they had responsibility. This would prevent the original publishing node from having to know anything about the documents over which it was searching. The search results could even be returned directly to the client that would do the assembling.

Even in a browser, the fan out and in approach can be used to distribute a calculation over a number of cores through the use of web workers. A simple example might take the form of creating a potion. A potion might contain a number of ingredients that can be combined to create a final product. It is quite computationally complicated combining ingredients so we would like to farm the process out to a number of workers.

We start with a combiner that contains a `combine()` method as well as a `complete()` function that is called once all the distributed ingredients are combined:

```
class Combiner {
  constructor() {
    this.waitingForChunks = 0;
  }
  combine(ingredients) {
    console.log("Starting combination");
    if (ingredients.length > 10) {
      for (let i = 0; i < Math.ceil(ingredients.length / 2); i++) {
        this.waitingForChunks++;
        console.log("Dispatched chunks count at: " + this.
          waitingForChunks);
        var worker = new Worker("FanOutInWebWorker.js");
        worker.addEventListener('message', (message) => this.
          complete(message));
        worker.postMessage({ ingredients: ingredients.slice(i, i * 2)
          });
      }
    }
  }
  complete(message) {
    this.waitingForChunks--;
    console.log("Outstanding chunks count at: " + this.
      waitingForChunks);
    if (this.waitingForChunks == 0)
      console.log("All chunks received");
  }
};
```

In order to keep track of the number of workers outstanding, we use a simple counter. Because the main section of code is single threaded we have no risk of race conditions. Once the counter shows no remaining workers we can take whatever steps are necessary. The web worker looks like the following:

```
self.addEventListener('message', function (e) {
  var data = e.data;
  var ingredients = data.ingredients;
  combinedIngredient = new Westeros.Potion.CombinedIngredient();
  for (let i = 0; i < ingredients.length; i++) {
    combinedIngredient.Add(ingredients[i]);
  }
  console.log("calculating combination");
  setTimeout(combinationComplete, 2000);
}, false);

function combinationComplete() {
  console.log("combination complete");
  (self).postMessage({ event: 'combinationComplete', result:
    combinedIngredient });
}
```

In this case we simply put in a timeout to simulate the complex calculation needed to combine ingredients.

The sub problems that are farmed out to a number of nodes don't have to be identical problems. However, they should be sufficiently complicated that the cost savings of farming them out are not consumed by the overhead of sending out a message.

# Dead letter queues

No matter how hard I try I have yet to write any significant block of code that does not contain any errors. Nor have I been very good at predicting the wide range of crazy things users do with my applications. Why would anybody click that link 73 times in a row? I'll never know.

Dealing with failures in a messaging scenario is very easy. The core of the failure strategy is to embrace errors. We have exceptions for a reason and to spend all of our time trying to predict and catch exceptions is counter-productive. You'll invariably spend time building in catches for errors that never happen and miss errors that happen frequently.

In an asynchronous system, errors need not be handled as soon as they occur. Instead, the message that caused an error can be put aside to be examined by an actual human later. The message is stored in a dead letter, or error, queue. From there the message can easily be reprocessed after it has been corrected or the handler has been corrected. Ideally the message handler is changed to deal with messages exhibiting whatever property caused the errors. This prevents future errors and is preferable to fixing whatever generates the message as there is no guarantee that other messages with the same problem aren't lurking somewhere else in the system. The workflow of a message through the queue and error queue can be seen here:

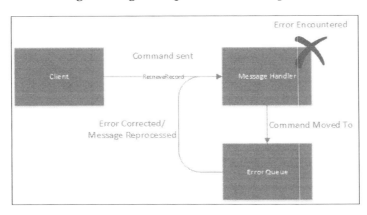

As more and more errors are caught and fixed, the quality of the message handlers increases. Having an error queue of messages ensures that nothing important, such as a BuySimonsBook message is missed. This means that getting to a correct system becomes a marathon instead of a sprint. There is no need to rush a fix into production before it is properly tested. Progress towards a correct system is constant and reliable.

Using a dead letter queue also improves the catching of intermittent errors. These are errors that result from an external resource being unavailable or incorrect. Imagine a handler that calls out to an external web service. In a traditional system, a failure in the web service guarantees failure in the message handler. However, with a message based system, the command can be moved back to the end of the input queue and tried again whenever it reaches the front of the queue. On the envelope we write down the number of times the message has been dequeued (processed). Once this dequeue count reaches a limit, like five, only then is the message moved into the true error queue.

This approach improves the overall quality of the system by smoothing over the small failures and stopping them from becoming large failures. In effect, the queues provide failure bulkheads to prevent small errors from overflowing and becoming large errors that might have an impact on the system as a whole.

# Message replay

When developers are working with a set of messages that produce an error, the ability to reprocess messages is also useful. Developers can take a snapshot of the dead letter queue and reprocess it in debug mode again and again until they have correctly processed the messages. A snapshot of a message can also make up a part of the testing for a message handler.

Even without there being an error, the messages sent to a service on a daily basis are representative of the normal workflows of users. These messages can be mirrored to an audit queue as they enter into the system. The data from the audit queue can be used for testing. If a new feature is introduced, then a normal day's workload can be played back to ensure that there has been no degradation in either correct behavior or performance.

Of course if the audit queue contains a list of every message, then it becomes trivial to understand how the application arrived at its current state. Frequently people implement history by plugging in a lot of custom code or by using triggers and audit tables. Neither of these approaches do as good of a job as messaging at understanding not only which data has changed, but why it has changed. Consider again the address change scenario, without messaging we will likely never know why an address for a user is different from the previous day.

Maintaining a good history of changes to system data is storage intensive but that cost is easily paid by allowing auditors to see how and why each change was made. Well-constructed messages also allow for the history to contain the intent of the user making the change.

While it is possible to implement this sort of messaging system, in a single process it is difficult. Ensuring that messages are properly saved in the event of errors is difficult, as the entire process that deals with messages may crash, taking the internal message bus with it. Realistically if the replaying of messages sounds like something worth investigating then external message busses are the solution.

# Pipes and filters

I mentioned earlier that messages should be considered immutable. This is not to say that messages cannot be rebroadcast with some properties changed or even broadcast as a new type of message. In fact, many message handlers may consume an event and then publish a new event after having performed some task.

As an example, you might consider the workflow for adding a new user to a system:

In this case, the `CreateUser` command triggers a `UserCreated` event. That event is consumed by a number of different services. One of these services passes on user information to a select number of affiliates. As this service runs, it publishes its own set of events, one for each affiliate that receives the new user's details. These events may, in turn, be consumed by other services which could trigger their own events. In this way changes can ripple through the entire application. However, no service knows more than what starts it and what events it publishes. This system has very low coupling. Plugging in new functionality is trivial and even removing functionality is easy: certainly easier than a monolithic system.

Systems constructed using messaging and autonomous components are frequently referred to as using **Service Oriented Architecture (SOA)** or Microservices. There remains a great deal of debate as to the differences, if indeed there are any, between SOA and Microservices.

The altering and rebroadcasting of messages can be thought of as being a pipe or a filter. A service can proxy messages through to other consumers just as a pipe would do or can selectively republish messages as would be done by a filter.

# Versioning messages

As systems evolve, the information contained in a message may also change. In our user creation example, we might have originally been asking for a name and e-mail address. However, the marketing department would like to be able to send e-mails addressed to Mr. Jones or Mrs. Jones so we need to also collect the user's title. This is where message versioning comes in handy.

We can now create a new message that extends the previous message. The message can contain additional fields and might be named using the version number or a date. Thus a message like `CreateUser` might become `CreateUserV1` or `CreateUser20140101`. Earlier I mentioned polymorphic messages. This is one approach to versioning messages. The new message extends the old so all the old message handlers still fire. However, we also talked about how there are no real polymorphic capabilities in JavaScript.

Another option is to use upgrading message handlers. These handlers will take in a version of the new message and modify it to be the old version. Obviously the newer messages need to have at least as much data in them as the old version or have data that permits converting one message type to another.

Consider a v1 message that looked like the following:

```
class CreateUserv1Message implements IMessage{
  __messageName: string
  UserName: string;
  FirstName: string;
  LastName: string;
  EMail: string;
}
```

Consider a v2 message that extended it adding a user title:

```
class CreateUserv2Message extends CreateUserv1Message implements
  IMessage{
  UserTitle: string;
}
```

Then we would be able to write a very simple upgrader or downgrader that looks like the following:

```
var CreateUserv2tov1Downgrader = (function () {
  function CreateUserv2tov1Downgrader (bus) {
    this.bus = bus;
  }
  CreateUserv2tov1Downgrader.prototype.processMessage = function
    (message) {
```

```
    message.__messageName = "CreateUserv1Message";
    delete message.UserTitle;
    this.bus.publish(message);
  };
  return CreateUserv2tov1Downgrader;
})();
```

You can see that we simply modify the message and rebroadcast it.

# Hints and tips

Messages create a well-defined interface between two different systems. Defining messages should be done by members of both teams. Establishing a common language can be tricky especially as terms are overloaded between different business units. What a sales department considers a customer may be totally different from what a shipping department considers a customer. Domain driven design provides some hints as to how boundaries can be established to avoid mixing terms.

There is a huge preponderance of queue technologies available. Each of them have a bunch of different properties around reliability, durability, and speed. Some of the queues support reading and writing JSON over HTTP: ideal for those interested in building JavaScript applications. Which queue is appropriate for your application is a topic for some research.

# Summary

Messaging and the associated patterns are large topics. Delving too deeply into messages will bring you in contact with **domain driven design (DDD)** and **command query responsibility segregation (CQRS)** as well as touching on high performance computing solutions.

There is substantial research and discussion ongoing as to the best way to build large systems. Messaging is one possible solution that avoids creating a big ball of mud that is difficult to maintain and fragile to change. Messaging provides natural boundaries between components in a system and the messages themselves provide for a consistent API.

Not every application benefits from messaging. There is additional overhead to building a loosely coupled application such as this. Applications that are collaborative, ones where losing data is especially undesirable, and those that benefit from a strong history story are good candidates for messaging. In most cases a standard CRUD application will be sufficient. It is still worthwhile to know about messaging patterns, as they will offer alternative thinking.

In this chapter we've taken a look at a number of different messaging patterns and how they can be applied to common scenarios. The differences between commands and events were also explored.

In the next chapter we'll look at some patterns for making testing code a little bit easier. Testing is jolly important so read on!

# 11
# Microservices

It seems like no book on programming these days is complete without at least some mention of microservices. For fear that this book could be singled out for ridicule as a non-conformant publication, a chapter has been included on microservices.

Microservices are billed as the solution to the problems of monolithic applications. Likely every application you've dealt with has been a monolith: that is, the application has a single logical executable and is perhaps split into layers such as a user interface, a service or application layer, and a data store. In many applications these layers might be a web page, a server side application, and a database. Monoliths have their issues as I'm sure you've encountered.

Maintaining a monolithic application quickly becomes an exercise in limiting the impact of change. Frequently in such applications a change to one, seemingly isolated, corner of the application has an unintended effect on some other part of the application. Although there are many patterns and approaches to describe well isolated components, these often fall by the wayside inside a monolith. Often we take shortcuts which may save time now but will return to make our lives terrible down the road.

Monolithic applications are also difficult to scale. Because we tend to have only three layers, we are limited to scaling each one of those layers. We can add more application servers if the middle tier is becoming slow or more web servers if the web tier is laggy. If the database is slow then we can increase the power of the database server. These scaling approaches are very large operations. If the only part of the application which is slow is signing up new users, then we really have no way to simply scale that one component. This means that components which are not frequently used (one might call these cold or cool components) must be able to scale as the whole application scales. This sort of scaling doesn't come for free.

Consider that scaling from a single web server to multiple web servers introduces the problem of sharing sessions between many web servers. If we were, instead, to divide our application into a number of services, of which each acts as the canonical source of truth for a piece of data, then we could scale these sections independently. A service for logging users in, another service for saving and retrieving their preferences, yet another for sending out reminder e-mails about abandoned shopping carts, each one responsible for its own functions and own data. Each service stands alone as a separate application and may run on a separate machine. In effect we have taken our monolithic application and sharded it into many applications. Not only does each service have an isolated function but it also has its own datastore and could be implemented using its own technology. The difference between a monolith and microservices can be seen here:

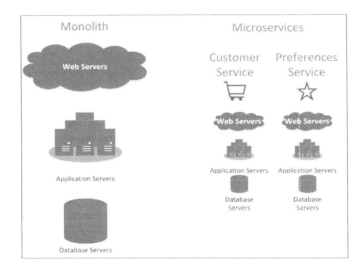

Applications are written more by composing services than by writing singular monolithic applications. The UI of an application can even be created by asking a number of services to provide visual components to be slotted into a composite UI by some form of composing service.

Node.js' lightweight approach to building applications with just the required components makes it an ideal platform to build lightweight microservices. Many microservice deployments make heavy use of HTTP to communicate between services while others rely more heavily on messaging systems such as **RabbitMQ** or **ZeroMQ**. These two communication methods may be mixed in deployments. One might split the technology used along the lines of using HTTP against services which are query-only, and messaging against services which perform some action. This is because messaging is more reliable (depending on your messaging system and configuration) than sending HTTP requests.

While it may seem that we've introduced a great deal of complexity into the system it is a complexity that is easier to manage with modern tooling. Very good tooling exists for managing distributed log files and for monitoring the performance of applications for performance issues. Isolating and running many applications with virtualization is more approachable than ever with containerization technologies.

Microservices may not be the solution to all our maintenance and scalability issues but they are certainly an approach that is viable for consideration. In this chapter we'll explore some of the patterns that may assist in using microservices:

- Façade
- Aggregate services
- Pipeline
- Message upgrader
- Service selector
- Failure patterns

Because microservices are a relatively new development, there are likely to be many more patterns which emerge as more and more applications are created with the microservice approach. There is some similarity between the Microservices approach and **Service Oriented Architecture (SOA)**. This means that there are likely some patterns from the SOA world which will be applicable in the microservices world.

# Façade

If you feel that you recognize the name of this pattern, then you're correct. We discussed this pattern way back in *Chapter 4, Structural Patterns*. In that application of the pattern we created a class which could direct the actions of a number of other classes providing a simpler API. Our example was that of an admiral who directed a fleet of ships. In the microservices world we can simply replace the concept of classes with that of services. After all, the functionality of a service is not that different from a microservice – they both perform a single action.

We might make use of a façade to coordinate the use of a number of other services. This pattern is a base pattern for many of the other patterns listed in this chapter. Coordinating services can be difficult, but by putting them behind a façade we can make the entire application much simpler. Let us consider a service which sends e-mails. Sending e-mails is quite a complex process which may involve a number of other services: a username to e-mail address translator, an anti-malware scanner, a spam checker, a formatter to message the e-mail body for various e-mail clients, and so forth.

Most clients who want to send e-mail don't want to concern themselves with all of these other services so a façade e-mail-sending service can be put in place which holds the responsibility of coordinating other services. The coordination pattern can be seen here:

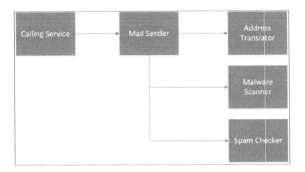

# Service selector

Along the same lines as a façade we have the service selector pattern. In this pattern we have a service which fronts a number of other services. Depending on the message which arrives, a different service could be selected to respond to the initial request. This pattern is useful in upgrade scenarios and for experimentation. If you're rolling out a new service and want to ensure that it will function correctly under load then you could make use of the service selector pattern to direct a small portion of your production traffic to the new service while monitoring it closely. Another application might be for directing specific customers or groups of customers to a different service. The distinguishing factor could be anything from directing people who have paid for your service toward faster end points, to directing traffic from certain countries to country-specific services. The service selector pattern can be seen in this illustration:

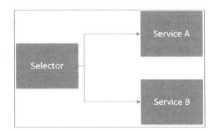

# Aggregate services

Data in a microservice architecture is owned by a single service, but there are many times when we might need to retrieve data from a number of different sources at once. Consider, again, a member of the Small Council in the land of Westeros. They may have a number of informants from whom they gather information about the workings of the kingdom. You can consider each informant to be its own microservice.

> Informants are a fantastic metaphor for microservices as each one is independent and holds its own data. Services may also fail from time to time just as informants may be captured and terminated. Messages are passed between informants just as they are among a collection of microservices. Each informant should know very little about how the rest of the informants work, and even, who they are – an abstraction which works for microservices too.

With the aggregate service pattern, we ask each one of a collection of nodes to perform some action or return some piece of data. This is a fairly common pattern even outside the microservice world and is a special case of the façade or even adapter pattern. The aggregator requests information from a number of other services and then waits for them to return. Once all the data has been returned, then the aggregator may perform some additional tasks such as summarizing the data or counting records. The information is then passed back to the caller. The aggregator can be seen in this illustration:

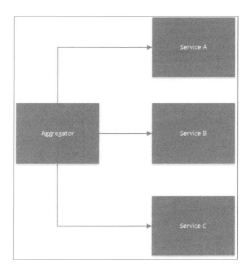

This pattern may also have some provision for dealing with slow-to-return services or failures of services. The aggregator service may return partial results or return data from a cache in the event that one of the child services reaches a timeout. In certain architectures, the aggregator could return a partial result and then return additional data to the caller when it becomes available.

# Pipeline

A pipeline is another example of a microservice connecting pattern. If you have made use of the shell on a *NIX system, then you have certainly piped the output of one command to another command. The programs on a *NIX system such as ls, sort, uniq, and grep are designed to perform just one task; their power comes from the ability to chain the tools together to build quite complex workflows. For instance, this command:

```
ls -1| cut -d \. -f 2 -s | sort |uniq
```

This command will list all the unique file extensions in the current directory. It does this by taking the list of files, then cutting them and taking the extension; this is then sorted and finally passed to uniq which removes duplicates. While I wouldn't suggest having a microservice for such trivial actions as sorting or deduplicating, you might have a series of services which build up more and more information.

Let's imagine a query service that returns a collection of company records:

```
| Company Id| Name | Address | City | Postal Code | Phone Number |
```

This record is returned by our company lookup service. Now we can pass this record onto our sales accounting service which will add a sales total to the record:

```
| Company Id| Name | Address | City | Postal Code | Phone Number | 2016
orders Total |
```

Now that record can be passed onto a sales estimate service, which further enhances the record with an estimate of 2017 sales:

```
| Company Id| Name | Address | City | Postal Code | Phone Number | 2016
orders Total | 2017 Sales Estimate |
```

This sort of progressive enhancement could be reversed too by a service that stripped out information which shouldn't be presented to the users. The record might now become the following:

```
| Name | Address | City | Postal Code | Phone Number | 2016 orders Total
| 2017 Sales Estimate |
```

Here we have dropped the company identifier because it is an internal identifier. A microservice pipeline should be bidirectional so that a quantum of information is passed into each step in the pipeline and then passed back out again through each step. This affords services the opportunity to act upon the data twice, manipulating it as they see fit. This is the same approach used in many web servers where modules such as PHP are permitted to act upon the request and the response. A pipeline can be seen illustrated here:

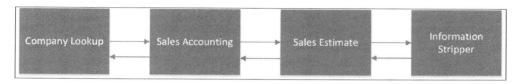

# Message upgrader

One of the highest-risk activities with some monolithic applications is upgrading. To do so you basically need to upgrade the entire application at once. With even a medium-sized application there are far too many aspects to reasonably test. Thus at some point you simply need to cut over from the old system to the new system. With a microservice approach, the cutover can be done for each individual service. Smaller services mean that the risk can be spread out over a long time and, should something go wrong, the source of the error can be more quickly pinpointed: the singular new component.

At issue are the services which are still talking to the old version of the upgraded service. How can we continue to serve these services without having to update all those services too? If the interface to the service remains unchanged, say our service calculates the distance between two points on the earth and we change it from using a simple Pythagorean approach to using haversine (a formula to find the distance between two spots on a sphere), then there may be no need to make changes to the input and output formats. Frequently, however, this approach isn't available to us as the message format must change. Even in the previous example there is a possibility of changing the output message. Haversine is more accurate than a Pythagorean approach so we could have more significant digits requiring a larger data type. There are two good approaches to deal with this:

1.  Continue to use the old version of our service and the new version. We can then slowly move the client services over to the new service as time permits. There are problems with this approach: we now need to maintain more code. Also, if the reason we change the service out was one which would not permit us to continue to run it (a security problem, termination of a dependent service, and so on) then we are at something of an impasse.

2. Upgrade messages and pass them on. In this approach we take the old message format and upgrade it to the new format. This is done by, you guessed it, another service. This service's responsibility is to take in the old message format and emit the new message format. At the other end you might need an equivalent service to downgrade messages back to the expected output format for older services.

Upgrader services should have a limited lifespan. Ideally we would want to make updates to the services which depend on deprecated services as quickly as possible. The small code footprint of microservices, coupled with the ability to rapidly deploy services, should make these sorts of upgrade much easier than those used to a monolithic approach might expect. An example message upgrader service can be seen here:

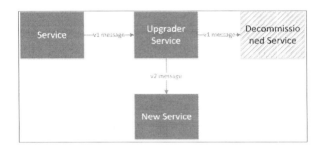

# Failure patterns

We have already touched upon some of the ways of dealing with failures in microservices in this chapter. There are, however, a couple of more interesting approaches we should consider. The first of these is service degradation.

# Service degradation

This pattern could also be called graceful degradation and is related to progressive enhancement. Let us hark back to the example of replacing the Pythagorean distance function with the haversine equivalent. If the haversine service is down for some reason, the less demanding function could be used in its place without a huge impact on users. In fact, they may not notice it at all. It isn't ideal that users have a worse version of the service but it is certainly more desirable than simply showing the user an error message. When the haversine service returns to life then we can stop using the less desirable service. We could have multiple levels of fallback allowing several different services to fail while we continue to present a fully functional application to the end user.

Another good application of this form of degradation is to fall back to more expensive services. I once had an application that sent SMS messages. It was quite important that these messages actually be sent. We used our preferred SMS gateway provider the majority of the time but, if our preferred service was unavailable, something we monitored closely, then we would fail over to using a different provider.

# Message storage

We've already drawn a bit of a distinction between services which are query-only and those which actually perform some lasting data change. When one of these updating services fails there is still a need to run the data change code at some point in the future. Storing these requests in a message queue allows them to be run later without risk of losing any of the ever-so important messages. Typically, when a message causes an exception it is returned to the processing queue where it can be retried.

There is an old saying that insanity is doing the same thing over again and expecting a different outcome. However, there are many transient errors which can be solved by simply performing the same action over again. Database deadlocks are a prime example of this. Your transaction may be killed to resolve a deadlock, in which case performing it again is, in fact, the recommended approach. However, one cannot retry messages ad infinitum so it is best to choose some relatively small number of retry attempts, three or five. Once this number has been reached then the message can be sent to a dead letter or poison message queue.

Poison messages, or dead letters as some call them, are messages which have actual legitimate reasons for failing. It is important to keep these messages around not only for debugging purposes but because the messages may represent a customer order or a change to a medical record: not data you can afford to lose. Once the message handler has been corrected these messages can be replayed as if the error never happened. A storage queue and message reprocessor can be seen illustrated here:

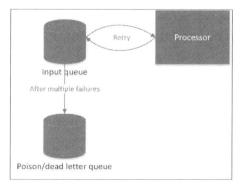

# Message replay

Although not a real production pattern, a side-effect of having a message-based architecture around all the services which change data is that you can acquire the messages for later replay outside of production. Being able to replay messages is very handy for debugging complex interactions between numerous services as the messages contain almost all the information to set up a tracing environment identical to production. Replay capabilities are also very useful for environments where one must be able to audit any data changes to the system. There are other methods to address such audit requirements but a very solid message log is simply a delight to work with.

# Indempotence of message handling

The final failure pattern we'll discuss is idempotence of message handling. As systems grow larger it is almost certain that a microservices architecture will span many computers. This is even more certain due to the growing importance of containers, which can, ostensibly, be thought of as computers. Communicating between computers in a distributed system is unreliable; thus, a message may end up being delivered more than once. To handle such an eventuality one might wish to make messaging handling idempotent.

 For more about the unreliability of distributed computing, I cannot recommend any paper more worth reading than *Falacies of Distributed Computing Explained* by Arnon Rotem-Gal-Oz at http://rgoarchitects.com/Files/fallacies.pdf.

Idempotence means that a message can be processed many times without changing the outcome. This can be harder to achieve than one might realize, especially with services which are inherently non-transactional such as sending e-mails. In these cases, one may need to write a record that an e-mail has been sent to a database. There are some scenarios in which the e-mail will be sent more than once, but a service crashing in the critical section between the e-mail being sent and the record of it being written is unlikely. The decision will have to be made: is it better to send an e-mail more than once or not send it at all?

# Hints and tips

If you think of a microservice as a class and your microservice web as an application, then it rapidly becomes apparent that many of the same patterns we've seen elsewhere in the book are applicable to microservices. Service discovery could be synonymous with dependency injection. Singleton, decorator, proxy; all of them could be applicable to the microservice world just as they are within the boundaries of a process.

One thing to keep in mind is that many of these patterns are somewhat chatty, sending significant data back and forth. Within a process there is no overhead to passing around pointers to data. The same is not true of microservices. Communicating over the network is likely to incur a performance penalty.

# Summary

Microservices are a fascinating idea and one which is more likely to be realized in the next few years. It is too early to tell if this is simply another false turn on the way to properly solving software engineering or a major step in the right direction. In this chapter we've explored a few patterns which may be of use should you embark upon a journey into the microservices world. Because we're only on the cusp of microservices becoming mainstream, it is likely that, more than any other chapter of this book, the patterns here will quickly become dated and found to be suboptimal. Remaining vigilant with regard to developments and being aware of the bigger picture when you're developing is highly advisable.

# 12
# Patterns for Testing

Throughout this book we've been pushing the idea that JavaScript is no longer a toy language with which we can't do useful things. Real world software is being written in JavaScript right now and the percentage of applications using JavaScript is only likely to grow over the next decade.

With real software comes concerns about correctness. Manually testing software is painful and, weirdly, error-prone. It is far cheaper and easier to produce unit and integration tests that run automatically and test various aspects of the application.

There are countless tools available for testing JavaScript, from test runners to testing frameworks; the ecosystem is a rich one. We'll try to maintain a more or less tool-agnostic approach to testing in this chapter. This book does not concern itself with which framework is the best or friendliest. There are overarching patterns that are common to testing as a whole. It is those that we'll examine. We will touch on some specific tools but only as a shortcut to having to write all our own testing tools.

In this chapter we'll look at the following topics:

- Fake objects
- Monkey patching
- Interacting with the user interface

## The testing pyramid

We computer programmers are, as a rule, highly analytical people. This means that we're always striving to categorize and understand concepts. This has led to our developing some very interesting global techniques that can be applied outside computer programming. For instance, agile development has applications in general society but can trace its roots back to computing. One might even argue that the idea of patterns owes much of its popularity to it being used by computer programmers in other walks of life.

This desire to categorize has led to the concept of testing code being divided up into a number of different types of tests. I've seen as many as eight different categories of tests from unit tests, right the way up to workflow tests and GUI tests. This is, perhaps, an overkill. It is much more common to think about having three different categories of test: unit, integration, and user interface:

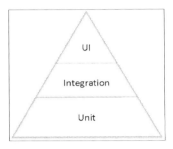

Unit tests form the foundation of the pyramid. They are the most numerous, the easiest to write, and the most granular in the errors they give. An error in a unit test will allow you to find the individual method that has an error in it. As we move up the pyramid, the number of tests falls along with the granularity while the complexity of each test increases. At a higher level, when a test fails we might only be able to say: "There is an issue with adding an order to the system".

# Testing in the small with unit tests

To many, unit testing is a foreign concept. This is understandable as it is a topic which is poorly taught in many schools. I know that I've done six years of higher education in computing science without it being mentioned. It is unfortunate because delivering a quality product is a pretty important part of any project.

For those who know about unit testing, there is a big barrier to adoption. Managers, and even developers, frequently see unit testing, and automated testing as a whole, as a waste of time. After all you cannot ship a unit test to your customer nor do most customers care whether their product has been properly unit tested.

Unit testing is notoriously difficult to define. It is close enough to integration testing that people slip back and forth between the two easily. In the seminal book; *The Art of Unit Testing*, *Roy Osherove*, the author defines a unit test as:

> *A unit test is an automated piece of code that invokes a unit of work in the system and then checks a single assumption about the behavior of that unit of work.*

The exact size of a unit of work is up for some debate. Some people restrict it to a single function or a single class, while others allow a unit of work to span multiple classes. I tend to think that a unit of work that spans multiple classes can actually be broken into smaller, testable units.

The key to unit testing is that it tests a small piece of functionality and it quickly tests the functionality in a repeatable, automated fashion. Unit tests written by one person should be easily runnable by any other member of the team.

For unit testing we want to test small pieces of functionality because we believe that if all the components of a system work correctly then the system as a whole will work. This is not the whole truth. The communication between modules is just as likely to fail as a function within the unit. This is why we want to write tests on several levels. Unit tests check that the code we're writing right now is correct. Integration testing tests entire workflows through the application and will uncover problems in the interaction of units.

The test-driven development approach suggests writing tests at the same time as we write code. While this gives us great confidence that the code we're writing is correct, the real advantage is that it helps drive good architecture. When code has too many interdependencies it is far harder to test than well-separated modular code. A lot of the code that developers write goes unread by anybody ever again. Unit tests provide a useful way of keeping developers on the right path even in cases where they know that nobody will ever see their code. There is no better way to produce a quality product than to tell people they are going to be checked on it, even if the checker happens to be an automated test.

Tests can be run both while developing new code and in an automatic fashion on the build machines. If every time a developer checks in a change, the entire project is built and tested, then some reassurance can be provided that the newly checked-in code is correct. From time to time the build will break and that will be a flag that something that was just added was in error. Often the code that is broken may not even be proximal to the code changed. An altered return value may percolate through the system and manifest itself somewhere wholly unexpected. Nobody can keep anything more than the most trivial system in their mind at any one time. Testing acts as a sort of second memory, checking and rechecking assumptions made previously.

Failing the build as soon as an error occurs shortens the time it takes between an error being made in the code and it being found and fixed. Ideally the problem will still be fresh in the developer's mind so the fix can easily be found. If the errors were not discovered until months down the road, the developer will certainly have forgotten what s/he was working on at the time. The developer may not even be around to help solve the problem, throwing somebody who has never seen the code in to fix it.

# Arrange-Act-Assert

When building tests for any piece of code, a very common approach to follow is that of Arrange-Act-Assert. This describes the different steps that take place inside a single unit test.

The first thing we do is set up a test scenario (arrange). This step can consist of a number of actions and may involve putting in place fake objects to simulate real objects as well as creating new instances of the subject under test. If you find that your test setup code is long or involved, it is likely a smell and you should consider refactoring your code. As mentioned in the previous section, testing is helpful for driving not just correctness but also architecture. Difficult-to-write tests are indicative that the architecture is not sufficiently modular.

Once the test is set up then the next step is to actually execute the function we would like to test (act). The act step is usually very short, in many cases no more than a single line of code.

The final part is to check to make sure that the result of the function or the state of the world is as you would expect (assert).

A very simple example of this might be a castle builder:

```
class CastleBuilder {
  buildCastle(size) {
    var castle = new Castle();
    castle.size = size;
    return castle;
  }
}
```

This class simply builds a new castle of a specific size. We want to make sure that no shenanigans are going on and that when we build a castle of size `10` we get a castle of size `10`:

```
function When_building_a_castle_size_should_be_correctly_set() {
  var castleBuilder = new CastleBuilder();
  var expectedSize = 10;
  var builtCastle = castleBuilder.buildCastle(10);
  assertEqual(expectedSize, builtCastle.size);
}
```

# Assert

You may have noticed that in the last example we made use of a function called `assertEquals`. An assert is a test that, when it fails, throws an exception. There is currently no built-in assert functionality in JavaScript, although there is a proposal in the works to add it.

Fortunately, building an assert is pretty simple:

```
function assertEqual(expected, actual){
  if(expected !== actual)
  throw "Got " + actual + " but expected " + expected;
}
```

It is helpful to mention, in the error, the actual value as well as the expected value.

There is a great number of assertion libraries in existence. Node.js ships with one, creatively called `assert.js`. If you end up using a testing framework for JavaScript it is likely that it will also contain an assertion library.

# Fake objects

If we think of the interdependencies between objects in an application as a graph it becomes quickly apparent that there are a number of nodes that have dependencies on, not just one, but many other objects. Attempting to place an object with a lot of dependencies under test is challenging. Each of the dependent objects must be constructed and included in the test. When these dependencies interact with external resources such as the network or file system, the problem becomes intractable. Pretty soon we're testing the entire system at a time. This is a legitimate testing strategy, known as **integration testing**, but we're really just interested in ensuring that the functionality of a single class is correct.

Integration testing tends to be slower to execute than unit tests.

The subject of a test can have a large dependency graph that makes testing it difficult. You can see an example here:

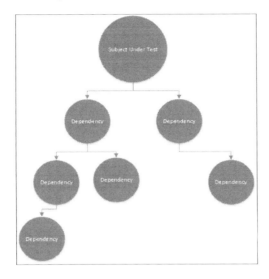

We need to find a way to isolate the class under test so that we don't have to recreate all the dependencies, including the network. We can think of this approach as adding bulkheads to our code. We will insert bulkheads to stop tests from flowing over from one class to many. These bulkheads are similar to how oil tankers maintain separation to limit the impact of spills and maintain weight distribution as can be seen here:

*Image courtesy of `http://www.reactivemanifesto.org/`.

To this end we can use fake objects that have a limited set of functionalities in place of the real objects. We'll look at three different methods of creating fake objects.

The first is the, rather niftily named, test spy.

# Test spies

A spy is an approach that wraps all the methods of an object and records the inputs and outputs from that method as well as the number of calls. By wrapping the calls, it is possible to examine exactly what was passed in and what came out of the function. Test spies can be used when the exact inputs into a function are not known beforehand.

In other languages, building test spies requires reflection and can be quite complicated. We can actually get away with making a basic test spy in no more than a couple of lines of code. Let's experiment.

To start we'll need a class to intercept:

```
var SpyUpon = (function () {
  function SpyUpon() {
  }
  SpyUpon.prototype.write = function (toWrite) {
    console.log(toWrite);
  };
  return SpyUpon;
})();
```

Now we would like to spy on this function. Because functions are first class objects in JavaScript we can simply rejigger the SpyUpon object:

```
var spyUpon = new SpyUpon();
spyUpon._write = spyUpon.write;
spyUpon.write = function (arg1) {
  console.log("intercepted");
  this.called = true;
  this.args = arguments;
  this.result = this._write(arg1, arg2, arg3, arg4, arg5);
  return this.result;
};
```

Here we take the existing function and give it a new name. Then we create a new function that calls the renamed function and also records some things. After the function has been called we can examine the various properties:

```
console.log(spyUpon.write("hello world"));
console.log(spyUpon.called);
console.log(spyUpon.args);
console.log(spyUpon.result);
```

Running this code in node gets us the following:

```
hello world
7
true
{ '0': 'hello world' }
7
```

Using this technique, it is possible to get all sorts of insight into how a function is used. There are a number of libraries that support creating test spies in a more robust way than our simple version here. Some provide tools for recording exceptions, the number of times called, and the arguments for each call.

# Stubs

A **stub** is another example of a fake object. We can use stubs when we have some dependencies in the subject under test that need to be satisfied with an object that returns a value. They can also be used to provide a bulkhead to stop computationally expensive or I/O reliant functions from being run.

Stubs can be implemented in much the same way that we implemented spies. We just need to intercept the call to the method and replace it with a version that we wrote. However, with stubs we actually don't call the replaced function. It can be useful to keep the replaced function around just in case we need to restore the functionality of the stubbed out class.

Let's start with an object that depends on another object for part of its functionality:

```
class Knight {
  constructor(credentialFactory) {
    this.credentialFactory = credentialFactory;
  }
  presentCredentials(toRoyalty) {
    console.log("Presenting credentials to " + toRoyalty);
    toRoyalty.send(this.credentialFactory.Create());
    return {};
  }
}
```

This knight object takes a `credentialFactory` argument as part of its constructor. By passing in the object we exteriorize the dependency and remove the responsibility for creating `credentialFactory` from the knight. We've seen this sort of inversion of control previously and we'll look at it in more detail in the next chapter. This makes our code more modular and testing far easier.

Now when we want to test the knight without worrying about how a credential factory works, we can use a fake object, in this case a stub:

```
class StubCredentialFactory {
  constructor() {
    this.callCounter = 0;
  }
  Create() {
    //manually create a credential
  };
}
```

This stub is a very simple one that simply returns a standard new credential. Stubs can be made quite complicated if there need to be multiple calls to it. For instance, we could rewrite our simple stub as the following:

```
class StubCredentialFactory {
  constructor() {
    this.callCounter = 0;
  }
  Create() {
    if (this.callCounter == 0)
      return new SimpleCredential();
    if (this.callCounter == 1)
      return new CredentialWithSeal();
    if (this.callCounter == 2)
      return null;
    this.callCounter++;
  }
}
```

This version of the stub returns a different sort of credential every time it is called. On the third call it returns null. As we set up the class using an inversion of control, writing a test is as simple as the following:

```
var knight = new Knight(new StubCredentialFactory());
knight.presentCredentials("Queen Cersei");
```

We can now execute the test:

```
var knight = new Knight(new StubCredentialFactory());
var credentials = knight.presentCredentials("Lord Snow");
assert(credentials.type === "SimpleCredentials");
credentials = knight.presentCredentials("Queen Cersei");
assert(credentials.type === "CredentialWithSeal");
credentials = knight.presentCredentials("Lord Stark");
assert(credentials == null);
```

Because there is no hard typing system in JavaScript, we can build stubs without worrying about implementing interfaces. There is also no need to stub an entire object but only the function in which we're interested.

# Mock

The final type of fake object is a **mock**. The difference between a mock and a stub is where the verification is done. With a stub, our test must check if the state is correct after the act. With a mock object, the responsibility for testing the asserts falls to the mock itself. Mocks are another place where it is useful to leverage a mocking library. We can, however, build the same sort of thing, simply, ourselves:

```
class MockCredentialFactory {
  constructor() {
    this.timesCalled = 0;
  }
  Create() {
    this.timesCalled++;
  }
  Verify() {
    assert(this.timesCalled == 3);
  }
}
```

This `mockCredentialsFactory` class takes on the responsibility of verifying the correct functions were called. This is a very simple sort of approach to mocking and can be used as such:

```
var credentialFactory = new MockCredentialFactory();
var knight = new Knight(credentialFactory);
var credentials = knight.presentCredentials("Lord Snow");
credentials = knight.presentCredentials("Queen Cersei");
credentials = knight.presentCredentials("Lord Stark");
credentialFactory.Verify();
```

This is a static mock that keeps the same behavior every time it is used. It is possible to build mocks that act as recording devices. You can instruct the mock object to expect certain behaviors and then have it automatically play them back.

The syntax for this is taken from the documentation for the mocking library; Sinon. It looks like the following:

```
var mock = sinon.mock(myAPI);
mock.expects("method").once().throws();
```

# Monkey patching

We've seen a number of methods for creating fake objects in JavaScript. When creating the spy, we made use of a method called **monkey patching**. Monkey patching allows you to dynamically change the behavior of an object by replacing its functions. We can use this sort of approach without having to revert to full fake objects. Any existing object can have its behavior changed in isolation using this approach. This includes built-in objects such as strings and arrays.

# Interacting with the user interface

A great deal of the JavaScript in use today is used on the client and is used to interact with elements that are visible on the screen. Interacting with the page flows through a model of the page known as **Document Object Model (DOM)**.

Every element on the page is represented in the DOM. Whenever a change is made to the page, the DOM is updated. If we add a paragraph to the page, then a paragraph is added to the DOM. Thus if our JavaScript code adds a paragraph, checking that it does so is simply a function of checking the DOM.

Unfortunately, this requires that a DOM actually exists and that it is formed in the same way that it is on the actual page. There are a number of approaches to testing against a page.

# Browser testing

The most naïve approach is to simply automate the browser. There are a few projects out there that can help with this task. One can either automate a fully-fledged browser such as Firefox, Internet Explorer, or Chrome, or one can pick a browser that is headless. The fully-fledged browser approach requires that a browser be installed on the test machine and that the machine be running in a mode that has a desktop available.

Many Unix-based build servers will not have been set up to show a desktop as it isn't needed for most build tasks. Even if your build machine is a Windows one, the build account frequently runs in a mode that has no ability to open a window. Tests using full browsers also have a tendency to break, to my mind. Subtle timing issues crop up and tests are easily interrupted by unexpected changes to the browser. It is a frequent occurrence that manual intervention will be required to unstick a browser that has ended up in an incorrect state.

Fortunately, efforts have been made to decouple the graphical portions of a web browser from the DOM and JavaScript. For Chrome this initiative has resulted in PhantomJS and for Firefox SlimerJS.

Typically, the sorts of test that require a full browser require some navigation of the browser across several pages. This is provided for in the headless browsers through an API. I tend to think of tests at this scale as integration tests rather than unit tests.

A typical test using PhantomJS and the CasperJS library that sits on top of the browser might look like the following:

```
var casper = require('casper').create();
casper.start('http://google.com', function() {
  assert.false($("#gbqfq").attr("aria-haspopup"));
  $("#gbqfq").val("redis");
  assert.true($("#gbqfq").attr("aria-haspopup"));
});
```

This would test that entering a value into the search box on Google changes the `aria-haspopup` property from `false` to `true`.

Testing things this way puts a great deal of reliance on the DOM not changing too radically. Depending on the selectors used to find elements on the page, a simple change to the style of the page could break every test. I like to keep tests of this sort away from the look of that page by never using CSS properties to select elements. Instead make use of IDs or, better yet, data-* attributes. We don't necessarily have the luxury of that when it comes to testing existing pages but certainly for new pages it is a good plan.

# Faking the DOM

Much of the time, we don't need a full page DOM to perform our tests. The page elements we need to test are part of a section on the page instead of the entire page. A number of initiatives exist that allow for the creation of a chunk of the document in pure JavaScript. `jsdom` for instance is a method for injecting a string of HTML and receiving back a fake window.

In this example, modified slightly from their README, they create some HTML elements, load JavaScript, and test that it returns correctly:

```
var jsdom = require("jsdom");
jsdom.env( '<p><a class="the-link" ref="https://github.com/tmpvar/
  jsdom">jsdom!</a></p>',
  ["http://code.jquery.com/jquery.js"],
```

```
    function (errors, window) {
        assert.equal(window.$("a.the-link").text(), "jsdom!");
    }
);
```

If your JavaScript is focused on a small section of the page, perhaps you're building custom controls or web components, then this is an ideal approach.

# Wrapping the manipulation

The final approach to dealing with graphical JavaScript is to stop interacting directly with elements on the page. This is the approach that many of the more popular JavaScript frameworks of today use. One simply updates a JavaScript model and this model then updates the page through the use of some sort of MV* pattern. We looked at this approach in some detail some chapters ago.

Testing in this case becomes quite easy. Our complicated JavaScript can simply be tested by building a model state prior to running the code and then testing to see if the model state after running the code is as we expect.

As an example we could have a model that looks like the following:

```
class PageModel{
    titleVisible: boolean;
    users: Array<User>;
}
```

The test code for it might look as simple as the following:

```
var model = new PageModel();
model.titleVisible = false;
var controller = new UserListPageController(model);
controller.AddUser(new User());
assert.true(model.titleVisible);
```

As everything on the page is manipulated, through the bindings to the model, we can be confident that changes in the model are correctly updating the page.

Some would argue that we've simply shifted the problem. Now the only place for errors is if the binding between the HTML and the model is incorrect. So we also need to test if we have bindings correctly applied to the HTML. This falls to higher-level testing that can be done more simply. We can cover far more with a higher-level test than with a lower-level one, although at the cost of knowing exactly where the error occurred.

You're never going to be able to test everything about an application but the smaller you can make the untested surface, the better.

# Tips and tricks

I have seen tests where people split up the Arrange-Act-Assert by putting in place comments:

```
function testMapping(){
  //Arrange
  ...
  //Act
  ...
  //Assert
  ...
}
```

You're going to wear your fingers to the bone typing those comments for every single test. Instead I just split them up with a blank line. The separation is clear and anybody who knows Arrange-Act-Assert will instantly recognize what it is that you're doing. You'll have seen the example code in this chapter split up in this fashion.

There are countless JavaScript testing libraries available to make your life easier. Choosing one may depend on your preferred style. If you like a gherkin-style syntax then cuumber.js might be for you. Otherwise try mocha, either on its own, or with the chai BDD style assertion library , which is is fairly nice. There are also testing frameworks such as Protractor which are specific to Angular apps (although you can use it to test other frameworks with a bit of work). I'd suggest taking a day and playing with a few to find your sweet spot.

When writing tests, I tend to name them in a way that makes it obvious that they are tests and not production code. For most JavaScript I follow camel case naming conventions such as `testMapping`. However, for test methods I follow an underscored naming pattern `When_building_a_castle_size_should_be_correctly_set`. In this way the test reads more like a specification. Others have different approaches to naming and there is no "right" answer, so feel free to experiment.

# Summary

Producing a quality product is always going to require extensive and repeated testing; this is exactly the sort of thing computers are really good at. Automate as much as possible.

Testing JavaScript code is an up-and-coming thing. The tooling around, mocking out objects, and even the tools for running tests are undergoing constant changes. Being able to use tools such as Node.js to run tests quickly and without having to boot up an entire browser is stunningly helpful. This is an area that is only going to improve over the next few years. I am enthused to see what changes come from it.

In the next chapter we'll take a look at some advanced patterns in JavaScript that you might not want to use every day but are very handy.

# 13

# Advanced Patterns

I hesitated when naming this chapter, *Advanced Patterns*. This isn't really about patterns that are more complicated or sophisticated than other patterns. It is about patterns that you wouldn't use very frequently. Frankly, coming from a static programming language background, some of them seem crazy. Nonetheless they are completely valid patterns and are in use within big name projects everywhere.

In this chapter we'll be looking at the following topics:

- Dependency injection
- Live post processing
- Aspect oriented programming
- Macros

## Dependency injection

One of the topics we've been talking about continuously during this book is the importance of making your code modular. Small classes are easier to test, provide better reuse, and promote better collaboration for teams. Modular, loosely coupled code is easier to maintain, as changes can be limited. You may remember the example of a ripstop we used earlier.

With modular code of this sort we see a lot of inversion of control. Classes have functionality inserted into them through passing additional classes by their creators. This moves the responsibility for how some portions of the child class work to the parent. For small projects, this is a pretty reasonable approach. As projects get more complicated and dependency graphs get more complicated, manually injecting the functionality becomes more and more difficult. We are still creating objects all over the code base, passing them into created objects so the coupling problem still exists, we've just shifted it up a level.

If we think of object creation as a service, then a solution to this problem presents itself. We can defer the object creation to a central location. This allows us to change the implementations for a given interface in one place, simply and easily. It also allows us to control object lifetime so that we can reuse objects or recreate them every time they are used. If we need to replace one implementation of an interface with another implementation, then we can be confident that we need to only change it in one location. Because the new implementation still fulfils the contract, that is the interface, then all the classes that make use of the interface can remain ignorant of the change.

What's more is that by centralizing object creation it becomes easier to construct objects that depend on other objects. If we look at a dependency graph for a module such as the `UserManager` variable, it is clear that it has a number of dependencies. These dependencies may have additional dependencies and so forth. To build a `UserManager` variable, we not only need to pass in the database, but also `ConnectionStringProvider`, `CredentialProvider`, and `ConfigFileConnectionStringReader`. Goodness, that is going to be a lot of work to create instances of all of these. If we, instead, register implementations of each of these interfaces in a registry, then we need only go to the registry to look up how to make them. This can be automated and the dependencies automatically get injected to all dependencies without a need to explicitly create any of them. This method of solving dependencies is commonly referred to as 'solving the transitive closure'.

A dependency injection framework handles the responsibility of constructing objects. On application set up the dependency injection framework is primed with a combination of names and objects. From this, it creates a registry or a container. When constructing an object through the container, the container looks at the signature of the constructor and attempts to satisfy the arguments on the constructor. Here is an illustration of a dependency graph:

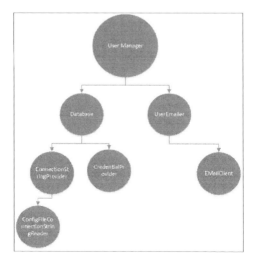

In more statically typed languages such as C# or Java, dependency injection frameworks are commonplace. They usually work by using reflection, a method of using code to extract structural information from other code. When building the container, one specifies an interface and one or more concrete classes that can satisfy the interface. Of course using interfaces and reflection to perform dependency injection requires that the language support both interfaces and introspection.

There is no way to do this in JavaScript. JavaScript has neither direct introspection nor a traditional object inheritance model. A common approach is to use variable names to solve the dependency problem. Consider a class that has a constructor like so:

```
var UserManager = (function () {
  function UserManager(database, userEmailer) {
    this.database = database;
    this.userEmailer = userEmailer;
  }
  return UserManager;
})();
```

The constructor takes two arguments that are very specifically named. When we construct this class through the dependency injection, these two arguments are satisfied by looking through the names registered with the container and passing them into the constructor. However, without introspection how can we extract the names of the parameters so we know what to pass into the constructor?

The solution is actually amazingly simple. The original text of any function in JavaScript is available by simply calling toString on it. So, for the constructor given in the preceding code, we can do just do this:

```
UserManager.toString()
```

Now we can parse the string returned to extract the names of the parameters. Care must be taken to parse the text correctly, but it is possible. The popular JavaScript framework, Angular, actually uses this method to do its dependency injection. The result remains relatively preformat. The parsing really only needs to be done once and the results cached, so no additional penalty is incurred.

I won't go through how to actually implement the dependency injection, as it is rather tedious. When parsing the function, you can either parse it using a string-matching algorithm or build a lexer and parser for the JavaScript grammar. The first solution seems easier but it is likely a better decision to try to build up a simple syntax tree for the code into which you're injecting. Fortunately, the entire method body can be treated as a single token, so it is vastly easier than building a fully-fledged parser.

If you're willing to impose a different syntax on the user of your dependency injection framework then you can even go so far as to create your own syntax. The Angular 2.0 dependency injection framework, di.js, supports a custom syntax for denoting both places where objects should be injected and for denoting which objects satisfy some requirement.

Using it as a class into which some code needs to be injected, looks like this code, taken from the di.js examples page:

```
@Inject(CoffeeMaker, Skillet, Stove, Fridge, Dishwasher)
export class Kitchen {
  constructor(coffeeMaker, skillet, stove, fridge, dishwasher) {
    this.coffeeMaker = coffeeMaker;
    this.skillet = skillet;
    this.stove = stove;
    this.fridge = fridge;
    this.dishwasher = dishwasher;
  }
}
```

The CoffeeMaker instance might look like the following code:

```
@Provide(CoffeeMaker)
@Inject(Filter, Container)
export class BodumCoffeeMaker{
  constructor(filter, container){

  ...
  }
}
```

You might have also noticed that this example makes use of the class keyword. This is because the project is very forward looking and requires the use of traceur.js to provide for ES6 class support. We'll learn about traceur.js file in the next chapter.

# Live post processing

It should be apparent now that running toString over a function in JavaScript is a valid way to perform tasks. It seems odd but, really, writing code that emits other code is as old as Lisp or possibly older. When I first came across how dependency injection works in AngularJS, I was both disgusted at the hack and impressed by the ingenuity of the solution.

If it is possible to do dependency injection by interpreting code on the fly, then what more could we do with it? The answer is: quite a lot. The first thing that comes to mind is that you could write domain specific languages.

We talked about DSLs in *Chapter 5, Behavioral Patterns,* and even created a very simple one. With the ability to load and rewrite JavaScript, we can take advantage of a syntax that is close to JavaScript but not wholly compatible. When interpreting the DSL, our interpreter would write out additional tokens needed to convert the code to actual JavaScript.

One of the nice features of TypeScript that I've always liked is that parameters to the constructors that are marked as public are automatically transformed into properties on the object. For instance, the TypeScript code that follows:

```
class Axe{
    constructor(public handleLength, public headHeight){}
}
```

Compiles to the following code:

```
var Axe = (function () {
    function Axe(handleLength, headHeight) {
        this.handleLength = handleLength;
        this.headHeight = headHeight;
    }
    return Axe;
})();
```

We could do something similar in our DSL. Starting with the `Axe` definition that follows:

```
class Axe{
    constructor(handleLength, /*public*/ headHeight){}
}
```

We've used a comment here to denote that `headHeight` should be public. Unlike the TypeScript version, we would like our source code to be valid JavaScript. Because comments are included in the `toString` function this works just fine.

The next thing to do is to actually emit new JavaScript from this. I've taken a naïve approach and used regular expressions. This approach would quickly get out of hand and probably only works with the well-formed JavaScript in the `Axe` class:

```
function publicParameters(func){
    var stringRepresentation = func.toString();
    var parameterString = stringRepresentation.match(/^function .*\
        ((.*)\)/)[1];
    var parameters = parameterString.split(",");
    var setterString = "";
    for(var i = 0; i < parameters.length; i++){
        if(parameters[i].indexOf("public") >= 0){
```

```
        var parameterName = parameters[i].split('/')[parameters[i].
          split('/').length-1].trim();
        setterString += "this." +  parameterName + " = " + parameterName
          + ";\n";
      }
    }
    var functionParts = stringRepresentation.match(/(^.*{)([\s\S]*)/);
    return functionParts[1] + setterString + functionParts[2];
  }

  console.log(publicParameters(Axe));
```

Here we extract the parameters to the function and check for those that have the
`public` annotation. The result of this function can be passed back into eval for
use in the current object or written out to a file if we're using this function in a
pre-processor. Typically use of eval in JavaScript is discouraged.

There are tons of different things that can be done using this sort of processing. Even
without string post-processing there are some interesting programming concept we
can explore by just wrapping methods.

# Aspect oriented programming

Modularity of software is a great feature, the majority of this book has been about
modularity and its advantages. However, there are some features of software that
span the entire system. Security is a great example of this.

We would like to have similar security code in all the modules of the application to
check that people are, in fact, authorized to perform some action. So if we have a
function of the sort:

```
var GoldTransfer = (function () {
  function GoldTransfer() {
  }
  GoldTransfer.prototype.SendPaymentOfGold = function (amountOfGold,
    destination) {
    var user = Security.GetCurrentUser();
    if (Security.IsAuthorized(user, "SendPaymentOfGold")) {
      //send actual payment
    } else {
      return { success: 0, message: "Unauthorized" };
    }
  };
  return GoldTransfer;
})();
```

We can see that there is a fair bit of code in place to check if a user is authorized. This same boilerplate code is used elsewhere in the application. In fact, with this being a high security application, the security checks are in place in every public function. All is well until we need to make a change to the common security code. This change needs to take place in every single public function in the application. We can refactor our application all we want, but the truth remains: we need to have at least some code in each of the public methods to perform a security check. This is known as a cross-cutting concern.

There are other instances of cross-cutting concerns in most large applications. Logging is a great example, as is database access and performance instrumenting. **Aspect oriented programming (AOP)** presents a way to minimize the repeated code through a process known as **weaving**.

An aspect is a piece of code that can intercept method calls and change them. On the .Net platform there is a tool called PostSharp that does aspect weaving and, on the Java platform, one called AspectJ. These tools hook into the build pipeline and modify the code after it has been transformed into instructions. This allows code to be injected wherever needed. The source code appears unchanged but the compiled output now includes calls to the aspect. Aspects solve the cross cutting concern by being injected into existing code. Here you can see the application of an aspect to a method through a weaver:

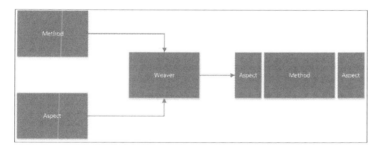

Of course we don't have the luxury of a design-time compile step in most JavaScript workflows. Fortunately, we've already seen some approaches that would allow us to implement cross cuts using JavaScript. The first thing we need is the wrapping of methods that we saw in the testing chapter. The second is the `tostring` abilities from earlier in this chapter.

There are some AOP libraries already in existence for JavaScript that may be a good bet to explore. However, we can implement a simple interceptor here. First let's decide on the grammar for requesting injection. We'll use the same idea of comments from earlier to denote methods that require interception. We'll just make the first line in the method a comment that reads `aspect(<name of aspect>)`.

To start we'll take a slightly modified version of our same `GoldTransfer` class from earlier:

```
class GoldTransfer {
  SendPaymentOfGold(amountOfGold, destination) {
    var user = Security.GetCurrentUser();
    if (Security.IsAuthorized(user, "SendPaymentOfGold")) {
    }
    else {
     return { success: 0, message: "Unauthorized" };
    }
  }
}
```

We've stripped out all the security stuff that used to exist in it and added a console log so we can see that it actually works. Next we'll need an aspect to weave into it:

```
class ToWeaveIn {
  BeforeCall() {
    console.log("Before!");
  }
  AfterCall() {
    console.log("After!");
  }
}
```

For this we use a simple class that has a `BeforeCall` and `AfterCall` method, one which is called before and one which is called after the original method. We don't need to use eval in this case so the interceptions are safer:

```
function weave(toWeave, toWeaveIn, toWeaveInName) {
  for (var property in toWeave.prototype) {
    var stringRepresentation = toWeave.prototype[property].toString();
    console.log(stringRepresentation);
    if (stringRepresentation.indexOf("@aspect(" + toWeaveInName + ")")
      >= 0) {
      toWeave.prototype[property + "_wrapped"] = toWeave.
        prototype[property];
      toWeave.prototype[property] = function () {
      toWeaveIn.BeforeCall();
      toWeave.prototype[property + "_wrapped"]();
      toWeaveIn.AfterCall();
    };
    }
  }
}
```

This interceptor can easily be modified to a shortcut and return something before the main method body is called. It can also be changed so that the output of the function can be modified by simply tracking the output from the wrapped method and then modifying it in the `AfterCall` method.

This is a fairly lightweight example of AOP. There are some frameworks in existence for JavaScript AOP, but perhaps the best approach is to make use of a precompiler or macro language.

# Mixins

As we saw much earlier in this book, the inheritance pattern for JavaScript is different from the typical pattern seen in languages like C# and Java. JavaScript uses prototype inheritance that allows adding functions to a class quite easily and from multiple sources. Prototype inheritance allows for adding methods from multiple sources in a similar fashion to the much-maligned multiple-inheritance. The primary criticism of multiple inheritance is that it is difficult to understand which overload of a method will be called in a situation. This problem is somewhat alleviated in a prototype inheritance model. Thus we can feel comfortable using the approach of adding functionality from several sources, which is known as mixins.

A mixin is a chunk of code which can be added to existing classes to expand their functionality. They make the most sense in scenarios where the functions need to be shared between disparate classes where an inheritance relationship is too strong.

Let's imagine a scenario where this sort of functionality would be handy. In the land of Westeros, death is not always as permanent as in our world. However, those who return from the dead may not be exactly as they were when they were alive. While much of the functionality is shared between `Person` and `ReanimatedPerson`, they are not close enough to have an inheritance relationship. In this code you can see the `extend` function of underscore used to add mixins to our two people classes. It is possible to do this without `underscore` but, as mentioned earlier, there are some complex edge cases around `extends` which make using a library handy:

```
var _ = require("underscore");
export class Person{
}
export class ReanimatedPerson{
}
export class RideHorseMixin{
  public Ride(){
```

```
        console.log("I'm on a horse!");
    }
}

var person = new Person();
var reanimatedPerson = new ReanimatedPerson();
_.extend(person, new RideHorseMixin());
_.extend(reanimatedPerson, new RideHorseMixin());

person.Ride();
reanimatedPerson.Ride();
```

Mixins provide a mechanism to share functionality between diverse objects but do pollute the prototype structure.

# Macros

Preprocessing code through macros is not a new idea. It was, and probably still is, very popular for C and C++. In fact, if you take a look at some of the source code for the Gnu utilities for Linux they are written almost entirely in macros. Macros are notorious for being hard to understand and debug. For a time, newly-created languages like Java and C# did not support macros for exactly this reason.

That being said, even more recent languages like Rust and Julia have brought the idea of macros back. These languages were influenced by the macros from the Scheme language, a dialect of Lisp. The difference between C macros and Lisp/Scheme macros is that the C versions are textual while the Lisp/Scheme ones are structural. This means that C macros are just glorified find/replace tools while Scheme macros are aware of the **abstract syntax tree** (AST) around them, allowing them to be much more powerful.

The AST for Scheme is a far simpler construct than that of JavaScript. Nonetheless, there is a very interesting project called Sweet.js that tries to create structural macros for JavaScript.

Sweet.js plugs into the JavaScript build pipeline and modified JavaScript source code using one or more macros. There are a number of fully-fledged JavaScript transpilers, that is compilers that emit JavaScript. These compilers are problematic for sharing code between multiple projects. Their code is so different that there is no real way to share it. Sweet.js supports multiple macros being expanded in a single step. This allows for much better code sharing. The reusable bits are a smaller size and more easy to run together.

A simple example of `Sweet.js` is as follows:

```
let var = macro {
  rule { [$var (,) ...] = $obj:expr } => {
    var i = 0;
    var arr = $obj;
    $(var $var = arr[i++]) (;) ...
  }

  rule { $id } => {
    var $id
  }
}
```

The macro here provides ECMAScript-2015-style deconstructors that split an array into tree fields. The macro matches an array assignment and also regular assignment. For regular assignment the macro simply returns the identity, while for assignment of an array it will explode the text and replace it.

For instance, if you run it over the following:

```
var [foo, bar, baz] = arr;
```

Then, the result will be the following:

```
var i = 0;
var arr$2 = arr;
var foo = arr$2[i++];
var bar = arr$2[i++];
var baz = arr$2[i++];
```

This is just one example macro. The power of macros is really quite spectacular. Macros can create an entirely new language or change very minor things. They can be easily plugged in to fit any sided requirement.

# Tips and tricks

Using name-based dependency injection allows for conflicts between names. In order to avoid conflicts it may be worth prefacing your injected arguments with a special character. For instance, AngularJS uses the $ sign to denote an injected term.

Several times in this chapter I've mentioned the JavaScript build pipeline. It may seem odd that we have to build an interpreted language. However, there are certain optimizations and process improvements that may result from building JavaScript. There are a number of tools that can be used to help building JavaScript. Tools such as Grunt and Gulp are specifically designed to perform JavaScript and web tasks but you can also make use of traditional build tools such as Rake, Ant, or even Make.

# Summary

In this chapter we covered a number of advanced JavaScript patterns. Of these patterns it's my belief that dependency injection and macros are the most useful to us. You may not necessarily want to use them on every project. When approaching problems simply being aware of the possible solutions may change your approach to the problem.

Throughout this book I have talked extensively about the next versions of JavaScript. However, you don't need to wait until some future time to make use of many of these tools. Today, there are ways to compile newer versions of JavaScript down to the current version of JavaScript. The final chapter will explore a number of these tools and techniques.

# 14
# ECMAScript-2015/2016 Solutions Today

I cannot count the number of times I have mentioned upcoming versions of JavaScript in this book, rest assured that it's a large number. It is somewhat frustrating that the language is not keeping pace with the requirements of application developers. Many of the approaches we've discussed become unnecessary with a newer version of JavaScript. There are, however, some ways to get the next version of JavaScript working today.

In this chapter we'll look at a couple of these, specifically:

- Typescript
- BabelJS

## TypeScript

There is no shortage of languages that compile to JavaScript. CoffeeScript is perhaps the best known example of one of these languages, although the Google web toolkit that compiles Java to JavaScript was also once very popular. Never ones to be left behind or use somebody else's solution, Microsoft released a language called TypeScript in 2012. It is designed to be a superset of JavaScript in the same way that C++ is a superset of C. This means that all syntactically valid JavaScript code is also syntactically valid TypeScript code.

Microsoft itself is making heavy use of TypeScript in some of its larger web properties. Both Office 365 and Visual Studio Online have significant code bases written in TypeScript. These projects actually predate TypeScript by a significant margin. The transition from JavaScript to TypeScript was reportedly quite easy due to the fact that it is a superset of JavaScript.

One of the design goals for TypeScript was to make it as compatible as possible with ECMAScript-2015 and future versions. This means that TypeScript supports some, although certainly not all, of the features of ECMAScript-2016, as well as a healthy chunk of ECMAScript-2015. Two significant features from ECMAScript-2016 which are partially supported by Typescript are decorators and async/await.

# Decorators

In an earlier chapter we explored **aspect oriented programming (AOP)**. With AOP we wrap function with interceptors. Decorators offer an easy way of doing this. Let's say that we have a class which dispatches messages in Westeros. Obviously there are no phones or internet there, so messages are dispatched via crows. It would be very helpful if we could spy on these messages. Our `CrowMessenger` class looks like the following:

```
class CrowMessenger {
  @spy
  public SendMessage(message: string) {
    console.log(`Send message is ${message}`);
  }
}
var c = new CrowMessenger();
var r = c.SendMessage("Attack at dawn");
```

You may note the `@spy` annotation on the `SendMessage` method. This is simply another function which intercepts and wraps the function. Inside of the spy we have access to the function descriptor. As you can see in the following code, we take the descriptor and manipulate it to capture the argument sent to the `CrowMessenger` class:

```
function spy(target: any, key: string, descriptor?: any) {
  if(descriptor === undefined) {
    descriptor = Object.getOwnPropertyDescriptor(target, key);
  }
  var originalMethod = descriptor.value;

  descriptor.value =  function (...args: any[]) {
    var arguments = args.map(a => JSON.stringify(a)).join();
    var result = originalMethod.apply(this, args);
    console.log(`Message sent was: ${arguments}`);
    return result;
  }
  return descriptor;
}
```

Spys would obviously be very useful for testing functions. Not only can we spy on the values here but we could replace the input and output to the function. Consider the following:

```
descriptor.value = function (...args: any[]) {
  var arguments = args.map(a => JSON.stringify(a)).join();
  var result = "Retreat at once";
  console.log(`Message sent was: ${arguments}`);
  return result;
}
```

Decorators can be used for purposes other than AOP. For instance, you could annotate the properties on an object as serializable and use the annotations to control custom JSON serialization. It is my suspicion that decorators will become more useful and powerful as decorators become supported. Already Angular 2.0 is making extensive use of decorators.

# Async/Await

In *Chapter 7, Reactive Programming*, we spoke about how the callback nature of JavaScript programming makes code very confusing. Nowhere is this more apparent than trying to chain together a series of asynchronous events. We rapidly fall into a trap of code, which looks like the following:

```
$.post("someurl", function(){
  $.post("someotherurl", function(){
    $.get("yetanotherurl", function(){
      navigator.geolocation.getCurrentPosition(function(location){
        ...
      })
    })
  })
})
```

Not only is this code difficult to read, it is nearly impossible to understand. The async/await syntax, which is borrowed from C#, allows for writing your code in a much more succinct fashion. Behind the scenes generators are used (or abused, if you like) to create the impression of true async/await. Let's look at an example. In the preceding code we made use of the geolocation API which returns the location of a client. It is asynchronous as it performs some IO with the user's machine to get a real world location. Our specification calls for us to get the user's location, post it back to the server, and then get an image:

```
navigator.geolocation.getCurrentPosition(function(location){
  $.post("/post/url", function(result){
    $.get("/get/url", function(){
```

```
        });
      });
    });
```

If we now introduce async/await, this can become the following:

```
async function getPosition(){
  return await navigator.geolocation.getCurrentPosition();
}
async function postUrl(geoLocationResult){
  return await $.post("/post/url");
}
async function getUrl(postResult){
  return await $.get("/get/url");
}
async function performAction(){
  var position = await getPosition();
  var postResult = await postUrl(position);
  var getResult = await getUrl(postResult);
}
```

This code assumes that all async responses return promises which are a construct that contains a status and a result. As it stands, most async operations do not return promises but there are libraries and utilities to convert callbacks to promises. As you can see, the syntax is much cleaner and easier to follow than the callback mess.

# Typing

As well as the ECMAScript-2016 features we've mentioned in the preceding section, TypeScript has a rather intriguing typing system incorporated into it. One of the nicest parts of JavaScript is that it is a dynamically typed language. We've seen, repeatedly, how, not being burdened by types has saved us time and code. The typing system in TypeScript allows you to use as much or as little typing as you deem to be necessary. You can give variables a type by declaring them with the following syntax:

```
var a_number: number;
var a_string: string;
var an_html_element: HTMLElement;
```

Once a variable has a type assigned to it, the TypeScript compiler will use that not only to check that variable's usage, but also to infer what other types may be derived from that class. For example, consider the following code:

```
var numbers: Array<number> = [];
numbers.push(7);
```

```
numbers.push(9);
var unknown = numbers.pop();
```

Here, the TypeScript compiler will know that unknown is a number. If you attempt to use it as something else, say as the following string:

```
console.log(unknown.substr(0,1));
```

Then the compiler will throw an error. However, you don't need to assign a type to any variable. This means that you can tune the degree to which the type checking is run. While it sounds odd, it is actually a brilliant solution for introducing the rigour of type checking without losing the pliability of JavaScript. The typing is only enforced during compilation, once the code is compiled to JavaScript, any hint that there was typing information associated with a field disappears. As a result, the emitted JavaScript is actually very clean.

If you're interested in typing systems and know words like contravariant and can discuss the various levels of gradual typing, then TypeScript's typing system may be well worth your time to investigate.

All the examples in this book were originally written in TypeScript and then compiled to JavaScript. This was done to improve the accuracy of the code and generally to save me from messing up quite so frequently. I'm horribly biased but I think that TypeScript is really well done and certainly better than writing pure JavaScript.

There is no support for typing in future versions of JavaScript. Thus, even with all the changes coming to future versions of JavaScript, I still believe that TypeScript has its place in providing compile time type checking. I never cease to be amazed by the number of times that the type checker has saved me from making silly mistakes when writing TypeScript.

# BabelJS

An alternative to TypeScript is to use the BabelJS compiler. This is an open source project ECMAScript-2015 and beyond to the equivalent ECMAScript 5 JavaScript. A lot of the changes put in place for ECMAScript-2015 are syntactic niceties, so they can actually be represented in ECMAScript 5 JavaScript, although not as succinctly or as pleasantly. We've seen that already using class-like structures in ES 5. BabelJS is written in JavaScript, which means that the compilation from ECMAScript-2015 to ES 5 is possible directly on a web page. Of course, as seems to be the trend with compilers, the source code for BabelJS makes use of ES 6 constructs, so BabelJS must be used to compile BabelJS.

At the time of writing, the list of ES6 functions that are supported by BabelJS are extensive:

- Arrow functions
- Classes
- Computed property names
- Default parameters
- Destructuring assignment
- Iterators and for of
- Generator comprehension
- Generators
- Modules
- Numeric literals
- Property method assignment
- Object initializer shorthand
- Rest parameters
- Spread
- Template literals
- Promises

BabelJS is multi-purpose JavaScript compiler, so compiling ES-2015 code is simply one of the many things it can do. There are numerous plugins which provide a wide array of interesting functionality. For instance, the "Inline environmental variable" plugin inserts compile time variables, allowing for conditional compilation based on environments.

There is already a fair bit of documentation available on how each of these features work so we won't go over all of them.

Setting up Babel JS is a fairly simple exercise if you already have node and npm installed:

```
npm install -g babel-cli
```

This will create a BabelJS binary which can do compilation like so:

```
babel  input.js --o output.js
```

For most use cases you'll want to investigate using build tools such as Gulp or Grunt, which can compile many files at once and perform any number of post-compilation steps.

# Classes

By now you should be getting sick of reading about different ways to make classes in JavaScript. Unfortunately for you I'm the one writing this book so let's look at one final example. We'll use the same castle example from earlier.

Modules within files are not supported in BabelJS. Instead, files are treated as modules, which allows for dynamic loading of modules in a fashion not unlike `require.js`. Thus we'll drop the module definition from our castle and stick to just the classes. One other feature that exists in TypeScript and not ES 6 is prefacing a parameter with `public` to make it a public property on a class. Instead we make use of the `export` directive.

Once we've made these changes, the source ES6 file looks like the following:

```
export class BaseStructure {
  constructor() {
    console.log("Structure built");
  }
}

export class Castle extends BaseStructure {
  constructor(name){
    this.name = name;
    super();
  }
  Build(){
    console.log("Castle built: " + this.name);
  }
}
```

The resulting ES 5 JavaScript looks like the following:

```
"use strict";

var _createClass = function () { function defineProperties(target,
props) { for (var i = 0; i < props.length; i++) { var descriptor
= props[i]; descriptor.enumerable = descriptor.enumerable ||
false; descriptor.configurable = true; if ("value" in descriptor)
descriptor.writable = true; Object.defineProperty(target, descriptor.
key, descriptor); } } return function (Constructor, protoProps,
staticProps) { if (protoProps) defineProperties(Constructor.
prototype, protoProps); if (staticProps) defineProperties(Constructor,
staticProps); return Constructor; }; }();
```

```javascript
Object.defineProperty(exports, "__esModule", {
  value: true
});

function _possibleConstructorReturn(self, call) { if (!self) { throw
  new ReferenceError("this hasn't been initialised - super() hasn't
  been called"); } return call && (typeof call === "object" || typeof
  call === "function") ? call : self; }

function _inherits(subClass, superClass) { if (typeof superClass
  !== "function" && superClass !== null) { throw new TypeError("Super
  expression must either be null or a function, not " + typeof
  superClass); } subClass.prototype = Object.create(superClass &&
  superClass.prototype, { constructor: { value: subClass, enumerable:
  false, writable: true, configurable: true } }); if (superClass)
  Object.setPrototypeOf ? Object.setPrototypeOf(subClass, superClass)
  : subClass.__proto__ = superClass; }

function _classCallCheck(instance, Constructor) { if (!(instance
  instanceof Constructor)) { throw new TypeError("Cannot call a class
  as a function"); } }

var BaseStructure = exports.BaseStructure = function BaseStructure() {
  _classCallCheck(this, BaseStructure);
  console.log("Structure built");
};

var Castle = exports.Castle = function (_BaseStructure) {
  _inherits(Castle, _BaseStructure);
  function Castle(name) {
    _classCallCheck(this, Castle);
    var _this = _possibleConstructorReturn(this, Object.
      getPrototypeOf(Castle).call(this));
    _this.name = name;
    return _this;
  }
  _createClass(Castle, [{
    key: "Build",
    value: function Build() {
      console.log("Castle built: " + this.name);
    }
  }]);
  return Castle;
}(BaseStructure);
```

Right away it is apparent that the code produced by BabelJS is not as clean as the code from TypeScript. You may also have noticed that there are some helper functions employed to handle inheritance scenarios. There are also a number of mentions of `"use strict";`. This is an instruction to the JavaScript engine that it should run in strict mode.

Strict mode prevents a number of dangerous JavaScript practices. For instance, in some JavaScript interpreters it is legal to use a variable without declaring it first:

```
x = 22;
```

This will throw an error if x has not previously been declared:

```
var x = 22;
```

Duplicating properties in objects is disallowed, as well as double declaring a parameter. There are a number of other practises that `"use strict";` will treat as errors. I like to think of `"use strict";` as being similar to treating all warnings as errors. It isn't, perhaps, as complete as `-Werror` in GCC but it is still a good idea to use strict mode on new JavaScript code bases. BabelJS simply enforces that for you.

# Default parameters

Not a huge feature but a real nicety in ES 6 is the introduction of default parameters. It has always been possible to call a function in JavaScript without specifying all the parameters. Parameters are simply populated from left to right until there are no more values and all remaining parameters are given undefined.

Default parameters allow setting a value other than undefined for parameters that aren't filled out:

```
function CreateFeast(meat, drink = "wine"){
  console.log("The meat is: " + meat);
  console.log("The drink is: " + drink);
}
CreateFeast("Boar", "Beer");
CreateFeast("Venison");
```

This will output the following:

```
The meat is: Boar
The drink is: Beer
The meat is: Venison
The drink is: wine
```

The JavaScript code produced is actually very simple:

```
"use strict";
function CreateFeast(meat) {
  var drink = arguments.length <= 1 || arguments[1] === undefined ?
    "wine" : arguments[1];
  console.log("The meat is: " + meat);
  console.log("The drink is: " + drink);
}
CreateFeast("Boar", "Beer");
CreateFeast("Venison");
```

# Template literals

On the surface, template literals seem to be a solution for the lack of string interpolation in JavaScript. In some languages, such as Ruby and Python, you can inject substitutions from the surrounding code directly into a string without having to pass them into some sort of string formatting function. For instance, in Ruby you can do the following:

```
name= "Stannis";
print "The one true king is ${name}"
```

This will bind the ${name} parameter to the name from the surrounding scope.

ES6 supports template literals that allow something similar in JavaScript:

```
var name = "Stannis";
console.log(`The one true king is ${name}`);
```

It may be difficult to see but that string is actually surrounded by backticks and not quotation marks. Tokens to bind to the scope are denoted by ${}. Within the braces you can put complex expressions such as:

```
var army1Size = 5000;
var army2Size = 3578;
console.log(`The surviving army will be ${army1Size > army2Size ?
  "Army 1": "Army 2"}`);
```

The BabelJS compiled version of this code simply substitutes appending strings for the string interpolation:

```
var army1Size = 5000;
var army2Size = 3578;
console.log(("The surviving army will be " + (army1Size > army2Size ?
  "Army 1" : "Army 2")));
```

Template literals also solve a number of other problems. New line characters inside of a template literal are legal, meaning that you can use template literals to create multiline strings.

With the multiline string idea in mind, it seems like template literals might be useful for building domain specific languages: a topic we've seen a number of times already. The DSL can be embedded in a template literal and then values from outside plugged in. An example might be using it to hold HTML strings (certainly a DSL) and inserting values in from a model. These could, perhaps, take the place of some of the template tools in use today.

# Block bindings with let

The scoping of variables in JavaScript is weird. If you define a variable inside a block, say inside an `if` statement, then that variable is still available outside of the block. For example, see the following code:

```
if(true)
{
  var outside = 9;
}
console.log(outside);
```

This code will print 9, even though the variable outside is clearly out of scope. At least it is out of scope if you assume that JavaScript is like other C-syntax languages and supports block level scoping. The scoping in JavaScript is actually function level. Variables declared in code blocks like those found attached to `if` and `for` loop statements are hoisted to the beginning of the function. This means that they remain in scope for the entirety of the function.

ES 6 introduces a new keyword, `let`, which scopes variables to the block level. This sort of variable is ideal for use in loops or to maintain proper variable values inside an `if` statement. Traceur implements support for block scoped variables. However, the support is experimental at the moment due to performance implications.

Consider the following code:

```
if(true)
{
  var outside = 9;
  et inside = 7;
}
console.log(outside);
console.log(inside);
```

This will compile to the following:

```
var inside$__0;
if (true) {
  var outside = 9;
  inside$__0 = 7;
}
console.log(outside);
console.log(inside);
```

You can see that the inner variable is replaced with a renamed one. Once outside the block, the variable is no longer replaced. Running this code will report that inside is undefined when the `console.log` method occurs.

# In production

BabelJS is a very powerful tool for replicating many of the structures and features of the next version of JavaScript today. However, the code generated is never going to be quite as efficient as having native support for the constructs. It may be worth benchmarking the generated code to ensure that it continues to meet the performance requirements of your project.

# Tips and tricks

There are two excellent libraries for working with collections functionally in JavaScript: Underscore.js and Lo-Dash. Used in combination with TypeScript or BabelJS they have a very pleasant syntax and provide immense power.

For instance, finding all the members of a collection that satisfy a condition using Underscore looks like the following:

```
_.filter(collection, (item) => item.Id > 3);
```

This code will find all the items where the ID is greater than 3.

Either of these libraries is one of the first things I add to a new project. Underscore is actually bundled with backbone.js, an MVVM framework.

Tasks for Grunt and Gulp exist for compiling code written in TypeScript or BabelJS. There is, of course, also good support for TypeScript in much of Microsoft's development tool chain, although BabelJS is currently not supported directly.

# Summary

As the functionality of JavaScript expands, the need for third party frameworks and even transpilers starts to drop off. The language itself replaces many of these tools. The end game for tools like jQuery is that they are no longer required as they have been absorbed into the ecosystem. For many years the velocity of web browsers has been unable to keep pace with the rate of change of people's desires.

There is a large effort behind the next version of AngularJS but great efforts are being made to align the new components with the upcoming web component standards. Web components won't fully replace AngularJS but Angular will end up simply enhancing web components.

Of course the idea that there won't be a need for any frameworks or tools is ridiculous. There is always going to be a new method of solving a problem and new libraries and frameworks will show up. The opinions of people on how to solve problems is also going to differ. That's why there is space in the market for the wide variety of MVVM frameworks that exist.

Working with JavaScript can be a much more pleasant experience if you make use of ES6 constructs. There are a couple of possible approaches to doing so, which of these is best suited to your specific problem is a matter for closer investigation.

# Index

## L

lazy instantiation
  about 135
  implementing 135, 136
live post processing 244-246

## M

macros 250, 251
mediator
  about 95
  implementing 95, 96
memento
  about 97, 98
  caretaker player 97
  implementing 98-100
  originator player 97
  player 98
memoization
  about 131
  implementing 131, 133
message
  about 192, 193
  commands 193, 194
  events 194-196
  hints and tips 210
message handling
  indempotence 222
message storage 221
message upgrader 219, 220
microservices
  about 213-215
  hints and tips 223
mixins 249, 250
mock 234
Model View Controller (MVC)
  about 150-155
  code 155-159
Model View Presenter (MVP)
  about 159, 160
  code 161-163
Model View ViewModel (MVVM)
  about 163, 164
  code 164, 165, 166
  model and view, changes
      transferring 166, 168

  tips and tricks 169
  view changes, observing 168
modules 30-33
monkey patching 26, 235
multithreading 182-184

## O

observer pattern
  about 100, 101
  implementing 101, 102

## P

Palo Alto Research Center (PARC) 19
pattern
  behavioral pattern 81
  hints and tips 79, 117
  structural patterns 57
pipeline 218
plugins
  about 177
  d3 179-181
  jQuery 177-179
promise pattern 187-189
prototype
  about 54
  building 25-28
  implementing 54, 55
proxy pattern
  about 76
  implementing 77-79
publish-subscribe model
  about 199-202
  fan out and in 202-205

## R

RabbitMQ 214
Reactive Extensions
  URL 141
request-reply
  about 196-199

## S

service degradation 220, 221
Service Oriented Architecture (SOA) 215

Printed in Great Britain
by Amazon